Postmodern Debates

READERS IN CULTURAL CRITICISM
General Editor: *Catherine Belsey*

Posthumanism	*Neil Badmington*
Postmodern Debates	*Simon Malpas*
Reading the Past	*Tamsin Spargo*
Reading Images	*Julia Thomas*
Gender	*Anna Tripp*

Readers in Cultural Criticism
Series Standing Order
ISBN 0–333–78660–2 hardcover
ISBN 0–333–75236–8 paperback
(outside North America only)

You can receive future titles in this series as they are published by placing a
standing order.
Please contact your bookseller or, in case of difficulty, write to us at the address below
with your name and address, the title of the series and the ISBN quoted above.

Customer Services Department, Macmillan Distribution Ltd
Houndmills, Basingstoke, Hampshire RG21 6XS, England

Postmodern Debates

Edited by Simon Malpas

palgrave

First published 2001 by
PALGRAVE
Houndmills, Basingstoke, Hampshire RG21 6XS and
175 Fifth Avenue, New York, N. Y. 10010
Companies and representatives throughout the world

PALGRAVE is the new global academic imprint of St. Martin's Press LLC
Scholarly and Reference Division and Palgrave Publishers Ltd (formerly
Macmillan Press Ltd).

ISBN 0–333–76535–4 hardback
ISBN 0–333–76536–2 paperback

This book is printed on paper suitable for recycling and
made from fully managed and sustained forest sources.

A catalogue record for this book is available
from the British Library.

Library of Congress Cataloging-in-Publication Data
Postmodern debates / edited by Simon Malpas.
        p. cm. — (Readers in cultural criticism)
    Includes bibliographical references and index.
    ISBN 0–333–76536–2
        1. Postmodernism—Social aspects. I. Malpas, Simon. II. Readers in cultural
    criticism (Palgrave (Firm))

HM449 .P65 2001
306′.01—dc21
                                                              2001021731

10   9   8   7   6   5   4   3   2   1
10   09   08   07   06   05   04   03   02   01

Typeset on 10/12 Times by
Kolam Information Services Pvt Ltd, Pondicherry, India.

Printed and bound in Great Britain by
Creative Print & Design (Wales),
Ebbw Vale

Contents

Contents

POSTMODERNITY, IDENTITY, GENDER

THE POSTCOLONIAL AND THE POSTMODERN

THE POLITICS OF POSTMODERNITY

General Editor's Preface

Culture is the element we inhabit as subjects.

Culture embraces the whole range of practices, customs and representations of a society. In their rituals, stories and images, societies identify what they perceive as good and evil, proper, sexually acceptable, racially other. Culture is the location of values, and the study of cultures shows how values vary from one society to another, or from one historical moment to the next.

But culture does not exist in the abstract. On the contrary, it is in the broadest sense of the term textual, inscribed in the paintings, operas, sculptures, furnishings, fashions, bus tickets and shopping lists which are the currency of both aesthetic and everyday exchange. Societies invest these artefacts with meanings, until in many cases the meanings are so 'obvious' that they pass for nature. Cultural criticism denaturalises and defamiliarises these meanings, isolating them for inspection and analysis.

The subject is what speaks, or, more precisely, what signifies, and subjects learn in culture to reproduce or to challenge the meanings and values inscribed in the signifying practices of the society that shapes them.

If culture is pervasive and constitutive for us, if it resides in the documents, objects and practices that surround us, if it circulates as the meanings and values we learn and reproduce as good citizens, how in these circumstances can we practise cultural *criticism*, where criticism implies a certain distance between the critic and the culture? The answer is that cultures are not homogeneous; they are not even necessarily coherent. There are always other perspectives, so that cultures offer alternative positions for the subjects they also recruit. Moreover, we have a degree of power over the messages we reproduce. A minor modification changes the script, and may alter the meaning; the introduction of a negative constructs a resistance.

The present moment in our own culture is one of intense debate. Sexual alignments, family values, racial politics, the implications of economic differences are all hotly contested. And positions are taken up not only in explicit discussions at political meetings, on television and in the pub. They are often reaffirmed or challenged implicitly in films and advertisements, horoscopes and lonely-hearts columns. Cultural criticism analyses all these forms in order to assess their hold on our consciousness.

There is no interpretative practice without theory, and the more sophisti-cated the theory, the more precise and perceptive the reading it makes possible. Cultural theory is as well defined now as it has ever been, and as strongly contested as our social values. There could not, in consequence, be a more exciting time to engage in the theory and practice of Cultural Criticism.

Catherine Belsey
Cardiff University

Acknowledgements

I should like to offer my sincere thanks to my colleagues and students at Manchester Metropolitan University for all of their interest in and assistance with the production of this book. In particular, thanks are due to Catherine Belsey for her unfailingly generous editorial advice and support, the late Antony Easthope for the encouragement and enthusiasm he showed for this project, Barry Atkins who has been instrumental in helping me to work out many of the arguments in the introduction, and the students of my MA Critical Theory classes whose critical discussions of the texts included here have been endlessly insightful.

The editor and publishers wish to thank the following for permission to use copyright material:

Jean Baudrillard, for material from *The Gulf War Did Not Take Place* by Jean Baudrillard, trans. Paul Patton (1995), pp. 31–2, 40–59, by permission of Indiana University Press and Power Publications, Power Institute, Sydney; Homi K. Bhabha, for material from *The Locations of Culture: the Postcolonial and the Postmodern* by Homi K. Bhabha, Routledge (1994), pp. 1–9, by permission of Taylor & Francis Books Ltd; Judith Butler, for material from *Gender Trouble: Feminism and the Subversion of Identity* by Judith Butler (1990), pp. 142–9, by permission of Taylor & Francis, Inc/ Routledge, Inc; Jacques Derrida, for 'The Deconstruction of Actuality: An Interview with Jacques Derrida', *Radical Philosophy*, trans. Jonathan Ree (1994), pp. 28–30, originally published in *Passages*, September (1993), by permission of *Radical Philosophy* and *Passages*; Terry Eagleton, for material from *Ideology: An Introduction* by Terry Eagleton (1991), pp. xi–xii, 199– 213, by permission of Verso; Jürgen Habermas, for 'Modernity: An Unfinished Project' from Maurizio Passerin d'Entrèves and Seyla Benhabib (eds), *Habermas and the Unfinished Project of Modernity*, trans. Nicholas Walker, Polity (1996), pp. 38–55, by permission of Suhrkamp Verlag and Blackwell Publishers; bell hooks, for material from *Yearning: Race, Gender and Cultural Politics* by bel hooks (1990), pp. 23–31, by permission of South End Press; Linda Hutcheon, for material from *The Politics of Postmodernism* by

Linda Hutcheon, Routledge (1989), pp. 141–50, 167–8, by permission of Taylor & Francis Books Ltd; Alice A. Jardine, for material from *Gynesis: Configurations of Women and Modernity* by Alice Jardine (1985), pp. 65–79. Copyright © 1985 by Cornell University Press, by permission of Cornell University Press; Fredric Jameson, for 'Postmodernism and Consumer Society' from Hal Foster (ed.), *Postmodern Culture* (1985), pp. 111–25, by permission of Pluto Press; Ernesto Laclau, for 'Politics and the Limits of Modernity' from Andrew Ross (ed.), *Universal Abandon? The Politics of Postmodernism* (1988), pp. 63–82, by permission of Edinburgh University Press; Jean-François Lyotard, for material from *Postmodern Fables* by Jean-François Lyotard, trans. Georges Van Den Abbeele (1997), pp. 83–101. Copyright © 1993 Editions Galilee, English language copyright © 1997 by the Regents of the University of Minnesota, by permission of the University of Minnesota Press; and 'Answering the Question: What is Postmodernism?' from Ihab Hassan (ed.), *Innovation/Renovation: New Perspectives on the Humanities*, trans. by Regis Durand (1983), by permission of The University of Wisconsin Press; Richard Rorty, for 'We Anti-Representationalists', *Radical Philosophy*, 60 (1992), 40–2, by permission of *Radical Philosophy*.

Every effort has been made to trace the copyright holders but if any have been inadvertently overlooked the publishers will be pleased to make the necessary arrangement at the first opportunity.

1

Introduction

Simon Malpas

The postmodern is neither a contemporary fashion nor a unified movement. More than anything else, it is a space for debate. Whether they are for it or against it, so many of the different theories about meaning, identity and politics in today's world revolve around the postmodern that it has become a site of intense and often heated discussion across the cultural spectrum. It is therefore important for anybody approaching cultural criticism to have a working knowledge of postmodernity and postmodernism if they want to examine how the world might be experienced and understood now. More than any other contemporary critical idea, the postmodern (and its cognates postmodernism and postmodernity) is concerned with how people live today, with the issues that face individuals and societies across the world.

The aim of this book is to bring together some of the debates between prominent thinkers in critical theory, philosophy and cultural studies in order to introduce readers to the importance of the issues at stake in postmodern theory. Rather than attempting to give an account of a unified movement, which the postmodern is certainly not, this book explores appropriations of the term by thinkers whose projects and political views are often at odds. Postmodern theory has become a space in which practically the whole range of different forms of modern critical enquiry intersect: many feminists are concerned with the implications of postmodernity, as are writers on race and colonialism, political theorists and philosophers. Each group brings different interests and discussions to bear on the postmodern, and draws different conclusions about its usefulness. These thinkers and discussions will be the focus of this book, which sets out to treat the postmodern as a context for debates about truth, politics, meaning and identity, with the aim of encouraging readers to think through some of the consequences of postmodern theories for contemporary culture. The purpose of this introduction is to provide a general outline of some of the key characteristics of postmodernism and postmodernity, and to dispel some of the myths that have grown up around the extensive use of these terms in the popular media.

1

POPULAR POSTMODERNISM

During the last 15 or 20 years, the postmodern has become a term that, although often poorly understood, is almost impossible to avoid. Outside of academia, it is most commonly encountered in the media. More so, perhaps, than any other critical or theoretical movement, postmodernism has become a part of the popular cultures of late twentieth-century Europe and America. At the beginning of the 1990s, 'postmodernism' was a word that anyone with an interest in culture simply couldn't escape. Each new development in the arts, in architecture, literature, and in culture generally, seemed to be greeted with the epithet, 'postmodern'. Panels of pundits on television and radio art shows hailed or dismissed every new fashion by determining just how post-modern it was. It was difficult to know just what this postmodernism might be, but there was no doubt that it was 'now'. Whether it was good or bad seemed hardly to matter: one could take one's pick, defining postmodernism as either the most up-to-date, radical and chic innovation of a world that just kept on getting better, or, alternatively, using it to mark the decline of artistic standards in an ever expanding, market-oriented culture for which saleability was the only marker of aesthetic value.

As a media buzz-word, though, 'postmodernism' subsequently seemed to have fallen a little out of fashion. For some pundits, it came to seem too common and too open to debate to be a safe slogan with which to pepper their conversation in the hope of appearing up to the minute. The term began to mark mystification in the face of what is new: statements like, 'this book is postmodern (whatever that might mean . . .)', have become useful ways of hedging one's bets in a culture that seems far less certain of the status of its critical judgements than it did a decade ago.

However, the postmodern has always been much more than a journalistic term. Indeed, the media frenzy about postmodernism has frequently served to cover up the complex and important critical work that is being done on postmodern culture in a range of humanities disciplines. The idea of the postmodern that tends to prevail in media discussions is one based purely on a model of artistic production. In this model, postmodernism is the latest aesthetic movement that follows on from modernism and is more experi-mental, more self-knowing, more fashionable, than the work of people like Virginia Woolf or James Joyce, who themselves came to transform the realism of nineteenth-century art.[1] Such fashion-based ideas of postmodern-ism fail to address the deeper and more radical changes that are taking place in the world today.

This idea of a purely stylistic postmodernism also tends to efface the work of writers in other areas of the humanities such as history, sociology, politics, philosophy and anthropology. In contradistinction to postmodernism, a notion of postmodernity has come to be important in all of these areas, challenging traditional means of thinking about the subject matter of each of the disciplines and breaking down some of the boundaries between them. There is a tendency to differentiate between postmodernism as an artistic movement and postmodernity as the general social condition that is studied in these disciplines. In the latter case, postmodernity marks the transformation that has taken place in society during the last few decades with the rise of new forms of capitalism, the development of communications technology such as the internet, the collapse of the Soviet Union which saw the end of the Cold War, and the emergence of voices from different cultures to disrupt the traditional white, male, European ideas of a universal human nature referred to as mankind or simply 'Man'.[2]

However, any strong opposition between postmodernism and postmodernity is probably too reductive because it splits artistic and cultural movements off from the society in which they are produced, and presents them as separate areas of interest in a way that practically all of the writers contained in this book set out to challenge. As Fredric Jameson writes in the third essay in this volume, the postmodern 'is not just another word for the description of a particular style. It is also . . . a periodising concept whose function is to correlate the emergence of new formal features in culture with the emergence of a new type of social life and a new economic order'.[3] One of the issues at stake in many of the essays, then, is how we might relate this cultural style to society, postmodernism to postmodernity, in a useful and productive way. These attempts to describe the links between artistic presentation and contemporary society have led thinkers to describe the postmodern as, variously, a 'condition', a 'cultural dominant' and a 'new horizon of our cultural, philosophical and political experience'.[4] In other words, in all of these cases, the postmodern concerns the way the world is for us now, both its social and political structures and also the means we might use to represent them. Instead of thinking of postmodernism as just a style and postmodernity as the state of everything else in the world, then, the essays in this book discuss the ramifications of the ways in which the two terms come together to form a complex postmodern condition that has a transformative effect across the whole range of arts and humanities disciplines.

The ideas of postmodernism and postmodernity that are prevalent in everyday culture, and which the media often use as labels to attach to anything new or different, are thus too reductive. They often function as a shorthand that covers over rather than opens up the important, complex and exciting issues that face today's culture. In order to engage with contemporary critical thought, a more nuanced idea of the postmodern is indispensable, and that is what this book sets out to provide.

But what is the postmodern? And how does it relate to the world in which we live today? As the different definitions offered by the essays included in this book will make clear, 'postmodern' is a very difficult term to pin down.

However, a crucial aspect of what is at stake for both postmodernism and postmodernity (which also provides some useful links between the two terms) is a transformation in the nature and status of narrative.

NARRATIVE AND METANARRATIVE

In the words of Jean-François Lyotard, one of the most important and influential writers about postmodernism, 'Simplifying to the extreme, I define *postmodern* as incredulity toward metanarratives'.[5] Despite the fact that Lyotard is 'simplifying', this is a complex idea. It is vitally important, though: at least in its 'simplified' form, this idea is shared by almost all of the writers whose work is included in this book, although the conclusions that each draws from it are very different. But what does it mean? What is a 'metanarrative'? And why do postmodernists distrust them?

A narrative recounts a series of events, tying together things that happen in order to present them in the form of a story. Although commonly associated with fiction, narratives also engage with events that actually take place: historical accounts of anything from agricultural crop rotation to the independence struggles of emerging nations in Africa are related as series of events linked to form narratives. In a similar manner, philosophical ideas such as René Descartes' 'I think, therefore I am' are presented as conclusions drawn from series of premises tied together by the causal links of a narrative sequence. Scientific and political studies such as Charles Darwin's *On the Origin of Species* or Karl Marx's and Friedrich Engels' *The Communist Manifesto* present their arguments and insights in the form of a narrative, in these cases as stories either of evolution or revolution. Even the stories that we tell about ourselves, or that others tell about us, are governed by narrative structures. Sigmund Freud's psychoanalysis, often referred to as the 'talking cure', is based on the process of a patient relating the story of the symptoms of his or her illness to the analyst: they describe their childhood, their dreams and experiences, and it is through the gaps in these narratives that repressed unconscious desires come to light. In this sense, it is through narrative that we gain ideas of who we are and an understanding of the world in which we live.

In each of the examples I have given, there are sets of rules that determine the form in which the events that are narrated should be linked together in order that the story can be told. These rules might take the form of logical progression in philosophy, temporal development in history, free association in psychoanalysis or cause and effect in science. Different genres of writing have traditionally had different sets of rules to define how narrative is used.[6] For example, one might recall the difference between poetry and history that Aristotle describes in the *Poetics*:

the poet's function is not to describe what has actually happened, but the kinds of things that might happen, that is, that could happen because they are, in the circumstances, either possible or necessary. The difference between the historian and the poet is not that the one writes in prose and the other in verse... The difference is that one tells of what has happened, the other of the kinds of things that might happen.[7]

In other words, while the historical narrative draws together events that have happened, the links in the poet's narrative are based on the probability of one event leading to another – even if neither of those events have happened or could ever happen. Of course, in modern culture the relations between different genres (and perhaps particularly fiction and history) are much more complex than this, but each type of speech or writing will be subject to rules that determine whether it is constructed in a way that is legitimate for the genre in which it appears.

The name given to those sets of rules is metalanguage or metanarrative. So, in other words, a metanarrative is the collection of rules that determine whether a given statement or narrative is legitimate within a particular genre of discourse. For example, the statement 'My love is like a red, red rose' might be thought of as highly evocative and moving within poetic discourse, but would not be considered acceptable for a textbook on botany. And this is not just the case for academic writing. Anything we say, write or hear is produced according to metanarrative rules that determine whether it makes sense, or is well formed, or not. Lyotard describes the relationship between languages and metalanguages in the following way:

languages are not employed haphazardly, however. Their use is subject to a condition we call pragmatic: each must formulate its own rules and petition the addressee to accept them. To satisfy this condition, an axiomatic is defined that includes a definition of the symbols used in the proposed language, a description of the form expressions in this langugage must take in order to gain acceptance (well formed expressions), and an enumeration of the operations that may be performed on the accepted expressions (axioms in the narrow sense).[8]

A metanarrative thus sets out the axioms (the principles or laws) that allow communication to take place, and determines the legitimacy of a narrative for a particular genre, as well as giving the rules to determine its truth or falsity.

These metanarratives are not simply natural sets of rules, however. Different rules are set up at different points of history by different philosophies that have different political interests, and are constantly in the process of transformation as new discoveries or ways of thinking emerge. For example, the philosophy of science charts the developments of scientific discovery and lays down the rules for what might constitute a properly scientific explanation. And, of course, these rules change: in medieval times science was based on forms of religious belief that are no longer prevalent or even plausible for modern sciences; during the Renaissance alchemy was considered by many to be a branch of science, but no mainstream scientist would today consider the attempt to turn lead into gold a properly scientific area of investigation. With Newtonian physics and Einstein's principles of relativity (not to mention modern quantum physics or chaos theory) the rules of scientific discourse change again to take account of new discoveries and ways of approaching the world. And it is not only the contents of the narrative that change as science develops, what counts as a scientific argument, what can be true or false, even the nature of what is considered evidence is also tranformed. In this way, the rules of the scientific metalanguage alter both the formal criteria for science and also the way in which science presents the world itself.

MODERNITY AND THE GRAND NARRATIVE

The idea that metanarratives develop as history progresses is the central tenet of what many of the writers in this book refer to as modernity. This idea is what allows Lyotard to distinguish between modernity and what he calls the 'classical age' which is based on 'the way that myth organises and distributes time, creating a rhythm of the beginning and end of the story it recounts, to the point of making them rhyme'.[9] Modernity, then, is based on the idea of progressive changes in the rules of narrative, whereas the classical age is constructed by the mythical narratives of a continual return to the same in which there is no historical development of metanarratives, just the continuous present of mythical time. Because of this notion of continual progressive change and development, modernity is frequently described as the period of the 'grand narrative'. According to Jürgen Habermas, 'modernity expresses the conviction that the future has already begun: It is the epoch that lives for the future, that opens itself up to the novelty of the future'.[10] If modernity is based on the idea that the world is in a constant state of change and progress, its aim is to generate a philosophical account of this change that will bring together the diverse events and experiences under the auspices of a grand narrative capable of presenting a link between the past, present and future. In the words of Immanuel Kant,

> Since the philosopher cannot presuppose any [conscious] individual purpose among men in their great drama, there is no other expedient for him except to try to see if he can discover a natural purpose in this idiotic

course of things human. In keeping with this purpose, it might be possible to have a history with a definite natural plan for creatures who have no plan of their own.[11]

For Kant then, human society, although potentially rational, is not so yet, and the task of the philosopher is to provide a 'definite natural plan' that will illustrate and explain how all of the confusing and apparently accidental events in the world make sense as part of a greater scheme of things. This approach to the world, which seeks a plan that will bring the past and present together in order to project a destiny for society in the future, is the basis of each of the different grand narratives of modernity.

But what exactly is a grand narrative? A grand narrative tells the story of the progress and development of narratives. If metanarratives give the formal rules for the legitimation of narratives, grand narratives legitimate their contents in relation to an overarching theme or idea. Thus, according to Lyotard, the term 'modernity' designates

> any science [in the widest sense meaning any system of knowledge] that legitimates itself with reference to a metanarrative of this kind making an explicit appeal to some grand narrative, such as the dialectics of Spirit, the hermeneutics of meaning, the emancipation of the rational or working subject, or the creation of wealth.[12]

The grand narratives that set up the links between different narratives produce the idea of progress that is the basis of history for modernity. Grand narratives tie everything together under a scheme that sets out to explain the world and people's place in it. One example of a grand narrative might be found in the Christian Bible, which sets out a version of the history of the world and predicts a future for humanity. In a grossly simplified form, it runs as follows: in the beginning God creates the world and humanity; after the original sin there is a fall from grace that is resolved through the teachings and martyrdom of Christ, and the possibility of redemption is held out with the idea of a second coming and the kingdom of Heaven on Earth.[13] Not only does this grand narrative give a history of the world, it provides a series of premises for interpreting events and sets out rules for behaviour that differentiate good from evil. In other words, it sets up the subject's place in the world, providing a system of beliefs and knowledges that will interpret anything that might happen. Other grand narratives include not only different religious systems, but political discourses from Marxism to liberalism or even fascism, and systems of ideas from Enlightenment philosophy to Darwinian evolution. Each of these produces a grand narrative according to which all other narratives can be interpreted and evaluated, albeit a very different one in each case, and gives a particular account of how the world works and how people should behave in it.

If modernity is the age of the grand narrative, the differences between the competing grand narratives set up different accounts of what, specifically, modernity is. It is therefore difficult to give, for example, a precise date when modernity begins, as different grand narratives locate its origin at different times. Some describe modernity as the Christian era that finds its first inter-preter in St Augustine during the fourth century.[14] Modernity has also been said to begin during the Renaissance with the idea of perspective in art and the birth of the modern subject in Descartes' philosophy which, combined with Copernicus' discovery that the Earth moves around the Sun, cast doubt on men's and women's image of themselves as at the centre of a created uni-verse.[15] Alternatively, it has been argued that modernity really gets underway at the beginning of the nineteenth century with the American, French and industrial revolutions, and their impact on the philosophies of Immanuel Kant and G. W. F. Hegel.[16] In any of these cases, and it is difficult to decide between them, the central feature of modernity in its broadest sense is the idea of a grand narrative of progress, whether it is Christian providence, scientific discovery or revolutionary upheaval. The narratives and metanarratives that construct experience are thereby given a historical, philosophical and political justification as being parts of a grand scheme of human development.

So, to recap briefly: the events, feelings and experiences that make up our lives are thought, described and even experienced in and as narratives. The rules of these narratives are given by metanarratives that indicate the sorts of statement that are legitimate for a particular narrative genre. The grand narratives of progress draw together all of the narratives and metanarratives in order to construct a historical, moral and political view of the world in which we live. Together, these three forms of narrative present the world to us, and are the basis from which knowledge, morality, identity, politics and freedom develop.

However, the postmodern marks a point at which the structure of the relationship between the narrative forms is called into question. To cite just one example of this idea, Jean-Luc Nancy's, with postmodernity the 'age of the grand narrative' has come to an end:

> history can no longer be presented as ... a 'grand narrative', the narrative of some grand, collective destiny of mankind (of Humanity, of Liberty, etc.), a narrative that was grand because it was great, and that was great because its ultimate destination was considered good. Our time is the time, when this history at least has been suspended: total war, genocide, the challenge of nuclear powers, implacable technology, hunger, and absolute misery, all these are, at the least, evident signs of self-destroying mankind, of self-annihilating history.[17]

This is a bleak view of the present, but Nancy's point about the death of the grand narratives that set up systems of beliefs and goals for the progress of the human race is indicative of the condition that the writers in this book will refer to as postmodernity. The question arises, then, what is this postmodernity? What is it that Lyotard identifies when he describes the postmodern as 'incredulity toward metanarratives'?

THE POSTMODERN CRISIS IN NARRATIVE

In relation to the overall structure of narrative that I have been setting out, metanarratives function like the keystone of an arch: the world-view that connects the particular, individual narratives that make up people's everyday experience to the universal grand narratives of modernity rests on the link that metanarratives form between the two. If these metanarratives arouse incredulity because they seem no longer to function adequately in postmodernity, then the whole structure of this arch is threatened with collapse because the link between individual events and the grand schemes of providence or progress has become uncertain. If this is the case, then the postmodern 'incredulity towards metanarratives' marks a radical transformation of the way human beings understand and relate to the world.

Just as there is little agreement about the date when modernity begins, the identification of a postmodern period is also problematic. For thinkers such as Jameson, postmodernism is the culture that comes into being with the development of the 'late capitalism' of multinational corporations and free-market economies in the West since the end of the Second World War. For Jean Baudrillard and others, it emerges with the developments in communications technology that have taken place during the last 20 years. However, for writers like Lyotard, the postmodern is less a period of history than a disruption of the historical periodisation of modernity's grand narratives. According to Diane Elam,

> Postmodernism does not simply happen after modernism but is a series of problems present to modernism in its continuing infancy... postmodernity is a rewriting of modernity, which has already been active *within* modernity for a long time. The 'post' (the effect) is already part of that to which it is 'post', is already contained within the supposed moment of historical cause (modernity).[18]

In this sense, modernity and postmodernity become difficult to separate along straightforward historical lines. Instead, they mark different responses to the whole problem of historical change and whether history can be usefully described in terms of the progress of a grand narrative. Modernity and the postmodern stand for different sets of approaches to the problems that face society, different political and philosophical perspectives about the state of the world. Regardless of whether one wants to follow Jameson, Baudrillard or Lyotard, or even move between the three perspectives, what is certain is that the postmodern crisis in narratives is a key aspect of many people's experience of the world today.

What might this incredulity towards metanarratives mean for the way we think about contemporary culture, though? And where does it come from? It is the different responses to these questions that mark the site of dispute that this book will cover. The consequences of each of the responses to the crisis in metanarratives are often very different: the ideas of subjectivity, politics, history and meaning which emerge from alternative readings of the crisis can lead in wholly different directions in the hands of each of the various writers. For some, the postmodern is a profoundly troubling development that has undermined traditional radical politics and leaves little room to struggle for a more egalitarian society in the future. This account of postmodernity is frequently a target for Marxist writers, who see it as a threat to socialist politics.[19] However, for others, the disruption of the rules of narrative allows new possibilities to emerge that were hidden by traditional ways of explaining the world, and new voices to be heard that were silenced in the grand narratives of modernity. This approach has been of particular interest to writers who set out to challenge universal concepts such as 'Man' from either feminist or postcolonial perspectives. Rather than taking sides, *Postmodern Debates* contains essays that approach postmodernity from either side of this problem. Its aim is to encourage readers to think through the issues for themselves and make their own minds up about an effective politics for the postmodern world.

This book is organised around a series of issues that form some of the central concerns of contemporary cultural theorists. The opening section contains four essays that make competing claims about what the postmodern is and whether it has radical or reactionary implications: Lyotard points to its potential to challenge traditional dogmas and open up new forms of politics, whereas Jameson and Jürgen Habermas remain sceptical about its complicity with capitalism. There are then a series of debates between different writers about the political implications postmodern theories have for specific contemporary issues. First, Baudrillard and Jacques Derrida present different accounts of the politics of representation in the aftermath of the Gulf War. Terry Eagleton and Richard Rorty discuss the importance of a concept of ideology for contemporary thought. Linda Hutcheon, Judith Butler and Alice Jardine present a series of different propositions and raise some crucial questions about the relationships between modernity, postmodernity and gender. bell hooks and Homi K. Bhabha then propose alternative accounts of whether the postmodern can provide a useful ground to challenge colonial and racial prejudice in today's world. In the final essay in the book, Ernesto Laclau produces a comprehensive discussion of the political potential of postmodernism which, rather than providing a conclusion, is itself in debate with the different ideas presented in the earlier chapters.

2

A Postmodern Fable

Jean-François Lyotard

'What a Human and his/her Brain – or rather the Brain and its Human – would resemble at the moment when they leave the planet forever, before its destruction; that, the story does not tell.'

So ends the fable we are about to hear.

The Sun is going to explode. The entire solar system, including the little planet Earth, will be transformed into a giant nova. Four and a half billion solar years have elapsed since the time this fable was told. The end of history has already been foreseen since that time.

Is this truly a fable? The lifetime of a star can be determined scientifically. A star is a furnace in the void that transforms elements by consuming them. Hence, a laboratory too. The furnace ends by extinguishing itself. The glare of the furnace can be analysed and its composition defined. It can thus be stated when the furnace will extinguish itself. So it is with that star called the Sun. The narrative of the end of the Earth is not in itself fictional, it's really rather realistic.

What the final words of this story cause us to ponder is not that the Earth will disappear with the Sun, but that something ought to escape the conflagration of the system and its ashes. And it's also that the fable hesitates to name the thing that ought to survive: is it the Human and his/her Brain, or the Brain and its Human? And, finally, how are we to understand the '*ought to escape*'? Is it a need, an obligation, an eventuality?

This uncertainty is no less realistic than the prediction of its coming to pass.

You can see the immense work yard the Earth will be for millennia prior to the Sun's death. Humanity, whatever might still be calling itself Humanity at that time, is meticulously preparing spaceships for the exodus. It has launched an entire hinterland of satellite stations to serve as relay points. It aims missiles. Over thousands of centuries, it draws up embarkation operations.

You can see the antlike busyness with some realism because some of the means are already realisable at the time the fable is told. There remain, there only remain, a few billion solar years to realise the other means. And, in particular, to make it so that what are today called human beings are capable of realising them. There remains much to be done, human beings *must* change a lot to get there. The fable says that they can get there (eventuality), that they are urged on to do it (need), that doing it is in their interest (obligation). But the fable cannot say what human beings will have become then.

Here, at present, is what the fable said:

'In the immensity of the cosmos, it happened that the energy distributed by chance into particles regrouped here and there into bodies. These bodies constituted isolated systems, galaxies, stars. They disposed of a finite quantity of energy. They used this energy to maintain themselves as stable systems. They never ceased transforming the particles of which they were made, thereby freeing new particles, especially photons and heat. But deprived of assignable energy, these systems were doomed to disappear in time. Energy came to be lacking. Distributed in them in a differential way to permit the work of transformation and the survival of the whole, the energy disorganised, returned to its most probable state, chaos, and spread out haphazardly into space. This process had already been identified for a long time under the name of entropy.

'In a minute part of the cosmic immensity, there was a minute galactic system named the Milky Way. And in the midst of the billions of stars that made it up, there was one star, called the Sun. Like all the closed systems, the Sun emitted heat, light, and radiation in the direction of the planets, over which it exerted its gravitational attraction. And as for all the closed systems, the life expectancy of the Sun was limited by entropy. At the time the fable was told, the Sun had more or less reached the midpoint of its life. It still had four and a half billion years before it would disappear.

'Among the planets, there was the Earth. And something unexpected took place on the surface of the Earth. Thanks to the fortuitous conjugation of various forms of energy – the molecules making up the elements of the Earth, especially water, the filtering of solar radiation by the atmosphere, the fluctuating temperature – it happened that more complex and more improbable systems (cells) synthesised themselves out of molecular systems. This was the first event whose enigmatic occurrence would condition the rest of the story, and even the possibility of its being recounted. The formation of so-called living cells meant, in effect, that differentiated systems of a certain order, the mineral realm, could under certain conditions, such as those then existing on the Earth's surface, produce differentiated systems of a higher order, the first algae. A process contrary to entropy was therefore possible.

'An especially remarkable sign of the complexifying represented by single-celled creatures was their ability to reproduce themselves by dividing into two parts almost identical to the original but independent of it. What was called scissiparity seemed to assure the perpetuation of single-celled systems in general, despite the disappearance of individuals.

'This is how life and death were born. As opposed to molecules, living systems were obligated, in order to survive, to consume external energy in a regular fashion (metabolism). On the one hand, this dependence made them extremely fragile, since they lived under the threat of a lack of energy appropriate for their metabolism. On the other hand, through this rush of external energy, they found themselves exempt from eventually disappearing, the predictable fate of isolated systems. Their life expectancy could be "negotiated", at least within certain limits.

'Another event came to affect living systems: sexual reproduction. This reproductive procedure was much more improbable than scissiparity, but it allowed the offspring to differ a lot more from their progenitors, since their ontogenesis proceeded from the more or less aleatory combination of two distinct genetic codes. The margin of uncertainty widened with each succeeding generation. Unexpected events had a greater chance of being produced. In particular, a "misreading" of the parental codes could give rise to genetic mutations.

'As for the following sequence in this story, it had already been recounted by a certain Mr Darwin. What he called evolution was remarkable in that it supposed no finality – no more than did the preceding sequence (which had led from physics to biology) – only the principle of the mechanical selection of the best "adapted" systems. New living systems would appear by chance. They found themselves confronted by the systems that were already existing, since all of them had to procure energy to survive. With energy sources being of a limited quantity, competition between systems was inevitable. So was born war. The most efficient systems had the best chances of being selected, mechanically.

'And so it was after some time (very brief by the standard of the astronomical clock) that the system called Humankind was selected. This was an extremely unlikely system – and exactly as unlikely as it is for a four-legged creature to stand up on the soles of its rear paws. The immediate implications of this stance are known: the hands are freed for grasping, the cranial cavity restores its balance along the vertical axis, offering a more spacious volume for the brain, the mass of cortical neurons grows and is diversified. Complex corporeal skills (*techniques*), especially manual ones, appeared at the same time as those symbolic skills we call human languages. These skills were supple and efficient prostheses that allowed the Human system, so unlikely and so precarious, to compensate for its weakness in the face of its adversaries.

'Along with these skills, something happened that was just as unexpected as what had happened with the appearance of single-celled life, which was endowed with the ability to reproduce by itself. In the same way, symbolic language, thanks to its recursiveness, had the ability to recombine its elements infinitely while still making sense, that is, giving something to think and to act upon. Symbolic language, being self-referential, had moreover the capacity to take itself as its own object, hence to provide its own memory and critique. Supported by these properties of language, material technique in turn underwent a mutation: it could refer to itself, build on itself, and improve its performance.

'Moreover, language allows humans to inflect the initially rigid (almost instinctual) forms by which they lived together in early communities. Less likely forms of organisation, each one different from the others, were born. They entered into competition. As for every living system, their success depended on their aptitude to discover, capture, and safeguard the energy sources they needed. In this regard, two great events marked the history of human communities, the Neolithic revolution and the Industrial Revolution. Each discovered new energy sources and new means of exploiting them, thereby affecting the structure of the social systems.

'For a long time (if you count in human time), techniques and collective institutions appeared by chance. The survival of the unlikely and fragile systems that were human groups thus remained out of their control. So it is that it happened that the most sophisticated techniques were considered as curiosities and neglected to the point of falling into oblivion. It also happened that communities that were more differentiated than others in political or economic matters were defeated by simpler but more vigorous systems (as had been the case among living species).

'Just as the properties of symbolic language allowed material skills to be conserved, corrected, and optimised in their efficiency, so it was with the modes of social organisation. The task of assuring the survival of communities required the ability to control the external or internal events that might strike a blow at their provisions of energy. Instances of authority, charged with this control, appeared in the social, economic, political, cognitive, and cultural fields.

'After a time, it happened that the systems labelled liberal democratic showed themselves to be the most appropriate at exercising these regulations. They in effect left the control programmes open to debate, they in principle allowed each unity to accede to decision functions, they thereby maximised the quantity of human energy useful to the systems. This flexibility turned out in the long run to be more efficient than the rigid fixation of roles in stable hierarchies. In opposition to the closed systems that had emerged in the course of human history, liberal democracies in their very core admitted a kind of competition between the units in the system. This space favoured the blossoming forth of new material, symbolic, and communitarian techniques. Of course, there thus resulted frequent crises that were sometimes dangerous for the survival of these systems. But, on the whole, the performativity of the latter found itself increased. This process was called progress. It induced an eschatological representation of the history of human systems.

'In the long run, the open systems won out completely over all the other systems (human, organic, and physical) locked in struggle on the surface of the planet Earth. Nothing appeared able to stop, or even guide, their development. Crises, wars, revolutions contributed to accelerate all this, especially by giving access to new sources of energy and by establishing new control over their exploitation. It even became necessary that the open systems temper their success over other systems in order to preserve the ensemble called an ecosystem from a catastrophic deregulation.

'Only the ineluctable disappearance of the entire solar system seemed like it ought to check the pursuit of development. In response to this challenge, the system already (at the time the fable was told) had begun to develop prostheses able to perpetuate it after the disappearance of the energy resources of solar origin that had contributed to the appearance and survival of living and, in particular, human systems.

'At the time this story was told, all research in progress was directed to this aim, that is, in a big lump: logic, econometrics and monetary theory, information theory, the physics of conductors, astrophysics and astronautics, genetic and dietetic biology and medicine, catastrophe theory, chaos theory, military strategy and ballistics, sports technology, systems theory, linguistics and potential literature. All of this research turns out, in fact, to be dedicated, closely or from afar, to testing and remodelling the so-called human body, or to replacing it, in such a way that the brain remains able to function with the aid only of the energy resources available in the cosmos. And so was prepared the final exodus of the negentropic system far from the Earth.

'What a Human and his/her Brain – or rather the Brain and its Human – would resemble at the moment when they leave the planet forever, before its destruction; that, the story does not say.'

Realism is the art of making reality, of knowing reality and knowing how to make reality. The story we just heard says that this art will still develop a lot in the future. Reality will be changed; making, knowing, and know-how will be changed. Between what we are and what the hero of the final exodus shall be, reality and the art of reality will have been at least as metamorphosed as they have been from the amoebae to us. The fable is realist because it recounts the story that makes, unmakes, and remakes reality. It is also realist because it takes note of the fact that this force has already greatly transformed reality and its art, and that, except for a catastrophe, this transformation ought to be pursued. It is realist, once more, insofar as it admits an inevitable obstacle to the pursuit of this transformation, the end of the solar system. Finally, is it realist when it predicts that this obstacle shall be overcome and that the force will evade disaster?

The fable tells the story of a conflict between two processes affecting energy. One leads to the destruction of every system, of every body, living or not, that exists on planet Earth and in the solar system. Inside this continuous and necessary entropic process, another process, contingent and discontinuous, at least for a long time, acts in the opposite direction through the increasing differentiation of these systems. The latter movement cannot put the brakes on the former (unless we find a way to furnish the Sun with motor fuel), but it can elude the catastrophe by abandoning its cosmic site, the solar system.

On Earth as elsewhere, entropy leads energy toward the most likely state, a kind of corpuscular *soup*, a cold chaos. Negative entropy combines energy, on the contrary, into differentiated systems, more complex ones, or let's say, more *developed* ones. Development is not an invention made by Humans. Humans are an invention of development. The hero of the fable is not the human species, but energy. The fable narrates a series of episodes marking now the success of what is most likely, death, and now the success of what is least likely and most precarious, and what is also the most efficient, the complex. It's a tragedy about energy. Like *Oedipus Rex*, it ends badly. Like *Oedipus at Colonus*, it admits a final remission.

The hero is not a subject. The word energy says nothing, except that there is some force. What happens to energy, its formation into systems, their death or survival, the appearance of more differentiated systems, it knows nothing and does not *want* any of it. It obeys blind, local laws and chance.

The human species is not the hero of the fable. It is a complex form of organising energy. Like the other forms, it is undoubtedly transitory. Other, more complex forms may appear that will win out over it. Perhaps one of these forms is preparing itself through techno-scientific development right from the time when the fable is being recounted. That's why the fable cannot begin to identify the system that will be the exile's hero. It can merely predict that this hero, if it succeeds in escaping the destruction of the solar system, *will have* to be more complex than the human species is at the time when the fable is being recounted, since this species does not then have the means of its exile, although it is the most complex organisation of energy we know in the Universe.

It will have to be more complex since it will have to be able to survive the destruction of the terrestrial context. It will not suffice for some living organism, in symbiosis with the specific energies it may find on Earth, that is to say, the human body, to continue to feed this system and especially the brain. It will have to be able to use directly the only forms of physical energy available in the cosmos: particles that are not already organised. That's why the fable lets it be understood that the exile's hero, destined to *survive* the destruction of terrestrial life, will not be a mere survivor, since it will not be alive in the sense we understand the word.

This condition is a necessary one, but at the time the fable is being recounted, no one can say how it will be met. There is uncertainty in this story because negative entropy acts in a contingent fashion and because the appearance of more complex systems – despite research and controls that are in themselves systematic – remain unforeseeable. This appearance can be facilitated but not ordered. One of the characteristics of the open systems the fable calls 'liberal democratic' is to leave open certain spaces of uncertainty that are apt to facilitate the appearance of more complex organisations, and this, in every realm. What we call research is a case, become trivial, of these spaces freed for invention and discovery. This case is itself the sign of a superior development, where necessity and chance are combined not only in the epistemological order, as Monod saw, but in the reality of a new alliance, in the terms of Prigogine and Isabelle Stengers. This alliance is not that of the objective with the subjective, but that of rule and chance, or of consecution and discontinuity.

Were there not such uncertain regions in the history of energy, the fable itself that tells this story would not be possible. For a fable is an organisation of language, and language is a very complex state of energy, a symbolic technical apparatus. Now, in order to be deployed, fabulation calls for a kind of spatio-temporal and material emptiness, in which linguistic energy is not invested in the direct constraints of its exploitation as making, knowing, and know-how.

In the fable, linguistic energy is expended for imagining. It therefore does fabricate a reality, that of the story it tells, but this reality is left in suspense with regard to its cognitive and technical use. It is exploited reflexively, that is, referred back to language in order to link on to its topic (which I am in the process of doing). This putting into suspense distinguishes poetics from practice and pragmatics. Fabulation maintains this reality in reserve and *apart* from its exploitation within the system. This reality is called imaginary. The existence of imaginary realities presupposes, in the system where it appears, zones that are neutralised, so to speak, in relation to the merely realist constraints of the said system's performativity. Rigid systems like a bent bow or even an instinctual programme (to borrow examples from living things we know) prohibit amoebae, sycamores, or eels from fabling, as a general rule.

Realism accepts and even requires the presence of the imaginary within it, and that the latter, far from being something foreign to reality, is one of its states, the nascent state. Science and technology themselves fable no less, and are no less poetic than painting, literature, or film. The only difference between them lies in the verification/falsification constraint of the hypothesis. The fable is a hypothesis that exempts itself from this constraint.

The fable we heard is neither recent nor original. But I claim that it is postmodern. Postmodern does not signify recent. It signifies how writing, in the broadest sense of thought and action, is situated after it has succumbed to the contagion of modernity and has tried to cure itself of it. Now, modernity is not recent either. It is not even an epoch. It is another state of writing, in the broad sense of the word.

The first traits of modernity can be seen to appear in the work done by Paul of Tarsis (the apostle), then by Augustine, to make an accommodation between the pagan classical tradition and Christian eschatology. A distinctive element of the modern imaginary is historicity, which is absent in the ancient imaginary. The moderns subordinate the legitimation of the collective subject called Europe or the West to the deployment of historical time. With Herodotus and Thucydides, Livy and Tacitus, the Ancients did, of course, invent *history* in opposition to myth and epic, the other narrative genres. And, on the other hand, with Aristotle, they elaborated the concept of *telos*, of the end as perfection, and teleological thinking. But eschatology, properly called, which governs the modern imaginary of historicity, is what the Christianity rethought by Paul and Augustine introduced into the core of Western thought. Eschatology recounts the experience of a subject affected by a lack, and prophesies that this experience will finish at the end of time with the remission of evil, the destruction of death, and the return to the Father's house, that is, to the full signifier.

Christian hope tied to this eschatology is regrounded in the rationality issuing from pagan classicism. It becomes reasonable to hope. And, reciprocally, Greek reason is transformed. It is no longer the equitable sharing of arguments between citizens deliberating over what must be thought and done in the ordeal of tragic destiny, political disorder, or ideological confusion. Modern reason is sharing with others, whoever they may be (slaves, women, immigrants), the experience proper to each of having sinned and having been acquitted. The ethics of *virtù* crown the ancient exercise of reason; that of *pardon*, its modern exercise. Classical consciousness is in conflict with the passionate disorders that shake up Mount Olympus. Modern consciousness, in full confidence, places its fate in the hands of a single just and good father.

This characterisation may appear too Christian. But over countless episodes, lay modernity maintains this temporal device, that of a 'great narrative', as one says, which *promises* at the end to reconcile the subject with itself and the overcoming of its separation. Although secularised, the Enlightenment narrative, Romanticist or speculative dialectics, and the Marxist narrative deploy the same historicity as Christianity, because they conserve the eschatological principle. The completion of history, be it always pushed back, will re-establish a full and whole relation with the law of the Other (capital *O*) as this relation was in the beginning: the law of God in the Christian paradise, the law of Nature in the natural right fantasised by Rousseau, the classless society, before family, property, and state, imagined by Engels. An immemorial past is always what turns out to be promised by way of an ultimate end. It is essential for the modern imaginary to project its legitimacy forward while founding it in a lost origin. Eschatology calls for an archaeology. This circle, which is also the hermeneutical circle, characterises *historicity* as the modern imaginary of time.

The fable we heard is a narrative, of course, but the history it recounts offers none of the principal traits of historicity.

First of all, it is a physical history, it is concerned only with energy and matter as a state of energy. Humankind is taken for a complex material system; consciousness, for an effect of language; and language, for a highly complex material system.

Then, the time that is put into play in this history is no more than diachrony. Succession is cut into clock units arbitrarily defined on the basis of supposedly uniform and regular physical movements. This time is not a temporality of consciousness that requires the past and the future, in their absence, to be nonetheless held as 'present' at the same time as the present. The fable admits such a temporality only for the systems endowed with symbolic language, which in effect allow memorisation and anticipation, that is, the presentifying of absence. As for the events ('it happened that...') that punctuate the fabulous history of energy, the latter neither awaits nor retains them.

In the third place, the end of this history is in no way directed toward the horizon of an emancipation. Of course, the end of the fable recounts the rescue of a very differentiated system, a kind of super-brain. That it can anticipate this outcome and prepare for it comes from the fact that it necessarily possesses a symbolic language of some sort, otherwise it would be less complex than our brain. The effect or the sentiment of a finality proceeds from this capacity of symbolic systems. They allow, of course, for more control of what comes to pass in the light of what has come to pass. But rather than a hermeneutic circle, the fable represents this effect as the result of a cybernetic loop regulated toward growth.

In the fourth place, for us today, the future the fable recounts in the past tense (not by chance) is not an object of hope. Hope is what belongs to a subject of history who promises him/herself – or to whom has been promised – a final perfection. The postmodern fable tells something completely different. The Human, or his/her brain, is a highly unlikely material (that is, energetic) formation. This formation is necessarily transitory since it is dependent on the conditions of terrestrial life, which are not eternal. The formation called Human or Brain will have been nothing more than an episode in the conflict between differentiation and entropy. The pursuit of greater complexity asks not for the perfecting of the Human, but its mutation or its defeat for the benefit of a better performing system. Humans are very mistaken in their presuming to be the motors of development and in confusing development with the progress of consciousness and civilisation. They are its products, vehicles, and witnesses. Even the criticisms they may make of development, its inequality, its inconsistency, its fatality, its inhumanity, even these criticisms are expressions of development and contribute to it. Revolution, wars, crises, deliberations, inventions, and discoveries are not the 'work of man' but effects and conditions of complexifying. These are always ambivalent for Humans, they bring them the best and the worst.

Without going any further, it can be seen clearly enough that the fable does not present the traits of a modern 'great narrative'. It does not respond to the demand for remission or emancipation. For lack of an eschatology, the conjugated mechanicalness and contingency of the story it tells leave thought suffering for lack of finality. This suffering is the postmodern state of thought, what is by agreement called in these times its crisis, its malaise, or its melancholia. The fable brings no remedy for this state, it proposes an explanation for it. An explanation is neither a legitimation nor a condemnation. The fable is unaware of good and evil. As for truth and falsehood, they are determined according to what is operational or not at the time judgement is made, under the regime of what has been called realism.

The *content* of the fable gives an explanation for the crisis, the fabulous narrative is by itself an expression of the crisis. The content, the meaning of what it is talking about, signifies the end of hopes (modernity's hell). The *form* of the narrative inscribes this content onto the narrative itself, reducing it in class to that of mere fable. A fable is exposed neither to argumentation nor to falsification. It is not even a critical discourse, but merely imaginary. This is how it exploits the space of indetermination the system keeps open for hypothetical thought.

This is also how it turns itself into the almost infantile expression of the crisis of thought today: the crisis of modernity, which is the state of postmodern thought. With no cognitive or ethico-political pretension, the fable grants itself a poetic or aesthetic status. It has worth only by its faithfulness to the postmodern affection, melancholia. It recounts its motive, first of all. But by the same token, every fable is melancholic, since it supplements reality.

It could be said that the fable we heard is the most pessimistic discourse the postmodern can hold forth about itself. It merely continues the discourses of Galileo, Darwin, and Freud: man is not the centre of the world, he is not the first (but the last) among creatures, he is not the master of discourse. All that's needed, in order for the fable to qualify as pessimistic, is the concept of an absolute evil, one that remains independent of the imaginaries produced by the human system.

But, after all, this fable asks not that it be believed, only that we reflect on it.

3

Postmodernism and Consumer Society

Fredric Jameson

The concept of postmodernism is not widely accepted or even understood today. Some of the resistance to it may come from the unfamiliarity of the works it covers, which can be found in all the arts: the poetry of John Ashbery, for instance, but also the much simpler talk poetry that came out of the reaction against complex, ironic, academic modernist poetry in the '60s; the reaction against modern architecture and in particular against the monumental buildings of the International Style, the pop buildings and decorated sheds celebrated by Robert Venturi in his manifesto, *Learning from Las Vegas*; Andy Warhol and Pop art, but also the more recent Photorealism; in music, the moment of John Cage but also the later synthesis of classical and 'popular' styles found in composers like Philip Glass and Terry Riley, and also punk and new-wave rock with such groups as the Clash, the Talking Heads and the Gang of Four; in film, everything that comes out of Godard – contemporary vanguard film and video – but also a whole new style of commercial or fiction films, which has its equivalent in contemporary novels as well, where the works of William Burroughs, Thomas Pynchon and Ishmael Reed on the one hand, and the French new novel on the other, are also to be numbered among the varieties of what can be called postmodernism.

This list would seem to make two things clear at once: first, most of the postmodernisms mentioned above emerge as specific reactions against the established forms of high modernism, against this or that dominant high modernism which conquered the university, the museum, the art gallery network, and the foundations. Those formerly subversive and embattled styles – Abstract Expressionism; the great modernist poetry of Pound, Eliot or Wallace Stevens; the International Style (Le Corbusier, Frank Lloyd Wright, Mies); Stravinsky; Joyce, Proust and Mann – felt to be scandalous or shocking by our grandparents are, for the generation which arrives at the gate in the 1960s, felt to be the establishment and the enemy – dead, stifling, canonical, the reified monuments one has to destroy to do anything new. This means that there will be as many different forms of postmodernism as there were high modernisms in place, since the former are at least initially specific and local reactions *against* those models. That obviously does not make the job of describing postmodernism as a coherent thing any easier, since the unity of this new impulse – if it has one – is given not in itself but in the very modernism it seeks to displace.

The second feature of this list of postmodernisms is the effacement in it of some key boundaries or separations, most notably the erosion of the older distinction between high culture and so-called mass or popular culture. This is perhaps the most distressing development of all from an academic stand-point, which has traditionally had a vested interest in preserving a realm of high or elite culture against the surrounding environment of philistinism, of schlock and kitsch, of TV series and *Reader's Digest* culture, and in transmit-ting difficult and complex skills of reading, listening and seeing to its initi-ates. But many of the newer postmodernisms have been fascinated precisely by that whole landscape of advertising and motels, of the Las Vegas strip, of the late show and Grade-B Hollywood film, of so-called paraliterature with its airport paperback categories of the gothic and the romance, the popular biography, the murder mystery and the science fiction or fantasy novel. They no longer 'quote' such 'texts' as a Joyce might have done, or a Mahler; they incorporate them, to the point where the line between high art and commer-cial forms seems increasingly difficult to draw.

A rather different indication of this effacement of the older categories of genre and discourse can be found in what is sometimes called contemporary theory. A generation ago there was still a technical discourse of professional philosophy – the great systems of Sartre or the phenomenologists, the work of Wittgenstein or analytical or common language philosophy – alongside which one could still distinguish that quite different discourse of the other academic disciplines – of political science, for example, or sociology or literary criticism. Today, increasingly, we have a kind of writing simply called 'theory' which is all or none of those things at once. This new kind of discourse, generally associated with France and so-called French theory, is becoming widespread and marks the end of philosophy as such. Is the work of Michel Foucault, for example, to be called philosophy, history, social theory or political science? It's undecidable, as they say nowadays; and I will suggest that such 'theoretical discourse' is also to be numbered among the manifestations of postmodernism.

Now I must say a word about the proper use of this concept: it is not just another word for the description of a particular style. It is also, at least in my use, a periodising concept whose function is to correlate the emergence of new formal features in culture with the emergence of a new type of social life and a new economic order – what is often euphemistically called modernisa-tion, postindustrial or consumer society, the society of the media or the spectacle, or multinational capitalism. This new moment of capitalism can be dated from the postwar boom in the United States in the late 1940s and early '50s or, in France, from the establishment of the Fifth Republic in 1958. The 1960s are in many ways the key transitional period, a period in which the new international order (neocolonialism, the Green Revolution, computerisation and electronic information) is at one and the same time set in place and is swept and shaken by its own internal contradictions and by external resistance. I want here to sketch a few of the ways in which the new postmodernism expresses the inner truth of that newly emergent social order of late capitalism, but will have to limit the description to only two of its significant features, which I will call pastiche and schizophrenia: they will give us a chance to sense the specificity of the postmodernist experience of space and time respectively.

One of the most significant features or practices in postmodernism today is pastiche. I must first explain this term, which people generally tend to confuse with or assimilate to that related verbal phenomenon called parody. Both pastiche and parody involve the imitation or, better still, the mimicry of other styles and particularly of the mannerisms and stylistic twitches of other styles. It is obvious that modern literature in general offers a very rich field for parody, since the great modern writers have all been defined by the invention or production of rather unique styles: think of the Faulknerian long sentence or of D. H. Lawrence's characteristic nature imagery; think of Wallace Stevens's peculiar way of using abstractions; think also of the mannerisms of the philosophers, of Heidegger for example, or Sartre; think of the musical styles of Mahler or Prokofiev. All of these styles, however different from each other, are comparable in this: each is quite unmistakable; once one is learned, it is not likely to be confused with something else.

Now parody capitalises on the uniqueness of these styles and seizes on their idiosyncrasies and eccentricities to produce an imitation which mocks the original. I won't say that the satiric impulse is conscious in all forms of parody. In any case, a good or great parodist has to have some secret sympathy for the original, just as a great mimic has to have the capacity to put himself/herself in the place of the person imitated. Still, the general effect of parody is – whether in sympathy or with malice – to cast ridicule on the private nature of these stylistic mannerisms and their excessiveness and eccentricity with respect to the way people normally speak or write. So there remains somewhere behind all parody the feeling that there is a linguistic norm in contrast to which the styles of the great modernists can be mocked.

But what would happen if one no longer believed in the existence of normal language, of ordinary speech, of the linguistic norm (the kind of clarity and communicative power celebrated by Orwell in his famous essay, say)? One could think of it in this way: perhaps the immense fragmentation and privatisation of modern literature – its explosion into a host of distinct private styles and mannerisms – foreshadows deeper and more general tendencies in social life as a whole. Supposing that modern art and modernism – far from being a kind of specialised aesthetic curiosity – actually anticipated social developments along these lines; supposing that in the decades since the emergence of the great modern styles society has itself begun to fragment in this way, each group coming to speak a curious private language of its own, each profession developing its private code or idiolect, and finally each individual coming to be a kind of linguistic island, separated from everyone else? But then in that case, the very possibility of any linguistic norm in terms of which one could ridicule private languages and idiosyncratic styles would vanish, and we would have nothing but stylistic diversity and heterogeneity.

That is the moment at which pastiche appears and parody has become impossible. Pastiche is, like parody, the imitation of a peculiar or unique style, the wearing of a stylistic mask, speech in a dead language: but it is a neutral practice of such mimicry, without parody's ulterior motive, without the satirical impulse, without laughter, without that still latent feeling that there exists something *normal* compared to which what is being imitated is rather comic. Pastiche is blank parody, parody that has lost its sense of humour: pastiche is to parody what that curious thing, the modern practice of a kind of blank irony, is to what Wayne Booth calls the stable and comic ironies of, say, the eighteenth century.

But now we need to introduce a new piece into this puzzle, which may help explain why classical modernism is a thing of the past and why postmodernism should have taken its place. This new component is what is generally called the 'death of the subject' or, to say it in more conventional language, the end of individualism as such. The great modernisms were, as we have said, predicated on the invention of a personal, private style, as unmistakable as your fingerprint, as incomparable as your own body. But this means that the modernist aesthetic is in some way organically linked to the conception of a unique self and private identity, a unique personality and individuality, which can be expected to generate its own unique vision of the world and to forge its own unique, unmistakable style.

Yet today, from any number of distinct perspectives, the social theorists, the psychoanalysts, even the linguists, not to speak of those of us who work in the area of culture and cultural and formal change, are all exploring the notion that that kind of individualism and personal identity is a thing of the past; that the old individual or individualist subject is 'dead'; and that one might even describe the concept of the unique individual and the theoretical basis of individualism as ideological. There are in fact two positions on all this, one of which is more radical than the other. The first one is content to say: yes, once upon a time, in the classic age of competitive capitalism, in the heyday of the nuclear family and the emergence of the bourgeoisie as the hegemonic social class, there was such a thing as individualism, as individual subjects. But today, in the age of corporate capitalism, of the so-called organisation man, of bureaucracies in business as well as in the state, of demographic explosion – today, that older bourgeois individual subject no longer exists.

Then there is a second position, the more radical of the two, what one might call the poststructuralist position. It adds: not only is the bourgeois individual subject a thing of the past, it is also a myth; it *never* really existed in the first place; there have never been autonomous subjects of that type. Rather, this construct is merely a philosophical and cultural mystification which sought to persuade people that they 'had' individual subjects and possessed this unique personal identity.

For our purposes, it is not particularly important to decide which of these positions is correct (or rather, which is more interesting and productive). What we have to retain from all this is rather an aesthetic dilemma: because if the experience and the ideology of the unique self, an experience and ideology which informed the stylistic practice of classical modernism, is over and done with, then it is no longer clear what the artists and writers of the present period are supposed to be doing. What is clear is merely that the older models – Picasso, Proust, T. S. Eliot – do not work any more (or are positively harmful), since nobody has that kind of unique private world and style to express any longer. And this is perhaps not merely a 'psychologic-al' matter: we also have to take into account the immense weight of seventy or eighty years of classical modernism itself. There is another sense in which the writers and artists of the present day will no longer be able to invent new styles and worlds – they've already been invented; only a limited number of combinations are possible; the most unique ones have been thought of already. So the weight of the whole modernist aesthetic tradition – now dead – also 'weighs like a nightmare on the brains of the living', as Marx said in another context.

Hence, once again, pastiche: in a world in which stylistic innovation is no longer possible, all that is left is to imitate dead styles, to speak through the masks and with the voices of the styles in the imaginary museum. But this means that contemporary or postmodernist art is going to be about art itself in a new kind of way; even more, it means that one of its essential messages will involve the necessary failure of art and the aesthetic, the failure of the new, the imprisonment in the past.

As this may seem very abstract, I want to give a few examples, one of which is so omnipresent that we rarely link it with the kinds of developments in high art discussed here. This particular practice of pastiche is not high-cultural but very much within mass culture, and it is generally known as the 'nostalgia film' (what the French neatly call *la mode rétro* – retrospective styling). We must conceive of this category in the broadest way: narrowly, no doubt, it consists merely of films about the past and about specific generational moments of that past. Thus, one of the inaugural films in this new 'genre' (if that's what it is) was Lucas's *American Graffiti*, which in 1973 set out to recapture all the atmosphere and stylistic peculiarities of the 1950s United States, the United States of the Eisenhower era. Polanski's great film *Chinatown* does something similar for the 1930s, as does Bertolucci's *The Conformist* for the Italian and European context of the same period, the fascist era in Italy; and so forth. We could go on listing these films for some time: why call them pastiche? Are they not rather work in the more traditional genre known as the historical film – work which can more simply be theorised by extrapolating that other well-known form which is the historical novel?

I have my reasons for thinking that we need new categories for such films. But let me first add some anomalies: supposing I suggested that *Star Wars* is also a nostalgia film. What could that mean? I presume we can agree that this is not a historical film about our own intergalactic past. Let me put it somewhat differently: one of the most important cultural experiences of the generations that grew up from the '30s to the '50s was the Saturday afternoon serial of the Buck Rogers type – alien villians, true American heroes, heroines in distress, the death ray or the doomsday box, and the cliffhanger at the end whose miraculous resolution was to be witnessed next Saturday afternoon. *Star Wars* reinvents this experience in the form of a pastiche: that is, there is no longer any point to a parody of such serials since they are long extinct. *Star Wars*, far from being a pointless satire of such now dead forms, satisfies a deep (might I even say repressed?) longing to experience them again: it is a complex object in which on some first level children and adolescents can take the adventures straight, while the adult public is able to gratify a deeper and more properly nostalgic desire to return to that older period and to live its strange old aesthetic artifacts through once again. This film is thus *metonymically* a historical or nostalgia film: unlike *American Graffiti*, it does not reinvent a picture of the past in its lived totality; rather, by reinventing the feel and shape of characteristic art objects of an older period (the serials), it seeks to reawaken a sense of the past associated with those objects. *Raiders of the Lost Ark*, meanwhile, occupies an intermediary position here: on some level it is *about* the '30s and '40s, but in reality it too conveys that period metonymically through its own characteristic adventure stories (which are no longer ours).

Now let me discuss another interesting anomaly which may take us further towards understanding nostalgia film in particular and pastiche generally. This one involves a recent film called *Body Heat*, which, as has abundantly been pointed out by the critics, is a kind of distant remake of *The Postman Always Rings Twice* or *Double Indemnity*. (The allusive and elusive plagiarism of older plots is, of course, also a feature of pastiche.) Now *Body Heat* is technically not a nostalgia film, since it takes place in a contemporary setting, in a little Florida village near Miami. On the other hand, this technical contemporaneity is most ambiguous indeed: the credits – always our first cue – are lettered and scripted in a '30s Art-Deco style which cannot but trigger nostalgic reactions (first to *Chinatown*, no doubt, and then beyond it to some more historical referent). Then the very style of the hero himself is ambiguous: William Hurt is a new star but has nothing of the distinctive style of the preceding generation of male superstars like Steve McQueen or even Jack Nicholson, or rather, his persona here is a kind of mix of their characteristics with an older role of the type generally associated with Clark Gable. So here too there is a faintly archaic feel to all this. The spectator begins to wonder why this story, which could have been situated anywhere, is set in a small Florida town, in spite of its contemporary reference. One begins to realise after a while that the small town setting has a crucial strategic function: it allows the film to do without most of the signals and references which we might associate with the contemporary world, with consumer society – the appliances and artifacts, the high rises, the object world of late capitalism. Technically, then, its objects (its cars, for instance) are 1980s products, but everything in the film conspires to blur that immediate contemporary reference and to make it possible to receive this too as nostalgia work – as a narrative set in some indefinable nostalgic past, an eternal '30s, say, beyond history. It seems to me exceedingly symptomatic to find the very style of nostalgia films invading and colonising even those movies today which have contemporary settings: as though, for some reason, we were unable today to focus our own present, as though we have become incapable of achieving aesthetic representations of our own current experience. But if that is so, then it is a terrible indictment of consumer capitalism itself – or at the very least, an alarming and pathological symptom of a society that has become incapable of dealing with time and history.

So now we come back to the question of why nostalgia film or pastiche is to be considered different from the older historical novel or film (I should also include in this discussion the major literary example of all this, to my mind the novels of E. L. Doctorow – *Ragtime*, with its turn-of-the-century atmosphere, and *Loon Lake*, for the most part about our 1930s. But these are, to my mind, historical novels in appearance only. Doctorow is a serious artist and one of the few genuinely Left or radical novelists at work today. It is no disservice to him, however, to suggest that his narratives do not represent our historical past so much as they represent our ideas or cultural stereotypes about that past.) Cultural production has been driven back inside the mind, within the monadic subject: it can no longer look directly out of its eyes at the real world for the referent but must, as in Plato's cave, trace its mental images of the world on its confining walls. If there is any realism left here, it is a 'realism' which springs from the shock of grasping that confinement and of realising that, for whatever peculiar reasons, we seem condemned to seek the historical past through our own pop images and stereotypes about that past, which itself remains forever out of reach.

I now want to turn to what I see as the second basic feature of postmodernism, namely its peculiar way with time – which one could call 'textuality' or 'écriture' but which I have found it useful to discuss in terms of current theories of schizophrenia. I hasten to forestall any number of possible misconceptions about my use of this word: it is meant to be descriptive and not diagnostic. I am very far indeed from believing that any of the most significant postmodernist artists – John Cage, John Ashbery, Philippe Sollers, Robert Wilson, Andy Warhol, Ishmael Reed, Michael Snow, even Samuel Beckett himself – are in any sense schizophrenics. Nor is the point some culture-and-personality diagnosis of our society and its art: there are, one would think, far more damaging things to be said about our social system than are available by the use of pop psychology. I'm not even sure that the view of schizophrenia I'm about to outline – a view largely developed in the work of the French psychoanalyst Jacques Lacan – is clinically accurate; but that doesn't matter either, for my purposes.

The originality of Lacan's thought in this area is to have considered schizophrenia essentially as a language disorder and to have linked schizophrenic experience to a whole view of language acquisition as the fundamental missing link in the Freudian conception of the formation of the mature psyche. He does this by giving us a linguistic version of the Oedipus complex in which the Oedipal rivalry is described in terms not of the biological individual who is the rival for the mother's attention, but rather of what he calls the Name-of-the-Father, paternal authority now considered as linguistic function. What we need to retain from this is the idea that psychosis, and more particularly schizophrenia, emerges from the failure of the infant to accede fully into the realm of speech and language.

As for language, Lacan's model is the now orthodox structuralist one, which is based on a conception of a linguistic sign as having two (or perhaps three) components. A sign, a word, a text, is here modelled as a relationship between a signifier – a material object, the sound of a word, the script of a text – and a signified, the *meaning* of that material word or material text. The third component would be the so-called 'referent', the 'real' object in the 'real' world to which the sign refers – the real cat as opposed to the concept of a cat or the sound 'cat'. But for structuralism in general there has been a tendency to feel that reference is a kind of myth, that one can no longer talk about the 'real' in that external or objective way. So we are left with the sign itself and its two components. Meanwhile, the other thrust of structuralism has been to try to dispel the old conception of language as naming (e.g., God gave Adam language in order to name the beasts and plants in the Garden), which involves a one-to-one correspondence between a signifier and a signified. Taking a structural view, one comes quite rightly to feel that sentences don't work that way: we don't translate the individual signifiers or words that make up a sentence back into their signifieds on a one-to-one basis. Rather, we read the whole sentence, and it is from the interrelationship of its words or signifiers that a more global meaning – now called a 'meaning-effect' – is derived. The signified – maybe even the illusion or the mirage of the signified and of meaning in general – is an effect produced by the interrelationship of material signifiers.

All of this puts us in the position of grasping schizophrenia as the breakdown of the relationship between signifiers. For Lacan, the experience of temporality, human time, past, present, memory, the persistence of personal identity over months and years – this existential or experiential feeling of time itself – is also an effect of language. It is because language has a past and a future, because the sentence moves in time, that we can have what seems to us a concrete or lived experience of time. But since the schizophrenic does not know language articulation in that way, he or she does not have our experience of temporal continuity either, but is condemned to live a perpetual present with which the various moments of his or her past have little connection and for which there is no conceivable future on the horizon. In other words, schizophrenic experience is an experience of isolated, disconnected, discontinuous material signifiers which fail to link up into a coherent sequence. The schizophrenic thus does not know personal identity in our sense, since our feeling of identity depends on our sense of the persistence of the 'I' and the 'me' over time.

On the other hand, the schizophrenic will clearly have a far more intense experience of any given present of the world than we do, since our own present is always part of some larger set of projects which force us selectively to focus our perceptions. We do not, in other words, simply globally receive the outside world as an undifferentiated vision: we are always engaged in using it, in threading certain paths through it, in attending to this or that object or person within it. The schizophrenic, however, is not only 'no one' in the sense of having no personal identity; he or she also does nothing, since to have a project means to be able to commit oneself to a certain continuity over time. The schizophrenic is thus given over to an undifferentiated vision of the world in the present, a by no means pleasant experience:

I remember very well the day it happened. We were staying in the country and I had gone for a walk alone as I did now and then. Suddenly, as I was passing the school, I heard a German song; the children were having a singing lesson. I stopped to listen, and at that instant a strange feeling came over me, a feeling hard to analyze but akin to something I was to know too well later – a disturbing sense of unreality. It seemed to me that I no longer recognized the school, it had become as large as a barracks; the singing children were prisoners, compelled to sing. It was as though the school and the children's song were apart from the rest of the world. At the same time my eye encountered a field of wheat whose limits I could not see. The yellow vastness, dazzling in the sun, bound up with the song of the children imprisoned in the smooth stone school-barracks, filled me with such anxiety that I broke into sobs. I ran home to our garden and began to play 'to make things seem as they usually were', that is, to return to reality. It was the first appearance of those elements which were always present in later sensations of unreality: illimitable vastness, brilliant light, and the gloss and smoothness of material things.[1]

Note that as temporal continuities break down, the experience of the present becomes powerfully, overwhelmingly vivid and 'material': the world comes before the schizophrenic with heightened intensity, bearing a mysterious and oppressive charge of affect, glowing with hallucinatory energy. But what might for us seem a desirable experience – an increase in our perceptions, a libidinal or hallucinogenic intensification of our normally humdrum and familiar surroundings – is here felt as loss, as 'unreality'.

What I want to underscore, however, is precisely the way in which the signifier in isolation becomes ever more material – or, better still, *literal* – ever more vivid in sensory ways, whether the new experience is attractive or terrifying. We can show the same thing in the realm of language: what the schizophrenic breakdown of language does to the individual words that remain behind is to reorient the subject or the speaker to a more literalising attention towards those words. Again, in normal speech, we try to see through the materiality of words (their strange sounds and printed appearance, my voice timbre and peculiar accent, and so forth) towards their meaning. As meaning is lost, the materiality of words becomes obsessive, as is the case when children repeat a word over and over again until its sense is lost and it becomes an incomprehensible incantation. To begin to link up with our earlier description, a signifier that has lost its signified has thereby been transformed into an image.

This long digression on schizophrenia has allowed us to add a feature that we could not quite handle in our earlier description – namely time itself. We must therefore now shift our discussion of postmodernism from the visual arts to the temporal ones – to music, poetry and certain kinds of narrative texts like those of Beckett. Anyone who has listened to John Cage's music may well have had an experience similar to those just evoked: frustration and desperation – the hearing of a single chord or note followed by a silence so long that memory cannot hold on to what went before, a silence then banished into oblivion by a new strange sonorous present which itself disappears. This experience could be illustrated by many forms of cultural production today. I have chosen a text by a younger poet, partly because his 'group' or 'school' – known as the Language Poets – has in many ways made the experience of temporal discontinuity – the experience described here in terms of schizophrenic language – central to their language experiments and to what they like to call the 'New Sentence'. This is a poem called 'China' by Bob Perelman (it can be found in his recent collection *Primer*, published by This Press in Berkeley, California):

We live on the third world from the sun. Number three. Nobody tells us what to do.

The people who taught us to count were being very kind.

It's always time to leave.

If it rains, you either have your umbrella or you don't.

The wind blows your hat off.

The sun rises also.

I'd rather the stars didn't describe us to each other; I'd rather we do it for ourselves.

Run in front of your shadow.

A sister who points to the sky at least once a decade is a good sister.

The landscape is motorized.

The train takes you where it goes.

Bridges among water.

Folks straggling along vast stretches of concrete, heading into the plane.

Don't forget what your hat and shoes will look like when you are nowhere to be found.

Even the words floating in air make blue shadows.

If it tastes good we eat it.

The leaves are falling. Point things out.

Pick up the right things.

Hey guess what? What? *I've learned how to talk.* Great.

The person whose head was incomplete burst into tears.

As it fell, what could the doll do? Nothing.

Go to sleep.

You look great in shorts. And the flag looks great too.

Everyone enjoyed the explosions.

Time to wake up.

But better get used to dreams.

Now one may object that this is not exactly schizophrenic writing in the clinical sense; it does not seem quite right to say that these sentences are free-floating material signifiers whose signifieds have evaporated. There does seem to be some global meaning here. Indeed, insofar as this is in some curious and secret way a political poem, it does seem to capture some of the excitement of the immense and unfinished social experiment of the new China, unparalleled in world history: the unexpected emergence, between the two superpowers, of 'number three'; the freshness of a whole new object-world produced by human beings in some new control over their own collective destiny; the signal event, above all, of a collectivity which has become a new 'subject of history' and which, after the long subjection of feudalism and imperialism, speaks in its own voice, for itself, for the first time ('Hey guess what?... I've learned how to talk.'). Yet such meaning floats over the text or behind it. One cannot, I think, read this text according to any of the older New-Critical categories and find the complex inner relationships and texture which characterised the older 'concrete universal' of classical modernisms such as Wallace Stevens's.

Perelman's work, and Language Poetry generally, owes something to Gertrude Stein and, beyond her, to certain aspects of Flaubert. So it is not inappropriate at this point to insert an old account of Flaubert's sentences by Sartre, which conveys a vivid feeling of the movement of such sentences:

> His sentence closes in on the object, seizes it, immobilizes it, and breaks its back, wraps itself around it, changes into stone and petrifies its object along with itself. It is blind and deaf, bloodless, not a breath of life; a deep silence separates it from the sentence which follows; it falls into the void, eternally, and drags its prey down into that infinite fall. Any reality, once described, is struck off the inventory.[2]

The description is a hostile one, and the liveliness of Perelman is historically rather different from this homicidal Flaubertian practice. (For Mallarmé, Barthes once observed in a similar vein, the sentence, the word, is a way of murdering the outside world.) Yet it conveys some of the mystery of sentences that fall into a void of silence so great that for a time one wonders whether any new sentence could possibly emerge to take their place.

But now the secret of this poem must be disclosed. It is a little like Photorealism, which looked like a return to representation after the anti-representational abstractions of Abstract Expressionism, until people began to realise that these paintings are not exactly realistic either, since what they represent is not the outside world but rather only a photograph of the outside world or, in other words, the latter's image. False realisms, they are really art about other art, images of other images. In the present case, the represented object is not really China after all: what happened was that Perelman came across a book of photographs in a stationery store in China-town, a book whose captions and characters obviously remained dead letters (or should one say material signifiers?) to him. The sentences of the poem are *his* captions to those pictures. Their referents are other images, another text, and the 'unity' of the poem is not *in* the text at all but outside it in the bound unity of an absent book.

Now I must try very rapidly in conclusion to characterise the relationship of cultural production of this kind to social life in this country today. This will also be the moment to address the principal objection to concepts of post-modernism of the type I have sketched here: namely that all the features we have enumerated are not new at all but abundantly characterised modernism proper or what I call high-modernism. Was not Thomas Mann, after all, interested in the idea of pastiche, and are not certain chapters of *Ulysses* its most obvious realisation? Did we not mention Flaubert, Mallarmé and Gertrude Stein in our account of postmodernist temporality? What is so new about all of this? Do we really need the concept of a *post*modernism?

One kind of answer to this question would raise the whole issue of period-isation and of how a historian (literary or other) posits a radical break between two henceforth distinct periods. I must limit myself to the sugges-tion that radical breaks between periods do not generally involve complete changes of content but rather the restructuration of a certain number of elements already given: features that in an earlier period or system were subordinate now become dominant, and features that had been dominant again become secondary. In this sense, everything we have described here can be found in earlier periods and most notably within modernism proper: my point is that until the present day those things have been secondary or minor features of modernist art, marginal rather than central, and that we have something new when they become the central features of cultural production.

But I can argue this more concretely by turning to the relationship between cultural production and social life generally. The older or classical modernism was an oppositional art; it emerged within the business society of the gilded age as scandalous and offensive to the middle-class public – ugly, dissonant, bohemian, sexually shocking. It was something to make fun of (when the police were not called in to seize the books or close the exhibi-tions): an offence to good taste and to common sense, or, as Freud and Marcuse would have put it, a provocative challenge to the reigning reality- and performance-principles of early twentieth-century middle-class society. Modernism in general did not go well with overstuffed Victorian furniture, with Victorian moral taboos, or with the conventions of polite society. This is to say that whatever the explicit political content of the great high modernisms, the latter were always in some mostly implicit ways dangerous and explosive, subversive within the established order.

If then we suddenly return to the present day, we can measure the immensity of the cultural changes that have taken place. Not only are Joyce and Picasso no longer weird and repulsive, they have become classics and now look rather realistic to us. Meanwhile, there is very little in either the form or the content of contemporary art that contemporary society finds intolerable and scandalous. The most offensive forms of this art – punk rock, say, or what is called sexually explicit material – are all taken in stride by society, and they are commercially successful, unlike the productions of the older high modernism. But this means that even if contemporary art has all the same formal features as the older modernism, it has still shifted its position fundamentally within our culture. For one thing, commodity production and in particular our clothing, furniture, buildings and other artifacts are now intimately tied in with styling changes which derive from artistic experimentation; our advertising, for example, is fed by postmodernism in all the arts and inconceivable without it. For another, the classics of high modernism are now part of the so-called canon and are taught in schools and universities – which at once empties them of any of their older subversive power. Indeed, one way of marking the break between the periods and of dating the emergence of postmodernism is precisely to be found there: in the moment (the early 1960s, one would think) in which the position of high modernism and its dominant aesthetics become established in the academy and are henceforth felt to be academic by a whole new generation of poets, painters and musicians.

But one can also come at the break from the other side, and describe it in terms of periods of recent social life. As I have suggested, non-Marxists and Marxists alike have come around to the general feeling that at some point following World War II a new kind of society began to emerge (variously described as postindustrial society, multinational capitalism, consumer society, media society and so forth). New types of consumption; planned obsolescence; an ever more rapid rhythm of fashion and styling changes; the penetration of advertising, television and the media generally to a hitherto unparalleled degree throughout society; the replacement of the old tension between city and country, centre and province, by the suburb and by universal standardisation; the growth of the great networks of superhighways and the arrival of automobile culture – these are some of the features which would seem to mark a radical break with that older prewar society in which high modernism was still an underground force.

I believe that the emergence of postmodernism is closely related to the emergence of this new moment of late, consumer or multinational capitalism. I believe also that its formal features in many ways express the deeper logic of that particular social system. I will only be able, however, to show this for one major theme: namely the disappearance of a sense of history, the way in which our entire contemporary social system has little by little begun to lose its capacity to retain its own past, has begun to live in a perpetual present and in a perpetual change that obliterates traditions of the kind which all earlier social formations have had in one way or another to preserve. Think only of the media exhaustion of news: of how Nixon and, even more so, Kennedy are figures from a now distant past. One is tempted to say that the very function of the news media is to relegate such recent historical experiences as rapidly as possible into the past. The informational function of the media would thus be to help us forget, to serve as the very agents and mechanisms for our historical amnesia.

But in that case the two features of postmodernism on which I have dwelt here – the transformation of reality into images, the fragmentation of time into a series of perpetual presents – are both extraordinarily consonant with this process. My own conclusion here must take the form of a question about the critical value of the newer art. There is some agreement that the older modernism functioned against its society in ways which are variously described as critical, negative, contestatory, subversive, oppositional and the like. Can anything of the sort be affirmed about postmodernism and its social moment? We have seen that there is a way in which postmodernism replicates or reproduces – reinforces – the logic of consumer capitalism; the more significant question is whether there is also a way in which it resists that logic. But that is a question we must leave open.

4

Modernity:
an Unfinished Project

Jürgen Habermas

Following the painters and the film-makers, the architects have now been admitted to the Venice Biennale as well. The response to this, the first architecture Biennale, was one of disappointment. The participants who exhibited in Venice formed an avant-garde with the fronts reversed. Under the slogan of 'the presence of the past' they sacrificed the tradition of modernity in the name of a new species of historicism: 'The fact that the entire modern movement was sustained through its engagement with the past, that Frank Lloyd Wright would be inconceivable without Japan, Le Corbusier without classical antiquity and Mediterranean architecture, and Mies van der Rohe without Schinkel and Behrens, all this is passed over in silence.' With this remark W. Pehnt, the critic on the *Frankfurter Allgemeine Zeitung*, supports his claim, one which provides a significant diagnosis of our times over and beyond its initial occasion: 'Postmodernity decisively presents itself as a form of Antimodernity.'[1]

This claim holds for an affective trend which has seeped into the pores of every intellectual domain and given rise to various theories of post-Enlightenment, of postmodernity, of post-history and so forth, in short to a new kind of conservatism. Adorno and his work stand in marked contrast to this trend.

So unreservedly did Adorno subscribe to the spirit of modernity that in the very attempt to distinguish authentic modernity from mere modernism he quickly sensed the affective response to the affront of modernity itself. It may not therefore be an entirely inappropriate way of expressing my gratitude for receiving the Adorno Prize if I pursue the question concerning the current attitude with respect to modernity. Is modernity as *passé* as the postmodernists argue? Or is the widely trumpeted arrival of postmodernity itself 'phony'? Is 'postmodern' a slogan which unobtrusively inherits the affective attitudes which cultural modernity has provoked in reaction to itself since the middle of the nineteenth century?

THE OLD AND THE NEW

Anyone who, like Adorno, conceives of 'modernity' as beginning around 1850 is perceiving it through the eyes of Baudelaire and avant-garde art. Let me elucidate this concept of cultural modernity with a brief look at its long prehistory, which has already been illuminated by Hans Robert Jauss.[2] The word 'modern' was first employed in the late fifth century in order to distinguish the present, now officially Christian, from the pagan and Roman past. With a different content in each case, the expression 'modernity' repeatedly articulates the consciousness of an era that refers back to the past of classical antiquity precisely in order to comprehend itself as the result of a transition from the old to the new. This is not merely true for the Renaissance, with which the 'modern age' begins *for us*; people also considered themselves as 'modern' in the age of Charlemagne, in the twelfth century, and in the Enlightenment – in short, whenever the consciousness of a new era developed in Europe through a renewed relationship to classical antiquity. In the process culminating in the celebrated *querelle des anciens et des modernes*, the dispute with the protagonists of a classicistic aesthetic taste in late seventeenth-century France, it was always *antiquitas*, the classical world, which was regarded as the normative model to be imitated. It was only the French Enlightenment's ideal of perfection and the idea, inspired by modern science, of the infinite progress of knowledge and the advance towards social and moral improvement that gradually lifted the spell exercised on the spirit of these *early* moderns by the classical works of antiquity. And finally, in opposing the classical and the romantic to one another, modernity sought its own past in an idealised vision of the Middle Ages. In the course of the nineteenth century *this* Romanticism produced a radicalised consciousness of modernity that detached itself from all previous historical connection and understood itself solely in abstract opposition to tradition and history as a whole.

At this juncture, what was considered modern was what assisted the spontaneously self-renewing historical contemporaneity of the *Zeitgeist* to find its own objective expression. The characteristic feature of such works is the moment of novelty, the New, which will itself be surpassed and devalued in turn by the innovations of the next style. Yet whereas the merely modish becomes outmoded once it is displaced into the past, the modern still retains a secret connection to the classical. The 'classical' has always signified that which endures through the ages. The emphatically 'modern' artistic product no longer derives its power from the authority of a past age, but owes it solely to the authenticity of a contemporary relevance that has now become past. This transformation of contemporary relevance into a relevance now past has both a destructive and a constructive aspect. As Jauss has observed, it is modernity itself that creates its own classical status – thus we can speak today of 'classical modernity' as if such an expression were obvious. Adorno opposes any attempted distinction between 'modernity' and 'modernism' because he believes that 'without the characteristic subjective mentality inspired by the New no objective modernity can crystallise at all'.[3]

THE MENTALITY OF AESTHETIC MODERNITY

The mentality of aesthetic modernity begins to take shape clearly with Baudelaire and with his theory of art, influenced as it was by Edgar Allan Poe. It then unfolded in the avant-garde artistic movements and finally attained its zenith with surrealism and the Dadaists of the Café Voltaire. This mentality is characterised by a set of attitudes which developed around a transformed consciousness of time. It is this consciousness that expresses itself in the spatial metaphor of the avant-garde – that is, an avant-garde that explores hitherto unknown territory, exposes itself to the risk of sudden and shocking encounters, conquers an as yet undetermined future, and must therefore find a path for itself in previously uncharted domains. But this forward orientation, this anticipation of an indefinite and contingent future, the cult of the New which accompanies it, all this actually signifies the glorification of a contemporariness that repeatedly gives birth to new and subjectively defined pasts. This new consciousness of time, which also found its way into philosophy with Bergson, expresses more than the experience of a mobilised society, of an accelerated history, of the disruption of everyday life. The new value which is now accorded to the ephemeral, the momentary and the transitory, and the concomitant celebration of dynamism, expresses precisely the yearning for a lasting and immaculate present. As a self-negating movement, modernism is a 'yearning for true presence'. This, according to Octavio Paz, 'is the secret theme of the finest modernist writers'.[4]

This also explains the abstract opposition of modernism to history, which thus forfeits the structure of an articulated process of cultural transmission ensuring continuity. Individual epochs lose their own distinctive features, and the present now assumes a heroic affinity either with what is most remote or what is closest to it: decadence recognises itself immediately in the barbaric, the wild and the primitive. The anarchistic intention of exploding the continuum of history accounts for the subversive force of an aesthetic consciousness which rebels against the norm-giving achievements of tradition, which is nourished on the experience of rebellion against everything normative, which neutralises considerations of moral goodness or practical utility, a consciousness which continually stages a dialectic of esoteric mystery and scandalous offence, narcotically fascinated by the fright produced by its acts of profanation – and yet at the same time flees from the trivialisation resulting from that very profanation. That is why for Adorno the wounds inflicted by disruption represent the seal of authenticity for modernity, the very thing through which modernity desperately negates the closed character of the eternally invariant; the act of explosion is itself one of the invariants of modernity. The zeal directed against the tradition becomes a devouring maelstrom. In this sense modernity is myth turned against itself; the timelessness of myth becomes the catastrophe of the moment which disrupts all temporal continuity.[5]

The consciousness of time articulated in avant-garde art is not simply an antihistorical one, of course. For it is directed only against the false normativity of a historical understanding essentially oriented towards the imitation of past models, something which has not been entirely eliminated even in Gadamer's philosophical hermeneutics. This time-consciousness avails itself of the objectified pasts made available by historical scholarship, but it simultaneously rebels against that neutralisation of criteria practised by a historicism which relegates history to the museum. It is in the same rebellious spirit that Walter Benjamin attempted to construe the relation of modernity to history in a *posthistorical* manner. He recalls the way in which the French Revolution conceived of itself: 'It evoked ancient Rome much as fashion evokes the costumes of the past. Fashion shows a flair for the topical, no matter where it stirs in the thickets of long ago.' And just as for Robespierre ancient Rome represented a past charged with 'nowness', so too the historian has to grasp the constellation 'into which his or her own era has entered with a particular earlier one'. This is how Benjamin grounds his concept of 'the present as the "time of the now" which is shot through with splinters of Messianic time'.[6]

This spirit of aesthetic modernity has aged since Benjamin's time. During the 1960s it was, of course, rehearsed once more. But with the 1970s now behind us, we have to confess that modernism finds almost no resonance today. Even during the 1960s Octavio Paz, a partisan for modernity, observed with some sadness that 'the avant-garde of 1967 repeats the deeds and the gestures of the avant-garde of 1917. We are witnessing the end of the idea of modern art.'[7] In the wake of Peter Bürger's work we now speak of post-avant-garde art, an expression that acknowledges the failure of the surrealist rebellion. Yet what is the significance of this failure? Does it indicate the demise of modernity? Does the post-avant-garde imply a transition to postmodernity?

In fact this is precisely how Daniel Bell, a well-known social theorist and the most brilliant of the American neoconservative thinkers, understands the situation. In an interesting book[8] Bell has developed the thesis that the crisis manifested in advanced Western societies can be traced back to the bifurcation between culture and society, between cultural modernity and the demands of the economic and administrative systems. Avant-garde art has supposedly penetrated the values of everyday life and thus infected the life-world with the modernist mentality. Modernism represents a great seduct-ive force, promoting the dominance of the principle of unrestrained self-realisation, the demand for authentic self-experience, the subjectivism of an overstimulated sensibility, and the release of hedonistic motivations quite incompatible with the discipline required by professional life, and with the moral foundations of a purposive-rational mode of life generally. Thus, like Arnold Gehlen in Germany, Bell locates the blame for the dissolution of the Protestant ethic, something which had already disturbed Max Weber, with an 'adversary culture', that is, with a culture whose modernism encourages hostility to the conventions and the values of everyday life as rationalised under economic and administrative imperatives.

Yet, on the other hand, this same reading claims that the impulse of modernity has definitely exhausted itself and that the avant-garde has run its course; although still propagated, the latter supposedly no longer repre-sents a creative force. Thus the question which concerns neoconservatism is how to establish norms that will restrain libertinism, restore discipline and the work ethic, and promote the virtues of individual competitiveness against the levelling effects of the welfare state. The only solution envisaged by Bell is some kind of religious renewal that would link up with quasi-naturally given traditions which are immune to criticism, which allow for the emergence of clearly defined identities, and which procure some existential sense of secur-ity for the individual.

CULTURAL MODERNITY AND SOCIAL MODERNISATION

Of course, it is not possible simply to conjure up authoritative beliefs from nowhere. That is why analyses of this kind only give rise, as the sole practical recommendation, to the sort of postulate we have also seen in Germany: namely, an intellectual and political confrontation with the intellectual representatives of cultural modernity. And here I quote Peter Steinfels, a perceptive observer of the new style which the neoconservatives succeeded in imposing on the intellectual scene in the 1970s:

> The struggle takes the form of exposing every manifestation of what could be considered an oppositionist mentality and tracing its 'logic' so as to link it to various expressions of extremism: drawing the connection between modernism and nihilism ... between government regulation and totalitar-ianism, between criticism of arms expenditures and subservience to Com-munism, between women's liberation or homosexual rights and the destruction of the family ... between the Left generally and terrorism, anti-Semitism, and fascism.[9]

Peter Steinfels is referring here only to the United States, but the parallels with our situation are very obvious. The personalising of debate and the degree of bitterness that characterise the abuse of intellectuals stirred up by those hostile to the Enlightenment cannot adequately be explained in psychological terms, since they are grounded rather in the internal conceptual weakness of neoconservative thought itself.

Neoconservatism displaces the burdensome and unwelcome consequences of a more or less successful capitalist modernisation of the economy on to cultural modernity. It obscures the connections between the processes of social modernisation, which it welcomes, on the one hand, and the crisis of motivation, which it laments, on the other, and fails to reveal the socio-structural causes of transformed attitudes to work, of consumer habits, of levels of demand and of the greater emphasis given to leisure time. Thus neoconservatism can directly attribute what appear to be hedonism, a lack of social identification, an incapacity for obedience, narcissism, and the withdrawal from competition for status and achievement to a culture which actually plays only a very mediated role in these processes. In place of these unanalysed causes, it focuses on those intellectuals who still regard themselves as committed to the project of modernity. It is true that Daniel Bell does perceive a further connection between the erosion of bourgeois values and the consumerism characteristic of a society which has become orientated towards mass production. But even Bell, seemingly unimpressed by his own argument, traces the new permissiveness back first and foremost to the spread of a lifestyle which originally emerged within the elite counter-cultures of bohemian artists. This is obviously only another variation on a misunderstanding to which the avant-garde itself had already fallen prey – the idea that the mission of art is to fulfil its implicit promise of happiness by introducing into society as a whole that artistic lifestyle that was defined precisely as its opposite.

Concerning the period in which aesthetic modernity emerged, Bell remarks that 'radical in economics, the bourgeoisie became conservative in morals and cultural taste'.[10] If this were true, one might see neoconservatism as a return to the old reliable pattern of the bourgeois mentality. But that is far too simple: the mood to which neoconservatism can appeal *today* by no means derives from a discontent with the antinomian consequences of a culture that has transgressed its boundaries and escaped from the museum back into life. This discontent is not provoked by the modernist intellectuals, but is rooted rather in much more fundamental reactions to a process of social modernisation which, under pressure from the imperatives of economic growth and state administration, intervenes further and further into the ecology of developed forms of social life, into the communicative infrastructure of the historical lifeworlds. Thus neopopulist protests are merely giving forceful expression to widespread fears concerning the possible destruction of the urban and the natural environments, and the destruction of humane forms of social life. Many different occasions for discontent and protest arise wherever a one-sided process of modernisation, guided by criteria of economic and administrative rationality, invades domains of life which are centred on the task of cultural transmission, social integration, socialisation and education, domains orientated towards quite *different* criteria, namely towards those of communicative rationality. But it is from just these social processes that the neoconservative doctrines distract our attention, only to project the causes which they have left shrouded in obscurity on to an intrinsically subversive culture and its representatives.

It is quite true that cultural modernity also generates its own aporias. And those intellectual positions which hasten to proclaim postmodernity, to recommend a return to premodernity, or which radically repudiate modernity altogether, all appeal to these aporias. Thus, apart from the problematic social consequences of *social* modernisation, it is true that certain reasons for doubt or despair concerning the project of modernity *also* arise from the *internal perspective* of cultural development.

THE PROJECT OF ENLIGHTENMENT

The idea of modernity is intimately bound up with the development of European art, but what I have called the project of modernity only comes into clear view when we abandon the usual concentration on art. Max Weber characterised cultural modernity in terms of the separation of substantive reason, formerly expressed in religious and metaphysical world-views, into three moments, now capable of being connected only formally with one another (through the form of argumentative justification). In so far as the world-views have disintegrated and their traditional problems have been separated off under the perspectives of truth, normative rightness and authenticity or beauty, and can now be treated in each case as questions of knowledge, justice or taste respectively, there arises in the modern period a differentiation of the value spheres of science and knowledge, of morality and of art. Thus scientific discourse, moral and legal enquiry, artistic production and critical practice are now institutionalised within the corresponding cultural systems as the concern of experts. And this professionalised treatment of the cultural heritage in terms of a single abstract consideration of validity in each case serves to bring to light the autonomous structures intrinsic to the cognitive-instrumental, the moral-practical and the aesthetic-expressive knowledge complexes. From now on there will also be *internal* histories of science and knowledge, of moral and legal theory, and of art. And although these do not represent linear developments, they none the less constitute learning processes. That is one side of the issue.

On the other side, the distance between these expert cultures and the general public has increased. What the cultural sphere gains through specialised treatment and reflection does not *automatically* come into the possession of everyday practice without more ado. For with cultural rationalisation, the lifeworld, once its traditional substance has been devalued, threatens rather to become *impoverished*. The project of modernity as it was formulated by the philosophers of the Enlightenment in the eighteenth century consists in the relentless development of the objectivating sciences, of the universalistic foundations of morality and law, and of autonomous art, all in accord with their own immanent logic. But at the same time it also results in releasing the cognitive potentials accumulated in the process from their esoteric high forms and attempting to apply them in the sphere of praxis, that is, to encourage the rational organisation of social relations. Partisans of the Enlightenment such as Condorcet could still entertain the extravagant expectation that the arts and sciences would not merely promote the control of the forces of nature, but also further the understanding of self and world, the progress of morality, justice in social institutions, and even human happiness.

Little of this optimism remains to us in the twentieth century. But the problem has remained, and with it a fundamental difference of opinion as before: should we continue to hold fast to the intentions of the Enlightenment, however fractured they may be, or should we rather relinquish the entire project of modernity? If the cognitive potentials in question do not merely result in technical progress, economic growth and rational administration, should we wish to see them checked in order to protect a life praxis still dependent on blind traditions from any unsettling disturbance?

Even among those philosophers who currently represent something of an *Enlightenment rearguard*, the project of modernity appears curiously fragmented. Each thinker puts faith in only one of the moments into which reason has become differentiated. Karl Popper, and I refer here to the theorist of the open society who has not yet allowed himself to be appropriated by the neoconservatives, holds firmly to the potentially enlightening capacity of scientific criticism when extended into the political domain. But for this he pays the price of a general moral scepticism and a largely indifferent attitude to the aesthetic dimension. Paul Lorenzen is interested in the question as to how an artificial language methodically constructed in accordance with practical reason can effectively contribute to the reform of everyday life. But his approach directs all science and knowledge along the narrow path of justification analogous to that of moral practice and he too neglects the aesthetic. In Adorno, on the other hand, the emphatic claim to reason has withdrawn into the accusatory gesture of the esoteric work of art, morality no longer appears susceptible to justification, and philosophy is left solely with the task of revealing, in an indirect fashion, the critical content sealed up within art.

The progressive differentiation of science and knowledge, morality and art, with which Max Weber characterised the rationalism of Western culture, implies *both* the specialised treatment of special domains *and* their detachment from the current of tradition, which continues to flow on in a quasi-natural fashion in the hermeneutic medium of everyday life. This detachment is the problem which is generated by the autonomous logic of the differentiated value spheres. And it is this detachment which has also provoked abortive attempts to 'sublate' the expert cultures which accompany it, a phenomenon most clearly revealed in the domain of art.

KANT AND THE AUTONOMY OF THE AESTHETIC

Simplifying considerably, one can trace a line of progressive autonomisation in the development of modern art. It was the Renaissance which first saw the emergence of a specific domain categorised exclusively in terms of the beautiful. Then, in the course of the eighteenth century, literature, the plastic arts and music were institutionalised as a specific domain of activity distinct from ecclesiastical and court life. Finally, around the middle of the nineteenth century, there also arose an aestheticist conception of art which obliged artists to produce their work in accordance with the conscious outlook of *l'art pour l'art*. The autonomy of the aesthetic was thereby explicitly constituted as a project.

In the initial phase of this process, therefore, there emerged the cognitive structures of a new domain, one quite distinct from the complex of science and knowledge and that of morality. And the task of clarifying these structures subsequently fell to philosophical aesthetics. Kant laboured energetically to define the distinctive character of the aesthetic domain. His point of departure here was the analysis of the judgement of taste, which is certainly directed towards something subjective, namely the free play of the imagination, but which manifests more than mere preference, being orientated rather towards intersubjective agreement.

Although aesthetic objects belong neither to the sphere of phenomena knowable by means of the categories of the understanding, nor to the sphere of free acts subject to the legislation of practical reason, works of art (and those of natural beauty) are accessible to *objective judgement*. The beautiful constitutes another domain of validity, alongside those of truth and morality, and it is this which grounds the *connection between art and the practice of art criticism*. For one 'speaks of beauty as if it were a property of things'.[11]

Beauty pertains, of course, only to the *representation* of a thing, just as the judgement of taste refers only to the relationship between the mental representation of an object and the feeling of pleasure or displeasure. It is only in the *medium of semblance* that an object can be perceived *as* an aesthetic object. And only as a fictive object can it so affect our sensibility as to succeed in presenting what evades the conceptual character of object-ivating thought and moral judgement. Kant describes the state of mind which is produced through the play of the representational faculties, and which is thus activated aesthetically, as one of *disinterested* pleasure. The quality of a *work* is therefore determined quite independently of any connections it might have with our practical relations to life.

Whereas the fundamental concepts of classical aesthetics already men-tioned – namely those of taste and criticism, beautiful semblance, disinter-estedness and the transcendent autonomy of the work of art – serve principally to distinguish the aesthetic domain from the other spheres of value and life practice, the concept of the *genius* which is required for the production of the work of art involves positive elements. Kant describes genius as 'the exemplary originality of the natural talents of a subject in the free employment of his or her cognitive faculties'.[12] If we detach the concept of genius from its romantic origins, we could freely paraphrase this thought as follows: the talented artist is capable of bestowing authentic expression on those experiences enjoyed through concentrated engagement with a decentred subjectivity which is released from the constraints of knowledge and action.

This autonomous character of the aesthetic – namely, the objectification of a self-experiencing decentred subjectivity, the exclusion of the spatio-temporal structures of everyday life, the rupturing of conventions attaching to the processes of perception and purposive activity, the dialectic of shock and revelation – could first emerge as a distinct consciousness of modernity only with the gestures of modernism, and only once two further conditions had been fulfilled. These conditions were, in the first place, the institutional-isation of artistic production dependent on the market and of a non-purpos-ive enjoyment of art mediated through the practice of art criticism; and in the second place, an aestheticist self-understanding on the part of artists, and also on the part of critics, who conceive of themselves less as representatives of the general public than as interpreters who form part of the process of artistic production itself. Now for the first time in painting and literature we discern the beginnings of a movement which some already see anticipated in the aesthetic criticism of Baudelaire: colours, lines, sounds and movements cease to be primarily for the purpose of representation; the media of repre-sentation, along with the techniques of production themselves, advance to become aesthetic objects in their own right. Thus Adorno can begin his *Aesthetic Theory* with the statement: 'It has now become self-evident, as far as art is concerned, that nothing is self-evident any more, either in art itself or in its relation to the whole, not even its right to exist.'

THE FALSE SUBLATION OF CULTURE

Of course, art's right to exist could not have been called into question by surrealism if modern art, and indeed especially modern art, did not also harbour a promise of happiness which concerned its 'relationship to the whole'. In Schiller the promise that aesthetic contemplation makes but fails to fulfil still possessed the explicit form of a utopia which points beyond art. This line of utopian aesthetic thought extends all the way to Marcuse's lament concerning the affirmative character of culture, expressed here as a critique of ideology. But even in Baudelaire, who repeats the *promesse de bonheur*, this utopia of reconciliation had turned into a critical reflection of the unreconciled nature of the social world. The more remote from life art becomes, the more it withdraws into the inviolable seclusion of complete aesthetic autonomy, the more painfully this lack of reconciliation is brought to conscious awareness. This pain is reflected in the boundless *ennui* of the outsider who identified himself with the Parisian rag-and-bone men.

Along such pathways of sensibility all those explosive energies gather which are finally discharged in rebellion, in the violent attempt to shatter the illusory autarchy of the sphere of art and thus to enforce reconciliation through this sacrifice. Adorno sees very clearly why the surrealist programme 'renounces art, without, however, being able to shake it off'.[13] All attempts to bridge the disjunction between art and life, fiction and praxis, illusion and reality, and to eliminate the distinction between artistic product and objects of utility, between something produced and something found, between premeditated configuration and spontaneous impulse, the attempt to declare everything art and everyone an artist, to abolish all criteria and to equate aesthetic judgements with the expression of subjective experience: all these undertakings, well analysed as they have been, can be seen today as nonsense experiments. They only succeed, against their own intention, in illuminating even more sharply the very structures of art which they had intended to violate: the medium of semblance, the autonomous transcendence of the work, the concentrated and premeditated character of artistic production, as well as the cognitive status of the judgement of taste.[14] Ironically, the radical attempt to sublate art reinstates those categories with which classical aesthetics had circumscribed its own domain, although it is also true that these categories have changed their character in the process.

The failure of the surrealist rebellion sets the seal of confirmation on a double error of a false sublation. On the one hand, once the vessels of an autonomously articulated cultural sphere are shattered, their contents are lost; once meaning has been desublimated and form dismantled, nothing remains and no emancipatory effect results. But the second error is even more fraught with consequences. In the communicative praxis of everyday life, cognitive interpretations, moral expectations, expressions and evaluations must interpenetrate one another. The processes of reaching understanding which transpire in the lifeworld require the resources of an inherited culture *in its entire range*. That is why a rationalised everyday life could not possibly be redeemed from the rigidity of cultural impoverishment by violently forcing open *one* cultural domain, in this case art, and establishing some connection with *one* of the specialised complexes of knowledge. Such an approach would only substitute one form of one-sidedness and abstraction with another.

There are also parallels in the domains of theoretical knowledge and morality to this programme and its unsuccessful practice of false sublation, although they are admittedly less clearly defined. It is certainly true that the sciences on the one hand and moral and legal theory on the other have, like art, become autonomous. But both these spheres remain closely connected with specialised forms of praxis, the former with a scientifically perfected technology, the latter with an organised practice of law and administration dependent on moral justification. And yet institutionalised scientific knowledge and the activity of moral-practical argument segregated within the legal system have become so remote from everyday life that here too the programme of *elevation* implied by the Enlightenment could be transformed into that of *sublation* instead.

The 'sublation of philosophy' is a slogan that has been current ever since the days of the Young Hegelians, and the question concerning the relationship of theory and praxis has been raised since Marx. And here the intellectuals have allied themselves with the workers' movement, of course. It was only at the margins of this social movement that sectarian groups found room to play out the programme of sublating philosophy in the way the surrealists played out the sublation of art. The consequences of dogmatism and moral rigorism here reveal the same error as before: once the praxis of everyday life, orientated as it is towards the unconstrained interplay between the cognitive, the moral-practical and the aesthetic-expressive dimensions, has become reified, it cannot be cured by being connected with any *one* of the cultural domains forcibly opened up. Nor should the imitation of the lifestyles of extraordinary representatives of these value spheres – in other words, by generalising the subversive forces which Nietzsche, Bakunin or Baudelaire expressed in their own lives – be confused with the institutionalisation and practical utilisation of knowledge accumulated through science, morality and art.

In specific situations it is quite true that terrorist activities may be connected with the overextension of one of these cultural moments, that is, with the inclination to aestheticise politics, to replace politics with moral rigorism, or to subjugate politics to dogmatic doctrines.

But these almost intangible connections should not mislead us into denouncing the intentions of an intransigent Enlightenment as the monstrous offspring of a 'terroristic reason'. Those who link the project of modernity with the conscious attitudes and spectacular public deeds of individual terrorists are just as short-sighted as those who claim that the incomparably more persistent and pervasive bureaucratic terrorism practised in obscurity, in the cellars of the military and the secret police, in prison camps and psychiatric institutions, represents the very essence of the modern state (and its positivistically eroded form of legal domination) simply because such terrorism utilises the coercive means of the state apparatus.

ALTERNATIVES TO THE FALSE SUBLATION OF CULTURE

I believe that we should learn from the aberrations which have accompanied the project of modernity and from the mistakes of those extravagant proposals of sublation, rather than abandoning modernity and its project. Perhaps we can at least *suggest* a possible escape from the aporias of cultural modernity if we take the reception of art as an example. Since the development of art criticism during the romantic period there have arisen certain contradictory tendencies, and they became more rigidly polarised with the emergence of the avant-garde movements. On the one hand, art criticism claims the role of a productive supplement to the work of art, while on the other it claims the role of an advocate who provides the interpretation required by the public at large. Bourgeois art addressed *both* of these expectations to its audience: on the one hand laypeople who enjoy art should educate themselves to become experts, while on the other they should behave as connoisseurs who are capable of relating their aesthetic experience back to the problems of their own life. Perhaps this second, apparently more innocuous mode of reception lost its radical character because its connection with the former mode remained obscure.

Of course, artistic production will inevitably degenerate semantically if it is not pursued as the specialised treatment of its own immanent problems, as an object of expert concern without regard for exoteric needs. All those who are involved (including the critic as a professionally trained recipient) engage in the problems they treat in terms of just one abstract criterion of validity. This sharply defined separation and the exclusive concentration on a single dimension breaks down, however, as soon as aesthetic experience is incorporated into the context of an individual life history or into a collective form of life. The reception of art by the layperson, or rather the person who is an expert in the field of everyday life, takes a *different course* from the reception of art by the professional critic who focuses principally on developments which are purely internal to art. Albrecht Wellmer has pointed out to me that an aesthetic experience which is not primarily translated into judgements of taste actually changes its functional character. For when it is related to problems of life or used in an exploratory fashion to illuminate a life-historical situation, it enters a language game which is no longer that of art criticism proper. In this case aesthetic experience not only revitalises those need interpretations in the light of which we perceive our world, but also influences our cognitive interpretations and our normative expectations, and thus alters the way in which all these moments *refer back and forth* to one another.

Peter Weiss narrates an example of the kind of exploratory, life-orientating power which can emanate from the encounter with a great painting at a crucial juncture in an individual's life. He has his protagonist wander through the streets of Paris after his dejected return from the Spanish Civil War and anticipate in imagination his imminent encounter with Géricault's painting of the shipwrecked sailors in the Louvre. A specific variant of the mode of artistic reception I am talking about here is even more precisely captured in the heroic effort of appropriation described by the same author in the first volume of his *Ästhetik des Widerstands* (Aesthetic of Resistance). He depicts a group of young people in Berlin in 1937, politically motivated workers who are eager to learn, who are acquiring the means of inwardly understanding the history, including the social history, of European painting through night school classes. Out of the obdurate stone of objective spirit they hew the fragments they are able to appropriate, drawing them into the experimental horizon of their own environment, one which is as remote from traditional education as it is from the existing regime, and turning them this way and that until they begin to glow:

> Our conception of culture only rarely cohered with what presented itself to us as a gigantic repository of commodities, of accumulated insights and discoveries. As propertyless people, we approached this hoard with initial trepidation, filled with awe, until it became clear to us that we had to supply our own evaluations to it all, that we could only make use of it as a totality if it actually spoke to us about our own conditions of life, about the difficulties and the peculiarities of our own processes of thought.[15]

Examples like this, where the *expert culture is appropriated from the perspective of the lifeworld,* successfully preserve something of the original intention of the doomed surrealist rebellion, and more of Brecht's, and even Benjamin's, experimental reflections on the reception of non-auratic works of art. And similar observations can be made concerning the spheres of science and morality when we consider that the human, social and behavioural sciences have not been *entirely* divorced from the structure of practically orientated knowledge even now, and further that the concentration of universalistic ethics on questions of justice represents an abstraction which cries out to be connected to those problems concerning the good life that it initially excluded.

However, a differentiated reconnection of modern culture with an every-day sphere of praxis that is dependent on a living heritage and yet is impoverished by mere traditionalism will admittedly only prove successful if the process of social modernisation can *also* be turned into *other* non-capitalist directions, if the lifeworld can develop institutions of its own in a way currently inhibited by the autonomous systemic dynamics of the economic and administrative system.

THREE CONSERVATISMS

Unless I am mistaken, the prospects for this are not encouraging. Virtually throughout the Western world a climate of opinion has arisen which promotes tendencies highly critical of modernism. The disillusionment provoked by the failure of programmes for the false sublation of art and philosophy, and the openly visible aporias of cultural modernity, have served as a pretext for various conservative positions. Let me briefly distinguish here the anti-modernism of the Young Conservatives from the premodernism of the Old Conservatives, on the one hand, and the postmodernism of the New Conservatives, on the other.

The *Young Conservatives* essentially appropriate the fundamental experience of aesthetic modernity, namely the revelation of a decentred subjectivity liberated from all the constraints of cognition and purposive action, from all the imperatives of labour and use value, and with this they break out of the modern world altogether. They establish an implacable opposition to modernism precisely through a modernist attitude. They locate the spontaneous forces of imagination and self-experience, of affective life in general, in what is most distant and archaic, and in Manichaean fashion oppose instrumental reason with a principle accessible solely to evocation, whether this is the will to power or sovereignty, Being itself or the Dionysian power for the poetic. In France this tradition leads from Georges Bataille through Foucault to Derrida. Over all these figures hovers, of course, the spirit of Nietzsche, newly resurrected in the 1970s.

The *Old Conservatives* do not allow themselves to be contaminated by cultural modernity in the first place. They observe with mistrust the collapse of substantive reason, the progressive differentiation of science, morality and art, the modern understanding of the world and its purely procedural canons of rationality, and recommend instead a return to positions *prior* to modernity (something which Max Weber regarded as a regression to the stage of material rationality). Here it is principally contemporary neo-Aristotelian-ism which has enjoyed some success, encouraged by the ecological question to renew the idea of a cosmological ethic. This tradition, which begins with Leo Strauss, has produced the interesting works of Hans Jonas and Robert Spaemann, for example.

It is the *New Conservatives* who relate most affirmatively to the achievements of modernity. They welcome the development of modern science so long as it only oversteps its own sphere in order to promote technological advance, capitalist growth and a rational form of administration. Otherwise, they recommend a politics directed essentially at defusing the explosive elements of cultural modernity. According to one claim, science, once properly understood, has already become meaningless as far as orientation in the lifeworld is concerned. According to another, politics should be immunised as much as possible from the demands of moral-practical legitimation. And a third claim affirms the total immanence of art, contests the idea of its utopian content, and appeals to its fictive character, precisely in order to confine aesthetic experience to the private sphere. One could mention the early Wittgenstein, Carl Schmitt in his middle period, and the later Gottfried Benn in this connection. With the definitive segregation of science, morality and art into autonomous spheres split off from the lifeworld and administered by specialists, all that remains of cultural modernity is what is left after renouncing the project of modernity itself. The resulting space is to be filled by traditions which are to be spared all demands for justification. Of course, it remains extremely difficult to see how such traditions could continue to survive in the modern world without the governmental support of ministries of culture.

Like every other typology, this too is a simplification, but it may be of some use for the analysis of contemporary intellectual and political controversies. For I fear that antimodernist ideas, coupled with an element of premodernism, are gaining ground in the circles of the greens and other alternative groups. On the other hand, in the changing attitudes within the political parties there is evidence of a similar turn, namely of an alliance between the advocates of postmodernity and those of premodernity. It seems to me that no one political party has a monopoly on neoconservative attitudes and the abuse of intellectuals. For this reason, especially after the clarifications you provided in your opening remarks, Mayor Wallmann, I have good reason to be grateful for the liberal spirit in which the City of Frankfurt has awarded me a prize which bears the name of Adorno, a son of this city who as a philosopher and a writer did more to shape the image of the intellectual than almost anyone else in the Federal Republic of Germany, and who has himself become an exemplary model for intellectuals.

5

Answering the Question:
What is Postmodernism?

Jean-François Lyotard

A DEMAND

This is a period of slackening – I refer to the colour of the times. From every direction we are being urged to put an end to experimentation, in the arts and elsewhere. I have read an art historian who extols realism and is militant for the advent of a new subjectivity. I have read an art critic who packages and sells 'Transavantgardism' in the marketplace of painting. I have read that under the name of postmodernism, architects are getting rid of the Bauhaus project, throwing out the baby of experimentation with the bathwater of functionalism. I have read that a new philosopher is discovering what he drolly calls Judaeo-Christianism, and intends by it to put an end to the impiety which we are supposed to have spread. I have read in a French weekly that some are displeased with *Mille Plateaux* [by Deleuze and Guattari] because they expect, especially when reading a work of philosophy, to be gratified with a little sense. I have read from the pen of a reputable historian that writers and thinkers of the 1960 and 1970 avant-gardes spread a reign of terror in the use of language, and that the conditions for a fruitful exchange must be restored by imposing on the intellectuals a common way of speaking, that of the historians. I have been reading a young philosopher of language who complains that Continental thinking, under the challenge of speaking machines, has surrendered to the machines the concern for reality, that it has substituted for the referential paradigm that of 'adlinguisticity' (one speaks about speech, writes about writing, intertextuality), and who thinks that the time has now come to restore a solid anchorage of language in the referent. I have read a talented theatrologist for whom postmodernism, with its games and fantasies, carries very little weight in front of political authority, especially when a worried public opinion encourages authority to a politics of totalitarian surveillance in the face of nuclear warfare threats.

I have read a thinker of repute who defends modernity against those he calls the neoconservatives. Under the banner of postmodernism, the latter would like, he believes, to get rid of the uncompleted project of modernism, that of the Enlightenment. Even the last advocates of *Aufklärung*, such as Popper or Adorno, were only able, according to him, to defend the project in a few particular spheres of life – that of politics for the author of *The Open Society*, and that of art for the author of *Ästhetische Theorie*. Jürgen Habermas (everyone had recognised him) thinks that if modernity has failed, it is in allowing the totality of life to be splintered into independent specialties which are left to the narrow competence of experts, while the concrete individual experiences 'desublimated meaning' and 'destructured form', not as a liberation but in the mode of that immense *ennui* which Baudelaire described over a century ago.

Following a prescription of Albrecht Wellmer, Habermas considers that the remedy for this splintering of culture and its separation from life can only come from 'changing the status of aesthetic experience when it is no longer primarily expressed in judgements of taste', but when it is 'used to explore a living historical situation', that is, when 'it is put in relation with problems of existence'. For this experience then 'becomes a part of a language game which is no longer that of aesthetic criticism'; it takes part 'in cognitive processes and normative expectations'; 'it alters the manner in which those different moments *refer* to one another'. What Habermas requires from the arts and the experiences they provide is, in short, to bridge the gap between cognitive, ethical, and political discourses, thus opening the way to a unity of experience.

My question is to determine what sort of unity Habermas has in mind. Is the aim of the project of modernity the constitution of sociocultural unity within which all the elements of daily life and of thought would take their places as in an organic whole? Or does the passage that has to be charted between heterogeneous language games – those of cognition, of ethics, of politics – belong to a different order from that? And if so, would it be capable of effecting a real synthesis between them?

The first hypothesis, of a Hegelian inspiration, does not challenge the notion of a dialectically totalising *experience*; the second is closer to the spirit of Kant's *Critique of Judgment*; but must be submitted, like the *Critique*, to that severe re-examination which postmodernity imposes on the thought of the Enlightenment, on the idea of a unitary end of history and of a subject. It is this critique which not only Wittgenstein and Adorno have initiated, but also a few other thinkers (French or other) who do not have the honour to be read by Professor Habermas – which at least saves them from getting a poor grade for their neoconservatism.

REALISM

The demands I began by citing are not all equivalent. They can even be contradictory. Some are made in the name of postmodernism, others in order to combat it. It is not necessarily the same thing to formulate a demand for some referent (and objective reality), for some sense (and credible transcendence), for an addressee (and audience), or an addressor (and subjective expressiveness) or for some communicational consensus (and a general code of exchanges, such as the genre of historical discourse). But in the diverse invitations to suspend artistic experimentation, there is an identical call for order, a desire for unity, for identity, for security, or popularity (in the sense of *Öffentlichkeit*, of 'finding a public'). Artists and writers must be brought back into the bosom of the community, or at least, if the latter is considered to be ill, they must be assigned the task of healing it.

There is an irrefutable sign of this common disposition: it is that for all those writers nothing is more urgent than to liquidate the heritage of the avant-gardes. Such is the case, in particular, of the so-called transavantgardism. The answers given by Achille Bonito Oliva to the questions asked by Bernard Lamarche-Vadel and Michel Enric leave no room for doubt about this. By putting the avant-gardes through a mixing process, the artist and critic feel more confident that they can suppress them than by launching a frontal attack. For they can pass off the most cynical eclecticism as a way of going beyond the fragmentary character of the preceding experiments; whereas if they openly turned their backs on them, they would run the risk of appearing ridiculously neoacademic. The *Salons* and the *Académies*, at the time when the bourgeoisie was establishing itself in history, were able to function as purgation and to grant awards for good plastic and literary conduct under the cover of realism. But capitalism inherently possesses the power to derealise familiar objects, social roles, and institutions to such a degree that the so-called realistic representations can no longer evoke reality except as nostalgia or mockery, as an occasion for suffering rather than for satisfaction. Classicism seems to be ruled out in a world in which reality is so destabilised that it offers no occasion for experience but one for ratings and experimentation.

This theme is familiar to all readers of Walter Benjamin. But it is necessary to assess its exact reach. Photography did not appear as a challenge to painting from the outside, any more than industrial cinema did to narrative literature. The former was only putting the final touch to the programme of ordering the visible elaborated by the quattrocento; while the latter was the last step in rounding off diachronies as organic wholes, which had been the ideal of the great novels of education since the eighteenth century. That the mechanical and the industrial should appear as substitutes for hand or craft was not in itself a disaster – except if one believes that art is in its essence the expression of an individuality of genius assisted by an elite craftsmanship.

The challenge lay essentially in that photographic and cinematographic processes can accomplish better, faster, and with a circulation a hundred thousand times larger than narrative or pictorial realism, the task which academicism had assigned to realism: to preserve various consciousnesses from doubt. Industrial photography and cinema will be superior to painting and the novel whenever the objective is to stabilise the referent, to arrange it according to a point of view which endows it with a recognisable meaning, to reproduce the syntax and vocabulary which enable the addressee to decipher images and sequences quickly, and so to arrive easily at the consciousness of his own identity as well as the approval which he thereby receives from others – since such structures of images and sequences constitute a communication code among all of them. This is the way the effects of reality, or if one prefers, the fantasies of realism, multiply.

If they too do not wish to become supporters (of minor importance at that) of what exists, the painter and novelist must refuse to lend themselves to such therapeutic uses. They must question the rules of the art of painting or of narrative as they have learned and received them from their predecessors. Soon those rules must appear to them as a means to deceive, to seduce, and to reassure, which makes it impossible for them to be 'true'. Under the common name of painting and literature, an unprecedented split is taking place. Those who refuse to re-examine the rules of art pursue successful careers in mass conformism by communicating, by means of the 'correct rules', the endemic desire for reality with objects and situations capable of gratifying it. Pornography is the use of photography and film to such an end. It is becoming a general model for the visual or narrative arts which have not met the challenge of the mass media.

As for the artists and writers who question the rules of plastic and narrative arts and possibly share their suspicions by circulating their work, they are destined to have little credibility in the eyes of those concerned with 'reality' and 'identity'; they have no guarantee of an audience. Thus it is possible to ascribe the dialectics of the avant-gardes to the challenge posed by the realisms of industry and mass communication to painting and the narrative arts. Duchamp's 'ready made' does nothing but actively and parodistically signify this constant process of dispossession of the craft of painting or even of being an artist. As Thierry de Duve penetratingly observes, the modern aesthetic question is not 'What is beautiful?' but 'What can be said to be art (and literature)?'

Realism, whose only definition is that it intends to avoid the question of reality implicated in that of art, always stands somewhere between academicism and kitsch. When power assumes the name of a party, realism and its neoclassical complement triumph over the experimental avant-garde by slandering and banning it – that is, provided the 'correct' images, the 'correct' narratives, the 'correct' forms which the party requests, selects, and propagates can find a public to desire them as the appropriate remedy for the anxiety and depression that public experiences. The demand for reality – that is, for unity, simplicity, communicability, etc. – did not have the same intensity nor the same continuity in German society between the two world wars and in Russian society after the Revolution: this provides a basis for a distinction between Nazi and Stalinist realism.

What is clear, however, is that when it is launched by the political apparatus, the attack on artistic experimentation is specifically reactionary: aesthetic judgement would only be required to decide whether such or such work is in conformity with the established rules of the beautiful. Instead of the work of art having to investigate what makes it an art object and whether it will be able to find an audience, political academicism possesses and imposes a priori criteria of the beautiful, which designate some works and a public at a stroke and forever. The use of categories in aesthetic judgement would thus be of the same nature as in cognitive judgement. To speak like Kant, both would be determining judgements: the expression is 'well formed' first in the understanding, then the only cases retained in experience are those which can be subsumed under this expression.

When power is that of capital and not that of a party, the 'transavantgardist' or 'postmodern' (in Jencks's sense) solution proves to be better adapted than the antimodern solution. Eclecticism is the degree zero of contemporary general culture: one listens to reggae, watches a western, eats McDonald's food for lunch and local cuisine for dinner, wears Paris perfume in Tokyo and 'retro' clothes in Hong Kong; knowledge is a matter for TV games. It is easy to find a public for eclectic works. By becoming kitsch, art panders to the confusion which reigns in the 'taste' of the patrons. Artists, gallery owners, critics, and public wallow together in the 'anything goes', and the epoch is one of slackening. But this realism of the 'anything goes' is in fact that of money; in the absence of aesthetic criteria, it remains possible and useful to assess the value of works of art according to the profits they yield. Such realism accommodates all tendencies, just as capital accommodates all 'needs', providing that the tendencies and needs have purchasing power. As for taste, there is no need to be delicate when one speculates or entertains oneself.

Artistic and literary research is doubly threatened, once by the 'cultural policy' and once by the art and book market. What is advised, sometimes through one channel, sometimes through the other, is to offer works which, first, are relative to subjects which exist in the eyes of the public they address, and second, works so made ('well made') that the public will recognise what they are about, will understand what is signified, will be able to give or refuse its approval knowingly, and if possible, even to derive from such work a certain amount of comfort.

The interpretation which has just been given of the contact between the industrial and mechanical arts, and literature and the fine arts is correct in its outline, but it remains narrowly sociologising and historicising – in other words, one-sided. Stepping over Benjamin's and Adorno's reticences, it must be recalled that science and industry are no more free of the suspicion which concerns reality than are art and writing. To believe otherwise would be to entertain an excessively humanistic notion of the mephistophelian functionalism of sciences and technologies. There is no denying the dominant existence today of techno-science, that is, the massive subordination of cognitive statements to the finality of the best possible performance, which is the technological criterion. But the mechanical and the industrial, especially when they enter fields traditionally reserved for artists, are carrying with them much more than power effects. The objects and the thoughts which originate in scientific knowledge and the capitalist economy convey with them one of the rules which supports their possibility: the rule that there is no reality unless testified by a consensus between partners over a certain knowledge and certain commitments.

This rule is of no little consequence. It is the imprint left on the politics of the scientist and the trustee of capital by a kind of flight of reality out of the metaphysical, religious, and political certainties that the mind believed it held. This withdrawal is absolutely necessary to the emergence of science and capitalism. No industry is possible without a suspicion of the Aristotelian theory of motion, no industry without a refutation of corporatism, of mercantilism, and of physiocracy. Modernity, in whatever age it appears, cannot exist without a shattering of belief and without discovery of the 'lack of reality' of reality, together with the invention of other realities.

What does this 'lack of reality' signify if one tries to free it from a narrowly historicised interpretation? The phrase is of course akin to what Nietzsche calls nihilism. But I see a much earlier modulation of Nietzschean perspectivism in the Kantian theme of the sublime. I think in particular that it is in the aesthetic of the sublime that modern art (including literature) finds its impetus and the logic of avant-gardes finds its axioms.

The sublime sentiment, which is also the sentiment of the sublime, is, according to Kant, a strong and equivocal emotion: it carries with it both pleasure and pain. Better still, in it pleasure derives from pain. Within the tradition of the subject, which comes from Augustine and Descartes and which Kant does not radically challenge, this contradiction, which some would call neurosis or masochism, develops as a conflict between the faculties of a subject, the faculty to conceive of something and the faculty to 'present' something. Knowledge exists if, first, the statement is intelligible, and second, if 'cases' can be derived from the experience which 'corresponds' to it. Beauty exists if a certain 'case' (the work of art), given first by the sensibility without any conceptual determination, the sentiment of pleasure independent of any interest the work may elicit, appeals to the principle of a universal consensus (which may never be attained).

Taste, therefore, testifies that between the capacity to conceive and the capacity to present an object corresponding to the concept, an undetermined agreement, without rules, giving rise to a judgement which Kant calls reflect-ive, may be experienced as pleasure. The sublime is a different sentiment. It takes place, on the contrary, when the imagination fails to present an object which might, if only in principle, come to match a concept. We have the Idea of the world (the totality of what is), but we do not have the capacity to show an example of it. We have the Idea of the simple (that which cannot be broken down, decomposed), but we cannot illustrate it with a sensible object which would be a 'case' of it. We can conceive the infinitely great, the infinitely powerful, but every presentation of an object destined to 'make visible' this absolute greatness or power appears to us painfully inadequate. Those are Ideas of which no presentation is possible. Therefore, they impart no knowledge about reality (experience); they also prevent the free union of the faculties which gives rise to the sentiment of the beautiful; and they prevent the formation and the stabilisation of taste. They can be said to be unpresentable.

I shall call modern the art which devotes its 'little technical expertise' (*son 'petit technique'*), as Diderot used to say, to present the fact that the unpre-sentable exists. To make visible that there is something which can be con-ceived and which can neither be seen nor made visible: this is what is at stake in modern painting. But how to make visible that there is something which cannot be seen? Kant himself shows the way when he names 'formlessness, the absence of form', as a possible index to the unpresentable. He also says of the empty 'abstraction' which the imagination experiences when in search for a presentation of the infinite (another unpresentable): this abstraction itself is like a presentation of the infinite, its 'negative presentation'. He cites the commandment, 'Thou shalt not make graven images' (Exodus), as the most sublime passage in the Bible in that it forbids all presentation of the Abso-lute. Little needs to be added to those observations to outline an aesthetic of sublime paintings. As painting, it will of course 'present' something though negatively; it will therefore avoid figuration or representation. It will be 'white' like one of Malevitch's squares; it will enable us to see only by making it impossible to see; it will please only by causing pain. One recognises in those instructions the axioms of avant-gardes in painting, inasmuch as they devote themselves to making an allusion to the unpresentable by means of visible presentations. The systems in the name of which, or with which, this task has been able to support or to justify itself deserve the greatest attention; but they can originate only in the vocation of the sublime in order to legitimise it, that is, to conceal it. They remain inexplicable without the incommensurability of reality to concept which is implied in the Kantian philosophy of the sublime.

It is not my intention to analyse here in detail the manner in which the various avant-gardes have, so to speak, humbled and disqualified reality by examining the pictorial techniques which are so many devices to make us believe in it. Local tone, drawing, the mixing of colours, linear perspective, the nature of the support and that of the instrument, the treatment, the display, the museum: the avant-gardes are perpetually flushing out artifices of presentation which make it possible to subordinate thought to the gaze and to turn it away from the unpresentable. If Habermas, like Marcuse, understands this task of derealisation as an aspect of the (repressive) 'desublimation' which characterises the avant-garde, it is because he confuses the Kantian sublime with Freudian sublimation, and because aesthetics has remained for him that of the beautiful.

THE POSTMODERN

What, then, is the postmodern? What place does it or does it not occupy in the vertiginous work of the questions hurled at the rules of image and narration? It is undoubtedly a part of the modern. All that has been received, if only yesterday (*modo, modo*, Petronius used to say), must be suspected. What space does Cézanne challenge? The Impressionists'. What object do Picasso and Braque attack? Cézanne's. What presupposition does Duchamp break with in 1912? That which says one must make a painting, be it cubist. And Buren questions that other presupposition which he believes had survived untouched by the work of Duchamp: the place of presentation of the work. In an amazing acceleration, the generations precipitate themselves. A work can become modern only if it is first postmodern. Postmodernism thus understood is not modernism at its end but in the nascent state, and this state is constant.

Yet I would like not to remain with this slightly mechanistic meaning of the word. If it is true that modernity takes place in the withdrawal of the real and according to the sublime relation between the presentable and the conceivable, it is possible, within this relation, to distinguish two modes (to use the musician's language). The emphasis can be placed on the powerlessness of the faculty of presentation, on the nostalgia for presence felt by the human subject, on the obscure and futile will which inhabits him in spite of everything. The emphasis can be placed, rather, on the power of the faculty to conceive, on its 'inhumanity' so to speak (it was the quality Apollinaire demanded of modern artists), since it is not the business of our understanding whether or not human sensibility or imagination can match what it conceives. The emphasis can also be placed on the increase of being and the jubilation which result from the invention of new rules of the game, be it pictorial, artistic, or any other. What I have in mind will become clear if we dispose very schematically a few names on the chessboard of the history of avant-gardes: on the side of melancholia, the German Expressionists, and on the side of *novatio*, Braque and Picasso, on the former Malevitch and on the latter Lissitsky, on the one Chirico and on the other Duchamp. The nuance which distinguishes these two modes may be infinitesimal; they often coexist in the same piece, are almost indistinguishable; and yet they testify to a difference (*un différend*) on which the fate of thought depends and will depend for a long time, between regret and assay.

The work of Proust and that of Joyce both allude to something which does not allow itself to be made present. Allusion, to which Paolo Fabbri recently called my attention, is perhaps a form of expression indispensable to the works which belong to an aesthetic of the sublime. In Proust, what is being eluded as the price to pay for this allusion is the identity of consciousness, a victim to the excess of time (*au trop de temps*). But in Joyce, it is the identity of writing which is the victim of an excess of the book (*au trop de livre*) or of literature.

Proust calls forth the unpresentable by means of a language unaltered in its syntax and vocabulary and of a writing which in many of its operators still belongs to the genre of novelistic narration. The literary institution, as Proust inherits it from Balzac and Flaubert, is admittedly subverted in that the hero is no longer a character but the inner consciousness of time, and in that the diegetic diachrony, already damaged by Flaubert, is here put in question because of the narrative voice. Nevertheless, the unity of the book, the odyssey of that consciousness, even if it is deferred from chapter to chapter, is not seriously challenged: the identity of the writing with itself throughout the labyrinth of the interminable narration is enough to connote such unity, which has been compared to that of *The Phenomenology of Mind*.

Joyce allows the unpresentable to become perceptible in his writing itself, in the signifier. The whole range of available narrative and even stylistic operators is put into play without concern for the unity of the whole, and new operators are tried. The grammar and vocabulary of literary language are no longer accepted as given; rather, they appear as academic forms, as rituals originating in piety (as Nietzsche said) which prevent the unpresentable from being put forward.

Here, then, lies the difference: modern aesthetics is an aesthetic of the sublime, though a nostalgic one. It allows the unpresentable to be put forward only as the missing contents; but the form, because of its recognisable consistency, continues to offer to the reader or viewer matter for solace and pleasure. Yet these sentiments do not constitute the real sublime sentiment, which is in an intrinsic combination of pleasure and pain: the pleasure that reason should exceed all presentation, the pain that imagination or sensibility should not be equal to the concept.

The postmodern would be that which, in the modern, puts forward the unpresentable in presentation itself; that which denies itself the solace of good forms, the consensus of a taste which would make it possible to share collectively the nostalgia for the unattainable; that which searches for new presentations, not in order to enjoy them but in order to impart a stronger sense of the unpresentable. A postmodern artist or writer is in the position of a philosopher: the text he writes, the work he produces are not in principle governed by pre-established rules, and they cannot be judged according to a determining judgement, by applying familiar categories to the text or to the work. Those rules and categories are what the work of art itself is looking for. The artist and the writer, then, are working without rules in order to formulate the rules of what *will have been done*. Hence the fact that work and text have the characters of an *event*; hence also, they always come too late for their author, or, what amounts to the same thing, their being put into work, their realisation (*mise en oeuvre*) always begin too soon. *Post modern* would have to be understood according to the paradox of the future (*post*) anterior (*modo*).

It seems to me that the essay (Montaigne) is postmodern, while the fragment (*The Athaeneum*) is modern.

Finally, it must be clear that it is our business not to supply reality but to invent allusions to the conceivable which cannot be presented. And it is not to be expected that this task will effect the last reconciliation between language games (which, under the name of faculties, Kant knew to be separated by a chasm), and that only the transcendental illusion (that of Hegel) can hope to totalise them into a real unity. But Kant also knew that the price to pay for such an illusion is terror. The nineteenth and twentieth centuries have given us as much terror as we can take. We have paid a high enough price for the nostalgia of the whole and the one, for the reconciliation of the concept and the sensible, of the transparent and the communicable experience. Under the general demand for slackening and for appeasement, we can hear the mutterings of the desire for a return of terror, for the realisation of the fantasy to seize reality. The answer is: Let us wage a war on totality; let us be witnesses to the unpresentable; let us activate the differences and save the honour of the name.

6

The Gulf War:
Is it Really Taking Place?

Jean Baudrillard

The media promote the war, the war promotes the media, and advertising competes with the war. Promotion is the most thick-skinned parasite in our culture. It would undoubtedly survive a nuclear conflict. It is our Last Judgement. But it is also like a biological function: it devours our substance, but it also allows us to metabolise what we absorb, like a parasitic plant or intestinal flora, it allows us to turn the world and the violence of the world into a consumable substance. So, war or promotion?

The war, along with the fake and presumptive warriors, generals, experts and television presenters we see speculating about it all through the day, watches itself in a mirror: am I pretty enough, am I operational enough, am I spectacular enough, am I sophisticated enough to make an entry onto the historical stage? Of course, this anxious interrogation increases the uncertainty with respect to its possible irruption. And this uncertainty invades our screens like a real oil slick, in the image of that blind seabird stranded on a beach in the Gulf, which will remain the symbol-image of what we all are in front of our screens, in front of that sticky and unintelligible event.

Two intense images, two or perhaps three scenes which all concern disfigured forms or costumes which correspond to the masquerade of this war: the CNN journalists with their gas masks in the Jerusalem studios; the drugged and beaten prisoners repenting on the screen of Iraqi TV; and perhaps that seabird covered in oil and pointing its blind eyes towards the Gulf sky. It is a masquerade of information: branded faces delivered over to the prostitution of the image, the image of an unintelligible distress. No images of the field of battle, but images of masks, of blind or defeated faces, images of falsification. It is not war taking place over there but the disfiguration of the world.

There is a profound scorn in the kind of 'clean' war which renders the other powerless without destroying its flesh, which makes it a point of honour to disarm and neutralise but not to kill. In a sense, it is worse than the other kind of war because it spares life. It is like humiliation: by taking less than life it is worse than taking life. There is undoubtedly a political error here, in so far as it is acceptable to be defeated but not to be put out of action. In this manner, the Americans inflict a particular insult by not making war on the other but simply eliminating him, the same as one would by not bargaining over the price of an object and thereby refusing any personal relationship with the vendor. The one whose price you accept without discussion despises you. The one whom you disarm without seeing is insulted and must be avenged. There is perhaps something of this in the presentation of those humiliated captives on television. It is in a sense to say to America: you who do not wish to see us, we will show you what you are like.

Just as the psychical or the screen of the psyche transforms every illness into a symptom (there is no organic illness which does not find its meaning elsewhere, in an interpretation of the ailment on another level: all the symptoms pass through a sort of black box in which the psychic images are jumbled and inverted, the illness becomes reversible, ungraspable, escaping any form of realistic medicine), so war, when it has been turned into information, ceases to be a realistic war and becomes a virtual war, in some way symptomatic. And just as everything psychical becomes the object of interminable speculation, so everything which is turned into information becomes the object of endless speculation, the site of total uncertainty. We are left with the symptomatic reading on our screens of the effects of the war, or the effects of discourse about the war, or completely speculative strategic evaluations which are analogous to those evaluations of opinion provided by polls. In this manner, we have gone in a week from 20% to 50% and then to 30% destruction of Iraqi military potential. The figure fluctuates exactly like the fortunes of the stock market. 'The land offensive is anticipated today, tomorrow, in a few hours, in any case sometime this week ... the climatic conditions are ideal for a confrontation, etc.' Whom to believe? There is nothing to believe. We must learn to read symptoms as symptoms, and television as the hysterical symptom of a war which has nothing to do with its critical mass. Moreover, it does not seem to have to reach its critical mass but remains in its inertial phase, while the implosion of the apparatus of information along with the accompanying tendency of the rate of information to fall seems to reinforce the implosion of war itself, with its accompanying tendency of the rate of confrontation to fall.

Information is like an unintelligent missile which never finds its target (nor, unfortunately, its anti-missile!), and therefore crashes anywhere or gets lost in space on an unpredictable orbit in which it eternally revolves as junk.

Information is only ever an erratic missile with a fuzzy destination which seeks its target but is drawn to every decoy – it is itself a decoy, in fact it scatters all over the environs and the result is mostly nil. The utopia of a targeted promotion or targeted information is the same as that of the targeted missile: it knows not where it lands and perhaps its mission is not to land but, like the missile, essentially to have been launched (as its name indicates). In fact, the only impressive images of missiles, rockets or satellites are those of the launch. It is the same with promotions or five year plans: the campaign launch is what counts, the impact or the end results are so uncertain that one frequently hears no more about them. The entire effect is in the programming, the success is that of the virtual model. Consider the Scuds: their strategic effectiveness is nil and their only (psychological) effect lies in the fact that Saddam succeeded in launching them.

The fact that the production of decoys has become an important branch of the war industry, just as the production of placebos has become an important branch of the medical industry and forgery a flourishing branch of the art industry – not to mention the fact that information has become a privileged branch of industry as such – all of this is a sign that we have entered a deceptive world in which an entire culture labours assiduously at its counterfeit. This also means that it no longer harbours any illusion about itself.

It all began with the leitmotif of precision, of surgical, mathematical and punctual efficacy, which is another way of not recognising the enemy as such, just as lobotomy is a way of not recognising madness as such. And then all that technical virtuosity finished up in the most ridiculous uncertainty. The isolation of the enemy by all kinds of electronic interference creates a sort of barricade behind which he becomes invisible. He also becomes 'stealthy', and his capacity for resistance becomes indeterminable. In annihilating him at a distance and as it were by transparency, it becomes impossible to discern whether or not he is dead.

The idea of a clean war, like that of a clean bomb or an intelligent missile, this whole war conceived as a technological extrapolation of the brain is a sure sign of madness. It is like those characters in Hieronymus Bosch with a glass bell or a soap bubble around their head as a sign of their mental debility. A war enclosed in a glass coffin, like Snow White, purged of any carnal contamination or warrior's passion. A clean war which ends up in an oil slick.

The French supplied the planes and the nuclear power stations, the Russians the tanks, the English the underground bunkers and runways, the Germans the gas, the Dutch the gas masks, while the Italians supplied the decoy equivalents of everything – tanks, bunkers, inflatable bombers, missiles with artificial thermal emissions, etc. Before so many marvels, one is drawn to compete in diabolical imagination: why not false gas masks for the Palestinians? Why not put the hostages at decoy strategic sites, a fake chemical factory for example?

Has a French plane been downed? The question becomes burning, it is our honour which is at stake. That would constitute a proof of our involvement, and the Iraqis appear to take a malicious pleasure in denying it (perhaps they have a more accurate idea of our involvement?). Whatever the situation, it will be necessary here too to set up decoys, simulated losses and *trompe l'oeil* victims (as with the fake destruction of civic buildings in Timisoara or Baghdad).

A war of high technological concentration but poor definition. Perhaps it has gone beyond its critical mass by too strong a concentration?

Fine illustration of the communication schema in which emitter and receiver on opposite sides of the screen, never connect with each other. Instead of messages, it is missiles and bombs which fly from one side to the other, but any dual or personal relation is altogether absent. Thus an aerial attack on Iraq may be read in terms of coding, decoding and feedback (in this case, very bad: we cannot even know what we have destroyed). This explains the tolerance of the Israelis: they have only been hit by abstract projectiles, namely missiles. The least live bombing attack on Israel would have provoked immediate retaliation.

Communication is also a clean relation: in principle, it excludes any violent or personal affect. It is strange to see this disaffection, this profound indifference to one another, played out at the very heart of violence and war.

The fact that the undetectable Stealth bombers should have begun the war by aiming at decoys and undoubtedly destroying fake objectives, that the Secret Services (also 'furtive') should have been so mistaken in so many ways about the realities of Iraqi weaponry, and the strategists so wrong about the effects of the intensive electronic war, all testifies to the illusionism of force once it is no longer measured against an adversary but against its abstract operation alone. All the generals, admirals and other meretricious experts should be sent to an inflatable strategic site, to see whether these decoys wouldn't in fact attract a real bomb on their heads.

Conversely, the Americans' innocence in admitting their mistake (declaring five months later that the Iraqi forces are almost intact while they themselves are not ready to attack) and all that counter-propaganda which adds to the confusion would be moving if it did not testify to the same strategic idiocy as the triumphal declarations at the outset, and did not further take us for complicit witnesses of this suspicious sincerity of the kind which says: you see, we tell you everything. We can always give credit to the Americans for knowing how to exploit their failures by means of a sort of *trompe l'oeil* candour.

A UN bedtime story: the UN awoke (or was awakened) from its glass coffin (the building in New York). As the coffin fell and was shattered (at the same time as the Eastern Bloc), she spat out the apple and revived, as fresh as a rose, only to find at once the waiting Prince Charming: the Gulf War, also fresh from the arms of the cold war after a long period of mourning. No doubt together they will give birth to a New World Order, or else end up like two ghosts locked in vampiric embrace.

Seeing how Saddam uses his cameras on the hostages, the caressed children, the (fake) strategic targets, on his own smiling face, on the ruins of the milk factory, one cannot help thinking that in the West we still have a hypocritical vision of television and information, to the extent that, despite all the evidence, we hope for their proper use. Saddam, for his part, knows what the media and information are: he makes a radical, unconditional, perfectly cynical and therefore perfectly instrumental use of them. The Romanians too were able to make a perfectly immoral and mystificatory use of them (from our point of view). We may regret this, but given the principle of simulation which governs all information, even the most pious and objective, and given the structural unreality of images and their proud indifference to the truth, these cynics alone are right about information when they employ it as an unconditional simulacrum. We believe that they immorally pervert images. Not so. They alone are conscious of the profound immorality of images, just as the Bokassas and Amin Dadas reveal, through the parodic and Ubuesque use they make of them, the obscene truth of the Western political and democratic structures they borrowed. The secret of the underdeveloped is to parody their model and render it ridiculous by exaggeration. We alone retain the illusion of information and of a right to information. They are not so naïve.

Never any acting out, or passage to action, but simply acting: roll cameras! But there is too much film, or none at all, or it was desensitised by remaining too long in the humidity of the cold war. In short, there is quite simply nothing to see. Later, there will be something to see for the viewers of archival cassettes and the generations of video-zombies who will never cease reconstituting the event, never having had the intuition of the non-event of this war.

   The archive also belongs to virtual time; it is the complement of the event 'in real time', of that instantaneity of the event and its diffusion. Moreover, rather than the 'revolution' of real time of which Virilio speaks, we should speak of an involution in real time; of an involution of the event in the instantaneity of everything at once, and of its vanishing in information itself. If we take note of the speed of light and the temporal short-circuit of pure war (the nanosecond), we see that this involution precipitates us precisely into the virtuality of war and not into its reality, it precipitates us into the absence of war. Must we denounce the speed of light?

Utopia of real time which renders the event simultaneous at all points on the globe. In fact, what we live in real time is not the event, but rather in larger than life (in other words, in the virtual size of the image) the spectacle of the degradation of the event and its spectral evocation (the 'spiritualism of information': event, are you there? Gulf War, are you there?) in the commentary, gloss, and verbose *mise en scène* of talking heads which only underlines the impossibility of the image and the correlative unreality of the war. It is the same aporia as that of *cinéma vérité* which seeks to short-circuit the unreality of the image in order to present us the truth of the object. In this manner, CNN seeks to be a stethoscope attached to the hypothetical heart of the war, and to present us with its hypothetical pulse. But this auscultation only provides a confused ultrasound, undecidable symptoms, and an assortment of vague and contradictory diagnoses. All that we can hope for is to see them die live (metaphorically of course), in other words that some event or other should overwhelm the information instead of the information inventing the event and commenting artificially upon it. The only real information revolution would be this one, but it is not likely to occur in the near future: it would presuppose a reversal of the idea we have of information. In the meantime, we will continue with the involution and encrustation of the event in and by information, and the closer we approach the live and real time, the further we will go in this direction.

The same illusion of progress occurred with the appearance of speech and then colour on screen: at each stage of this progress we moved further away from the imaginary intensity of the image. The closer we supposedly approach the real or the truth, the further we draw away from them both, since neither one nor the other exists. The closer we approach the real time of the event, the more we fall into the illusion of the virtual. God save us from the illusion of war.

At a certain speed, the speed of light, you lose even your shadow. At a certain speed, the speed of information, things lose their sense. There is a great risk of announcing (or denouncing) the Apocalypse of real time, when it is precisely at this point that the event volatilises and becomes a black hole from which light no longer escapes. War implodes in real time, history implodes in real time, all communication and all signification implode in real time. The Apocalypse itself, understood as the arrival of catastrophe, is unlikely. It falls prey to the prophetic illusion. The world is not sufficiently coherent to lead to the Apocalypse.

Nevertheless, in confronting our opinions on the war with the diametrically opposed opinions of Paul Virilio, one of us betting on apocalyptic escalation and the other on deterrence and the indefinite virtuality of war, we concluded that this decidedly strange war went in both directions at once. The war's programmed escalation is relentless and its non-occurrence no less inevitable: the war proceeds at once towards the two extremes of intensification and deterrence. The war and the non-war take place at the same time, with the same period of deployment and suspense and the same possibilities of de-escalation or maximal increase.

What is most extraordinary is that the two hypotheses, the apocalypse of real time and pure war along with the triumph of the virtual over the real, are realised at the same time, in the same space-time, each in implacable pursuit of the other. It is a sign that the space of the event has become a hyperspace with multiple refractivity, and that *the space of war has become definitively non-Euclidean.* And that there will undoubtedly be no resolution of this situation: we will remain in the undecidability of war, which is the undecidability created by the unleashing of the two opposed principles.

Soft war and pure war go boating.

There is a degree of popular good will in the micro-panic distilled by the airwaves. The public ultimately consents to be frightened, and to be gently terrorised by the bacteriological scenarios, on the basis of a kind of affective patriotism, even while it preserves a fairly profound indifference to the war. But it censors this indifference, on the grounds that we must not cut ourselves off from the world scene, that we must be mobilised at least as extras in order to rescue war: we have no other passion with which to replace it. It is the same with political participation under normal circumstances: this is largely second hand, taking place against a backdrop of spontaneous indifference. It is the same with God: even when we no longer believe, we continue to believe that we believe. In this hysterical replacement function, we identify at once those who are superfluous and they are many. By contrast, the few who advance the hypothesis of this profound indifference will be received as traitors.

By the force of the media, this war liberates an exponential mass of stupidity, not the particular stupidity of war, which is considerable, but the professional and functional stupidity of those who pontificate in perpetual commentary on the event: all the Bouvards and Pécuchets for hire, the would-be raiders of the lost image, the CNN types and all the master singers of strategy and information who make us experience the emptiness of television as never before. This war, it must be said, constitutes a merciless test. Fortunately, no one will hold this expert or general or that intellectual for hire to account for the idiocies or absurdities proffered the day before, since these will be erased by those of the following day. In this manner, everyone is amnestied by the ultra-rapid succession of phony events and phony discourses. The laundering of stupidity by the escalation of stupidity which reconstitutes a sort of total innocence, namely the innocence of washed and bleached brains, stupefied not by the violence but by the sinister insignificance of the images.

Chevènement in the desert: *Morituri te salutant!* Ridiculous. France with its old Jaguars and its presidential slippers.

Capillon on television: the benefit of this war will have been to recycle our military leaders on television. One shudders at the thought that in another time, in a real war, they were operational on the battlefield.

Imbroglio: that pacifist demonstration in Paris, thus indirectly for Saddam Hussein, who does want war, and against the French Government which does not want it, and which from the outset gives all the signs of refusing to take part, or of doing so reluctantly.

Deserted shops, suspended vacations, the slowdown of activity, the city turned over to the absent masses: it may well be that, behind the alibi of panic, this war should be the dreamed-for opportunity to soft-pedal, the opportunity to slow down, to ease off the pace. The crazed particles calm down, the war erases the guerrilla warfare of everyday life. Catharsis? No: renovation. Or perhaps, with everyone glued at home, TV plays out fully its role of social control by collective stupefaction: turning uselessly upon itself like a dervish, it affixes populations all the better for deceiving them, as with a bad detective novel which we cannot believe could be so pointless.

Iraq is being rebuilt even before it has been destroyed. Aftersales service. Such anticipation reduces even further the credibility of the war, which did not need this to discourage those who wanted to believe in it.

Sometimes a glimmer of black humour: the twelve thousand coffins sent along with the arms and ammunition. Here too, the Americans demonstrate their presumption: their projections and their losses are without common measure. But Saddam challenged them with being incapable of sacrificing ten thousand men in a war: they replied by sending twelve thousand coffins.

The overestimation of losses is part of the same megalomaniac light show as the publicised deployment of 'Desert Shield' and the orgy of bombardment. The pilots no longer even have any targets. The Iraqis no longer even have enough decoys to cater for the incessant raids. The same target must be bombed five times. Mockery.

The British artillery unleashed for twenty four hours. Long since there was nothing left to destroy. Why then? In order 'to cover the noise of the armoured columns advancing towards the front by the noise of the bombardment'. Of course, the effect of surprise must be maintained (it is February 21). The best part is that there was no longer anyone there, the Iraqis had already left. Absurdity.

Saddam is a mercenary, the Americans are missionaries. But once the mercenary is beaten, the missionaries become *de facto* the mercenaries of the entire world. But the price for becoming a perfect mercenary is to be stripped of all political intelligence and all will. The Americans cannot escape it: if they want to be the police of the world and the New World Order, they must lose all political authority in favour of their operational capacity alone. They will become pure executants and everyone else pure extras in the consensual and policed New World Order.

Whoever the dictator to be destroyed, any punitive force sure of itself is even more frightening. Having assumed the Israeli style, the Americans will henceforth export it everywhere and, just as the Israelis did, lock themselves into the spiral of unconditional repression.

For the Americans, the enemy does not exist as such. *Nothing personal.* Your war is of no interest to me, your resistance is of no interest to me. I will destroy you when I am ready. Refusal to bargain, whereas Saddam Hussein, for his part, bargains his war by overbidding in order to fall back, attempting to force the hand by pressure and blackmail, like a hustler trying to sell his goods. The Americans understand nothing in this whole psychodrama of bargaining, they are had every time until, with the wounded pride of the Westerner, they stiffen and impose their conditions. They understand nothing of this floating duel, this passage of arms in which, for a brief moment, the honour and dishonour of each is in play. They know only their virtue, and they are proud of their virtue. If the other wants to play, to trick and to challenge, they will virtuously employ their force. They will oppose the other's traps with their character armour and their armoured tanks. For them, the time of exchange does not exist. But the other, even if he knows that he will concede, cannot do so without another form of procedure. He must be recognised as interlocutor: this is the goal of the exchange. He must be recognised as an enemy: this is the whole aim of the war. For the Americans, bargaining is cheap whereas for the others it is a matter of honour, (mutual) personal recognition, linguistic strategy (language exists, it must be honoured) and respect for time (altercation demands a rhythm, it is the price of there being an Other). The Americans take no account of these primitive subtleties. They have much to learn about symbolic exchange.

By contrast, they are winners from an economic point of view. No time lost in discussion, no psychological risk in any duel with the other: it is a way of proving that time does not exist, that the other does not exist, and that all that matters is the model and mastery of the model.

From a military point of view, to allow this war to endure in the way they have (instead of applying an Israeli solution and immediately exploiting the imbalance of force while short-circuiting all retaliatory effects), is a clumsy solution lacking in glory and full of perverse effects (Saddam's aura among the Arab masses). Nevertheless, in doing this, they impose a suspense, a temporal vacuum in which they present to themselves and to the entire world the spectacle of their virtual power. They will have allowed the war to endure as long as it takes, not to win but to persuade the whole world of the infallibility of their machine.

The victory of the model is more important than victory on the ground. Military success consecrates the triumph of arms, but the programming success consecrates the defeat of time. War-processing, the transparency of the model in the unfolding of the war, the strategy of relentless execution of a programme, the electrocution of all reaction and any live initiative, including their own: these are more important from the point of view of general deterrence (of friends and foes alike) than the final result on the ground. Clean war, white war, programmed war: more lethal than the war which sacrifices human lives.

We are a long way from annihilation, holocaust and atomic apocalypse, the total war which functions as the archaic imaginary of media hysteria. On the contrary, this kind of preventative, deterrent and punitive war is a warning to everyone not to take extreme measures and inflict upon themselves what they inflict on others (the missionary complex): the rule of the game that says everyone must remain within the limits of their power and not make war by any means whatever. Power must remain virtual and exemplary, in other words, virtuous. The decisive test is the planetary apprenticeship in this regulation. Just as wealth is no longer measured by the ostentation of wealth but by the secret circulation of speculative capital, so war is not measured by being waged but by its speculative unfolding in an abstract, electronic and informational space, the same space in which capital moves.

While this conjuncture does not exclude all accident (disorder in the virtual), it is nevertheless true that the probability of the irruption of those extreme measures and mutual violence which we call war is increasingly low.

Saddam the hysteric. Interminable shit kicker. The hysteric cannot be crushed: he is reborn from his symptoms as though from his ashes. Confronted by a hysteric, the other becomes paranoid, he deploys a massive apparatus of protection and mistrust. He suspects the hysteric of bad faith, of ruse and dissimulation. He wants to constrain him to the truth and to transparency. The hysteric is irreducible. His means are decoys and the overturning of alliances. Confronted with this lubricity, this duplicity, the paranoid can only become more rigid, more obsessional. The most violent reproach addressed to Saddam Hussein by Bush is that of being a liar, a traitor, a bad player, a trickster. *Lying son of a bitch!* Saddam, like a good hysteric, has never given birth to his own war: for him, it is only a phantom pregnancy. By contrast, he has until now succeeded in preventing Bush from giving birth to his. And, with the complicity of Gorbachev, he almost succeeded in fucking him up the ass. But the hysteric is not suicidal, this is the advantageous other side to Saddam. He is neither mad nor suicidal. Perhaps he should be treated by hypnosis?

The Iraqis and the Americans have at least one thing in common, a heinous crime which they (and with them the West) share. Many things about this war are explained by this anterior crime from which both sides sought to profit with impunity. The secret expiation of this crime feeds the Gulf War in its confusion and its allure of the settling of accounts. Such is the shared agreement to forget it that little is spoken about this prior episode (even by the Iranians), namely the war against Iran. Saddam must avenge his failure to win, even though he was the aggressor and sure of his impunity. He must avenge himself against the West which trained him for it, while the Americans, for their part, must suppress him as the embarrassing accomplice in that criminal act.

For any government official or despot, power over his own people takes precedence over everything else. In the case of the Gulf War, this provides the only chance of a solution or a de-escalation. Saddam will prefer to concede rather than destroy his internal hegemony or sacrifice his army, etc. In this sense, sheltering his planes in Iran is a good sign: rather than an offensive sign, it is the ploy of a burglar who stashes his haul in order to retrieve it when he comes out of prison, thus an argument against any heroic or suicidal intention.

While one fraction of the intellectuals and politicians, specialists in the reserve army of mental labour, are whole-heartedly in favour of the war, and another fraction are against it from the bottom of their hearts, but for reasons no less disturbing, all are agreed on one point: this war exists, we have seen it. There is no interrogation into the event itself or its reality; or into the fraudulence of this war, the programmed and always delayed illusion of battle; or into the machination of this war and its amplification by information, not to mention the improbable orgy of material, the systematic manipulation of data, the artificial dramatisation...If we do not have practical intelligence about the war (and none among us has), at least let us have a sceptical intelligence towards it, without renouncing the pathetic feeling of its absurdity.

But there is more than one kind of absurdity: that of the massacre and that of being caught up in the illusion of massacre. It is just as in La Fontaine's fable: the day there is a real war you will not even be able to tell the difference. The real victory of the simulators of war is to have drawn everyone into this rotten simulation.

7

Deconstruction and Actuality

Jacques Derrida

This interview was conducted in Paris in August 1993, to mark the publication of Derrida's Spectres de Marx *(Paris, 1993), and was published in the monthly review* Passages *in September. This English translation appears in* Radical Philosophy *with permission.*

Passages: From Bogota to Santiago, from Prague to Sofia, not to mention Berlin or Paris, your work gives people an impression of being in touch with the moment, with actuality. Do you share that feeling? Are you a philosopher of the present? Or at least one of those who think their time?

Derrida: Who knows? How could anyone be sure? And anyway, being 'in touch with actuality' and 'thinking one's time' are not the same thing. Both of them imply *doing* something, over and above establishing facts or offering descriptions: taking part, participating, taking sides. That is when you 'make contact', and perhaps change things, if only slightly. But one 'intervenes', as they say, in a time which is not present to one, or given in advance. There are no pre-established norms which can guarantee that one is 'making contact with actuality', or 'thinking one's time' as you put it. And you often get one without the other. But I don't think I am capable of improvising an answer to this kind of question. We must stick to the time of our conversation – and of course time is limited. Now more than ever, thinking one's time – especially if there is a danger, or a hope, of speaking about it in public – means recognising and exploiting the fact that the time of this speaking is produced artificially. It is an *artifact*. In its actualisation, the time of such a public act is calculated and constrained, 'formatted' and 'initialised' by (to put it briefly) the organisations of the media – and these alone would deserve an almost infinite analysis. These days, anyone who wants to think their time, especially if they want to talk about it too, is bound to pay heed to a public space, and therefore to a political present which is constantly changing in form and content as a result of the tele-technology of what is confusedly called news, information or communication.

But your question referred not only to the present, but to actuality. Very schematically, let me quickly mention just two of the most actual features of the moment. They are too abstract to capture the most characteristic features of my own experience of 'actuality', or any other *philosophical* experience of it, but they do point to something of what constitutes actuality in general. I will try to designate them by two portmanteau terms: *artifactuality* and *actuvirtuality*. The first means that actuality is indeed *made*: it is important to know what it is made of, but it is even more necessary to recognise that it is made. It is not given, but actively produced; it is sorted, invested and performatively interpreted by a range of hierarchising and selective procedures – *factitious* or *artificial* procedures which are always subservient to various powers and interests of which their 'subjects' and agents (producers and consumers of actuality, always interpreters, and in some cases 'philosophers' too), are never sufficiently aware. The 'reality' of 'actuality' – however individual, irreducible, stubborn, painful or tragic it may be – only reaches us through fictional devices. The only way to analyse it is through a work of resistance, of vigilant counter-interpretation, etc. Hegel was right to tell the philosophers of his time to read the newspapers. Today, the same duty requires us to find out how news is *made*, and by whom: the daily papers, the weeklies, and the TV news as well. We need to insist on looking at them from the other end: that of the press agencies as well as that of the teleprompter. And we should never forget what this entails: whenever a journalist or a politician appears to be speaking to us directly, in our homes, and looking us straight in the eye, he or she is actually reading, from a screen, at the dictation of a 'prompter', and reading a text which was produced elsewhere, on a different occasion, possibly by other people, or by a whole network of nameless writers and editors.

Passages: Presumably there is a duty to develop a systematic critique of what you call *artifactuality*. You say we 'ought'...

Derrida: Yes, a critical culture, a kind of education. But I would not speak about this duty of ours as citizens and philosophers – I would never say 'ought' – without adding two or three crucial qualifications.

The first of these is about the question of *nationality*. (To respond briefly to one of the connotations of your first question, it sounded as if, coming back from abroad, you had fished it out of your diary for some reason: 'here's what they say about you abroad: so what do you make of that?' I would have liked to comment on this; but let it pass.) Amongst the filters which 'inform' the moment – and despite the accelerating pace and increasing ambiguity of internationalisation – nations, regions and provinces, or indeed the 'West', still have a dominance which overdetermines every other hierarchy (sport in the first place, then the 'politician' – though not the political – and finally the 'cultural', in decreasing order of supposed popularity, spectacularity, and comprehensibility). This leads to the discounting of a whole mass of events: all those, in fact, which are taken to be irrelevant to the (supposedly public) national interest, or the national language, or the national code or style. On the news, 'actuality' is automatically ethnocentric. Even when it has to do with 'human rights', it will exclude foreigners, sometimes within the same country, though not on the basis of nationalist passions, or doctrines, or policies. Some journalists make honourable attempts to escape from this pressure, but by definition they can never do enough, and in the end it does not depend on the professional journalists anyway. It is especially important to remember this now, when old nationalisms are taking new forms, and making use of the most 'advanced' media techniques (the official radio and TV of former Yugoslavia are only one example, though a particularly striking one). And it is worth noticing that some of them have felt it necessary to cast doubt on the critique of ethnocentrism, or (to simplify greatly) on the deconstruction of Eurocentrism. This is still considered acceptable, even now: it is as if they were completely blind to the deadly threats currently being issued, in the name of ethnicities, right at the centre of Europe, within a Europe whose only reality today – whose only 'actuality' – is economic and national, and whose only law, in alliances as in conflicts, is still that of the market.

But the tragedy, as always, lies in a contradiction, a double demand: the apparent internationalisation of sources of news and information is often based on the appropriation and monopolisation of channels of information, publication and distribution. Just think of what happened in the Gulf War. It may have represented an exemplary moment of heightened awareness, or even rebellion, but this should not be allowed to conceal the normality and constancy of this kind of violence in conflicts everywhere, not just the Middle East. Sometimes, then, this apparently international process of homogenisation may provoke 'national' resistance. That is the first complication.

A second qualification: this international artifactuality – the monopolisation of the 'actuality effect', and the centralisation of the artifactual power to 'create events' – may be accompanied by advances in 'live' communication, taking place in so-called 'real' time, in the present. The theatrical genre of the 'interview' is a propitiation, at least a fictive one, of this idolatry of 'immediate' presence and 'live' communication. The newspapers will always prefer to publish an interview, accompanied by photographs of the author, rather than an article which will face up to its responsibilities in reading, criticism and education. But how can we carry on criticising the mystifications of 'live' communication (videocameras, etc.) if we want to continue making use of it? In the first place, by continuing to point out, and *argue*, that 'live' communication and 'real time' are never pure: they do not furnish us with intuitions or transparencies, or with perceptions unmarked by technical interpretation or intervention. And any such argument inevitably makes reference to philosophy.

And finally – as I just mentioned – the necessary deconstruction of artifactuality should never be allowed to turn into an alibi or an excuse. It must not create an inflation of the image, or be used to neutralise every danger by means of what might be called the trap of the trap, the delusion of delusion: a denial of events, by which everything – even violence and suffering, war and death – is said to be constructed and fictive, and constituted by and for the media, so that nothing really ever happens, only images, simulacra, and delusions. The deconstruction of artifactuality should be carried as far as possible, but we must also take every precaution against this kind of critical neo-idealism. We must bear in mind not only that any coherent deconstruction is about singularity, about events, and about what is ultimately irreducible in them, but also that 'news' or 'information' is a contradictory and heterogeneous process. Information can transform and strengthen knowledge, truth and the cause of future democracy, with all the problems associated with them, and it must do so, just as it often has done in the past. However artificial and manipulative it may be, we have to hope that artifactuality will bend itself or lend itself to the coming of what is on its way, to the outcome which carries it along and towards which it is moving. And to which it is going to have to bear witness, whether it wants to or not.

Passages: A moment ago you mentioned another term, referring not to technology and artificiality, but to virtuality.

Derrida: If we had enough time I would want to stress another aspect of 'actuality' – of what is happening now, and what is happening *to actuality*. I would emphasise not only these *artificial* syntheses (synthetic images, synthetic voices, all the prosthetic supplements which can be substituted for real actuality) but also, and especially, a concept of *virtuality* (virtual images, virtual spaces, and therefore virtual outcomes or events). Clearly it is no longer possible to contrast virtuality with actual reality, along the lines of the serene old philosophical distinction between power and act, *dynamis* and *energeia*, the potentiality of matter and the determining form of a *telos*, and hence of *progress*, etc. Virtuality now reaches right into the structure of the eventual event and imprints itself there; it affects both the time and the space of images, discourses, and 'news' or 'information' – in fact everything which connects us to actuality, to the unappeasable reality of its supposed present. In order to 'think their time', philosophers today need to attend to the implications and effects of this virtual time – both to the new technical uses to which it can be put, and to how they echo and recall some far more ancient possibilities.

8

Ideology, Discourse and the Problems of 'Post-Marxism'

Terry Eagleton

Consider the following paradox. The last decade has witnessed a remarkable resurgence of ideological movements throughout the world. In the Middle East, Islamic fundamentalism has emerged as a potent political force. In the so-called Third World, and in one region of the British Isles, revolutionary nationalism continues to join battle with imperialist power. In some of the post-capitalist states of the Eastern bloc, a still tenacious neo-Stalinism remains locked in combat with an array of oppositional forces. The most powerful capitalist nation in history has been swept from end to end by a peculiarly noxious brand of Christian Evangelicalism. Throughout this period, Britain has suffered the most ideologically aggressive and explicit regime of living political memory, in a society which traditionally prefers its ruling values to remain implicit and oblique. Meanwhile, somewhere on the left bank, it is announced that the concept of ideology is now obsolete.

How are we to account for this absurdity? Why is it that in a world racked by ideological conflict, the very notion of ideology has evaporated without trace from the writings of postmodernism and poststructuralism?[1] The theoretical clue to this conundrum is a topic that shall concern us in this book. Very briefly, I argue that three key doctrines of postmodernist thought have conspired to discredit the classical concept of ideology. The first of these doctrines turns on a rejection of the notion of representation – in fact, a rejection of an *empiricist* model of representation, in which the representational baby has been nonchalantly slung out with the empiricist bathwater. The second revolves on an epistemological scepticism which would hold that the very act of identifying a form of consciousness as ideological entails some untenable notion of absolute truth. Since the latter idea attracts few devotees these days, the former is thought to crumble in its wake. We cannot brand Pol Pot a Stalinist bigot since this would imply some metaphysical certitude about what not being a Stalinist bigot would involve. The third doctrine concerns a reformulation of the relations between rationality, interests and power, along roughly neo-Nietzschean lines, which is thought to render the whole concept of ideology redundant. Taken together, these three theses have been thought by some enough to dispose of the whole question of ideology, at exactly the historical moment when Muslim demonstrators beat their foreheads till the blood runs, and American farmhands anticipate being swept imminently up into heaven, Cadillac and all.

Hegel remarks somewhere that all great historical events happen, so to speak, twice. (He forgot to add: the first time as tragedy, the second as farce.) The current suppression of the concept of ideology is in one sense a recycling of the so-called 'end of ideology' epoch which followed the Second World War; but whereas that movement was at least partially explicable as a traumatised response to the crimes of fascism and Stalinism, no such political rationale underpins the present fashionable aversion to ideological critique. Moreover, the 'end-of-ideology' school was palpably a creation of the political right, whereas our own 'post-ideological' complacency often enough sports radical credentials. If the 'end-of-ideology' theorists viewed all ideology as inherently closed, dogmatic and inflexible, postmodernist thought tends to see all ideology as teleological, 'totalitarian' and metaphysically grounded. Grossly travestied in this way, the concept of ideology obediently writes itself off.

[...]

Ideology is often felt to entail a 'naturalisation' of social reality; and this is another area in which the semiotic contribution has been especially illuminating. For the Roland Barthes of *Mythologies* (1957), myth (or ideology) is what transforms history into Nature by lending arbitrary signs an apparently obvious, unalterable set of connotations. 'Myth does not deny things, on the contrary, its function is to talk about them; simply it purifies them, it makes them innocent, it gives them a natural and eternal justification, it gives them a clarity which is not that of an explanation but of a statement of fact.'[2] The 'naturalisation' thesis is here extended to discourse as such, rather than to the world of which it speaks. The 'healthy' sign for Barthes is one which unashamedly displays its own gratuitousness, the fact that there is no internal or self-evident bond between itself and what it represents; and to this extent artistic modernism, which typically broods upon the 'unmotivated' nature of its own sign-systems, emerges as politically progressive. The 'unhealthy' – mythological or ideological – signifier is one which cunningly erases this radical lack of motivation, suppresses the semiotic labour which produced it, and so allows us to receive it as 'natural' and 'transparent', gazing through its innocent surface to the concept or signified to which it permits us magically immediate access. Literary realism, for Barthes and his disciples, is then exemplary of this deceptive transparency – a curiously formalist, trans-historical judgement on everything from Defoe to Dostoevsky, which in the 'wilder' versions of this richly suggestive case becomes an unmitigated disaster which ought really never to have happened.

It is just this spurious naturalisation of language which the literary critic Paul de Man sees as lying at the root of all ideology. What de Man terms the 'phenomenalist' delusion, in the words of his commentator Christopher Norris, is the idea that language 'can become somehow consubstantial with the world of natural objects and processes, and so transcend the ontological gulf between words (or concepts) and sensuous intuitions'.[3] Ideology is language which forgets the essentially contingent, accidental relations between itself and the world, and comes instead to mistake itself as having some kind of organic, inevitable bond with what it represents. For the essentially tragic philosophy of a de Man, mind and world, language and being, are eternally discrepant; and ideology is the gesture which seeks to conflate these quite separate orders, hunting nostalgically for a pure presence of the thing within the word, and so imbuing meaning with all the sensuous positivity of natural being. Ideology strives to bridge verbal concepts and sensory intuitions; but the force of truly critical (or 'deconstructive') thought is to demonstrate how the insidiously figural, rhetorical nature of discourse will always intervene to break up this felicitous marriage. 'What we call ideology', de Man observes in *The Resistance to Theory*, 'is precisely the confusion of linguistic with natural reality, of reference with phenomenalism.'[4] One might find exemplary instances of such a confusion in the thought of the later Heidegger, for whom certain words allow us a privileged access to 'Being'; in the contemporaneous literary criticism of F. R. Leavis; and in the poetry of Seamus Heaney. The flaw of this theory, as in the case of Barthes, lies in its unargued assumption that *all* ideological discourse operates by such naturalisation – a contention we have already seen reason to doubt. As often in the critique of ideology, one particular paradigm of ideological consciousness is surreptitiously made to do service for the whole varied array of ideological forms and devices. There are styles of ideological discourse other than the 'organicist' – the thought of Paul de Man, for example, whose gloomy insistence that mind and world can never harmoniously meet is among other things a coded refusal of the 'utopianism' of emancipatory politics.

It belongs to a poststructuralist or postmodernist perspective to see all discourse as traced through by the play of power and desire, and thus to view all language as ineradicably *rhetorical*. We should be properly suspicious of too hard-and-fast a distinction between some scrupulously neutral, purely informative sort of speech act, and those 'performative' pieces of language which are clearly engaged in cursing, cajoling, seducing, persuading and so on. Telling someone the time of day is as much a 'performative' as telling them to get lost, and no doubt involves some inscrutable play of power and desire for any analyst with enough useless ingenuity to pursue the matter. All discourse is aimed at the production of certain effects in its recipients, and is launched from some tendentious 'subject position'; and to this extent we might conclude with the Greek Sophists that everything we say is really a matter of rhetorical performance within which questions of truth or cognition are strictly subordinate. If this is so, then all language is 'ideological', and the category of ideology, expanded to breaking-point, once more collapses. One might add that the production of this effect is precisely part of the ideological intention of those who claim that 'everything is rhetorical'.

It is, however, a simple sleight-of-hand, or sheer intellectual disingenuousness, to imagine that all language is rhetorical to exactly the same degree. Once again, postmodernist 'pluralism' here stands convicted of violently homogenising quite different sorts of speech act. The assertion 'It's five o'clock' certainly involves interests of a kind, springing as it does from a particular way of slicing up temporality, and belonging as it does to some intersubjective context (that of telling someone the time) which is never innocent of authority. But it is merely perverse to imagine that such an utterance, in most circumstances at least, is as 'interested' as stating that by five o'clock all historical materialists must be washed in the blood of the Lamb or face instant execution. Someone who writes a doctoral thesis on the relations between race and social class in South Africa is by no means disinterested; why bother, for one thing, to write it in the first place? But such a piece of work normally differs from statements such as 'The white man will never surrender his heritage' in that it is open to being disproved. Indeed this is part of what we mean by a 'scientific' hypothesis, as opposed to a groan of alarm or a stream of invective. The pronouncement 'The white man will never surrender his heritage' *appears* as though it could be disproved, since it could be obtusely taken as a sociological prediction; but to take it this way would of course be wholly to miss its ideological force. There is no need to imagine that to enforce a working distinction between these two discursive genres is to surrender to the myth of some 'scientific disinterestedness' – a fantasy which no interesting philosopher of science has anyway entertained for the past half-century. The humanist's traditional patrician disdain for scientific enquiry is not rendered particularly more plausible by being dressed up in glamorously avant-garde guise.

If all language articulates specific interests, then it would appear that all language is ideological. But as we have seen already, the classical concept of ideology is by no means limited to 'interested discourse', or to the production of suasive effects. It refers more precisely to the processes whereby interests of a certain kind become masked, rationalised, naturalised, universalised, legitimated in the name of certain forms of political power; and much is to be politically lost by dissolving these vital discursive strategies into some undifferentiated, amorphous category of 'interests'. To claim that all language is at some level rhetorical is thus not the same as to claim that all language is ideological. As John Plamenatz points out in his work *Ideology*, someone who shouts 'Fire!' in a theatre is not engaging in ideological discourse. A mode of discourse may encode certain interests, for example, but may not be particularly intent on directly promoting or legitimating them; and the interests in question may in any case have no crucially relevant relation to the sustaining of a whole social order. Again, the interests at stake may not be in the least 'false' or specious ones, whereas we have seen that, for some theories of ideology at least, this would need to be so for a discourse to be dubbed ideological. Those who today press the sophistical case that all language is rhetorical, like Stanley Fish in *Doing What Comes Naturally*, are quite ready to acknowledge that the discourse in which they frame this case is nothing but a case of special pleading too; but if a Fish is genially prepared to admit that his own theorising is a bit of rhetoric, he is notably more reluctant to concede that it is a piece of *ideology*. For to do this would involve reflecting on the political ends which such an argument serves in the content of Western capitalist society; and Fish is not prepared to widen his theoretical focus to encompass such embarrassing questions. Indeed his response would no doubt have to be that he is himself so thoroughly a product of that society – which is undoubtedly true – that he is quite unable to reflect on his own social determinants – which is undoubtedly false.

It is via the category of 'discourse' that a number of theorists over recent years have made the steady trek from erstwhile revolutionary political positions to left reformist ones. This phenomenon is generally known as 'post-Marxism'; and it is worth inquiring into the logic of this long march from Saussure to social democracy.

In a number of works of political theory,[5] the English sociologists Paul Hirst and Barry Hindess firmly reject the kind of classical epistemology which assumes some match or 'correspondence' between our concepts and the way the world is. For if 'the way the world is' is itself always conceptually defined, then this age-old philosophical case would appear to be viciously circular. It is a rationalist fallacy, so Hindess and Hirst argue, to hold that what enables us to know is the fact that the world takes the shape of a concept – that it is somehow conveniently pre-structured to fit our cognition of it. As for a Paul de Man, there is no such congruence or internal bond between mind and reality, and so no privileged epistemological language which could allow us untroubled access to the real. For to determine that this language adequately measured the fit or non-fit between our concepts and the world, we would presumably need another language to guarantee the adequacy of *this* one, and so on in a potentially infinite regress of 'metalanguages'. Rather, objects should be considered not as external to a realm of discourse which seeks to approximate them, but as wholly internal to such discourses, constituted by them through and through.

This position – though Hindess and Hirst do not say so, perhaps being nervous or unaware of the fact – is a thoroughly Nietzschean one. There is no given order *in* reality at all, which for Nietzsche is just ineffable chaos; meaning is just whatever we arbitrarily construct by our acts of sense-making. The world does not spontaneously sort itself out into kinds, causal hierarchies, discrete spheres, as a philosophical realist would imagine; on the contrary, it is *we* who do all this by talking about it. Our language does not so much *reflect* reality as *signify* it, carve it into conceptual shape. The answer, then, to *what* exactly is being carved into conceptual shape is impossible to give: reality itself, before we come to constitute it through our discourses, is just some inarticulable *x*.

It is hard to know quite how far this anti-realist case can be pressed. Nobody believes that the world sorts itself into shape, independently of our descriptions of it, in the sense that the literary superiority of Arthur Hugh Clough to Alfred Lord Tennyson is just a 'given' distinction inscribed in reality before time began, grandly autonomous of anything we might come to say about the issue. But it seems plausible to believe that there is a given distinction between wine and wallabies, and that to be unclear on this point might be the occasion of some frustration on the part of someone looking for a drink. There may well be societies for which these things signify something entirely at odds with what they signify for us, or even certain bizarre cultural systems which saw no occasion to *mark* the distinction at all. But this does not mean that they would stock their off-licences with wallabies or encourage children to feed bottles of wine in their zoos. It is certainly true that we ourselves may not distinguish between certain sorts of plant which for another culture are uniquely different. But it would be impossible for an anthropologist to stumble upon a society which registered no distinction between water and sulphuric acid, since they would all be long in their graves.

Similarly, it is difficult to know how hard to press the case that our discourses do not reflect real causal connections in reality – an empiricist doctrine which a good many post-Marxists have rather surprisingly appropriated. It is certainly arguable that the Marxist claim that economic activity finally determines the shape of a society is just a causal relation which Marxists, for their own political reasons, want to construct, rather than a hierarchy already inscribed in the world waiting to be discovered. It is somewhat less persuasive to claim that the apparent causal relation between my lunging at you with a scimitar and your head dropping instantly to the ground is just one discursively constructed for particular ends.

Hindess and Hirst's 'anti-epistemological' thesis is intended among other things to undermine the Marxist doctrine that a social formation is composed of different 'levels', some of which exert more significant determinacy than others. For them, this is merely another instance of the rationalist illusion, which would view society as somehow already internally structured along the lines of the concepts by which we appropriate it in thought. There is, then, no such thing as a 'social totality', and no such thing as one sort of social activity being in general or in principle more determinant or causally privileged than another. The relations between the political, cultural, economic and the rest are ones *we* fashion for specific political ends within given historical contexts; they are in no sense relations which subsist independently of our discourse. Once again, it is not easy to see just how far this case should be extended. Does it mean, for instance, that we cannot in principle rule out the possibility that the Bolshevik revolution was triggered by Bogdanov's asthma or Radek's penchant for pork pies? If there are no causal hierarchies *in* reality, why should this not be so? What is it which *constrains* our discursive constructions? It cannot be 'reality', for that is simply a *product* of them; in which case it might appear that we are free, in some voluntarist fantasy, to weave any network of relations which strikes our fancy. It is clear in any case that what began as an argument about epistemology has now shifted to an opposition to revolutionary politics; for if the Marxist doctrine of 'last-instance' economic determinacy is discarded, then much in traditional revolutionary discourse will need to be radically revised. In place of this 'global' brand of analysis, Hindess and Hirst urge instead the pragmatic calculation of political effects within some particular social conjuncture, which is a good deal more palatable to Mr Neil Kinnock. This theory, coincidentally enough, was sponsored just at the historical point where the radical currents of the 1960s and early 1970s were beginning to ebb under the influence of an aggressive set of assaults from the political right. In this sense, it was a 'conjunctural' position in more senses than it proclaimed.

The thesis that objects are entirely internal to the discourses which constitute them raises the thorny problem of how we could ever judge that a discourse had constructed its object validly. How can anyone, on this theory, ever be wrong? If there can be no meta-language to measure the 'fit' between my language and the object, what is to stop me from constructing the object in any way I want? Perhaps the internal rigour and consistency of my arguments is the litmus test here; but magic and Satanism, not to speak of Thomistic theology, are perfectly capable of constructing their objects in internally coherent ways. Moreover, they may always produce effects which somebody, from some vantage-point somewhere, may judge to be politically beneficial. But if meta-language is an illusion, then there would seem no way of judging that any particular political perspective was more beneficial than any other. The pragmatist move here, in other words, simply pushes the question back a step: if what validates my social interpretations are the political ends they serve, how am I to validate these ends? Or am I just forced back here, aggressively and dogmatically, on asserting my interests over yours, as Nietzsche would have urged? For Hindess and Hirst, there can be no way of countering an objectionable political case by an appeal to the way things are with society, for the way things are is just the way you construct them to be. You must appeal instead to your political ends and interests – which means that it is now these, not the distinction between wine and wallabies, which are somehow sheerly 'given'. They cannot be derived from social reality, since social reality derives from *them*; and they are therefore bound to remain as mysteriously unfathered and self-referential as the work of art for a whole tradition of classical aesthetics.

Where interests derive from, in other words, is as opaque a matter for post-Marxism as where babies come from is for the small infant. The traditional Marxist case has been that political interests derive from one's location within the social relations of class-society; but this for post-Marxism would seem to entail the unSaussurean assumption that our political discourses 'reflect' or 'correspond' to something else. If our language is not just some passive reflection of reality, but actively constitutive of it, then this surely cannot be so. It cannot be that your place within a mode of production furnishes you with certain objective interests which your political and ideological discourses then simply 'express'. There can be no 'objective' interests spontaneously 'given' by reality; once again, interests are what we *construct*, and politics in this sense has the edge over economics.

That social interests do not lie around the place like slabs of concrete waiting to be stumbled over may be cheerfully conceded. There is no reason to suppose, as Hindess and Hirst rightly argue, that the mere occupancy of some place within society will automatically supply you with an appropriate set of political beliefs and desires, as the fact that by no means all women are feminists would readily attest. Social interests are indeed in no sense independent of anything we come to do or say; they are not some given 'signified', which has then merely to discover its appropriate signifier or mode of ideological discourse to come into its own. But this is not the only way of understanding the concept of 'objective interests'[Imagine an objective location within the social formation known as third galley slave from the front on the starboard side. This location brings along with it certain responsibilities, such as rowing non-stop for fifteen hours at a stretch and sending up a feeble chant of priase to the Emperor on the hour. To say that this social location comes readily inscribed with a set of interests is just to say that anyone who found himself occupying it would do well to get out of it, and that this would be no mere whim or quirk on his part. It is not necessarily to claim that this thought would spontaneously occur to a galley slave as soon as he had sat down, or to rule out the odd masochist who took a grisly relish in the whole affair and tried to row faster than the others. The view that the slave, *ceteris paribus*, would do well to escape is not one that springs from some God's-eye viewpoint beyond all social discourse; on the contrary, it is more likely to spring from the viewpoint of the League of Escaped Galley Slaves. There is no interest in question here that nobody could ever conceivably come to know about. When the galley slave engages in a spot of critical self-reflection, such as muttering to himself 'this is one hell of a job', then he might reasonably be said to be articulating in his discourse an objective interest, in the sense that he means that it is one hell of a job not just for him but for anyone whatsoever. There is no divine guarantee that the slave *will* arrive at the conclusion that there might be more agreeable ways of passing his time, or that he will not view his task as just retribution for the crime of existing, or as a creative contribution to the greater good of the empire. To say that he has an objective interest in emancipating himself is just to say that if he *does* feel this way, then he is labouring under the influence of false consciousness. It is to claim, moreover, that in certain optimal conditions – conditions relatively free of such coercion and mystification – the slave could be brought to recognise this fact. He would acknowledge that it was in fact in his interests to escape even before he came to realise this, and this is part of what he is now realising.

The galley slave might be instructed by the odd discourse theorist he encountered at various ports of call that the interests he had now begun to articulate were in no sense a mere passive reflection of social reality, and he would do well to take this point seriously. He would no doubt appreciate the force of it already, recalling the long years during which he held the view that being lashed to ribbons by the emperor's captain was an honour ill-befitting a worm such as himself, and remembering the painful inner struggle which brought him to his current, more enlightened opinions. He might well be brought to understand that 'oppression' is a discursive affair, in the sense that one condition is identifiable as oppressive only by contrast with some other less or non-oppressive state of affairs, and that all this is cognisable only through discourse. Oppression, in short, is a normative concept: someone is being oppressed not simply if they drag out a wretched existence, but if certain creative capacities they could feasibly realise are being actively thwarted by the unjust interests of others. And none of this can be determined other than discursively; you could not decide that a situation was oppressive simply by looking at a photograph of it. The galley slave, however, would no doubt be churlishly unimpressed by the suggestion that all this meant that he was not 'really' oppressed at all. He would be unlikely to greet such a judgement with the light-hearted playfulness beloved of some postmodernist theorists. Instead, he would doubtless insist that while what was in question here was certainly an interpretation, and thus always in principle controvertible, what the interpretation enforced was the *fact* that this situation was oppressive.

Post-Marxism is given to denying that there is any necessary relation between one's socio-economic location and one's politico-ideological interests. In the case of our galley slave, this claim is clearly false. It is certainly true, as post-Marxism properly insists, that the slave's politico-ideological position is not just some 'reflex' of his material conditions. But

his ideological views do indeed have an internal relation to that condition –
not in the sense that this condition is the automatic *cause* of them, but in the
sense that it is the *reason* for them. Sitting for fifteen hours a day in the third
row from the front is what his ideological opinions are *about*. What he says is
about what he does; and what he does is the reason for what he says. The
'real' here certainly exists prior to and independent of the slave's discourse, if
by the 'real' is meant that specific set of practices which provide the reason
for what he says, and form the referent of it. That these practices will be
interpretatively transformed when the slave arrives at his emancipatory
views is doubtless true; he will be led to theoretically revise those conditions
in a quite different light. This is the kernel of truth of the post-Marxist case:
that 'signifiers', or the means of political and ideological representation, are
always active in respect of what they signify. It is in this sense that politico-
ideological interests are not just the obedient, spontaneous expression of
'given' socio-economic conditions. What is represented is never some 'brute'
reality, but will be moulded by the practice of representation itself. Political
and ideological discourses thus produce their own signifieds, conceptualise
the situation in specific ways.

It is only a short step from here – a step which Hindess and Hirst rashly
take – to imagining that the *whole socio-economic situation* in question is
simply defined by political and ideological interests, with no reality beyond
this. Semiotically speaking, Hindess and Hirst have merely inverted the
empiricist model: whereas in empiricist thought the signifier is thought to
follow spontaneously from the signified – in the sense that the world
instructs us, so to speak, in how to represent it – it is now a question of the
signified following obediently from the signifier. The situation is just whatever political and ideological discourses define it as being. But this is to
conflate economic and political interests just as drastically as the most vulgar
Marxism. For the fact is that there are economic interests, such as desiring
better pay or conditions of work, which may not yet have achieved *political*
articulation. And such interests can be inflected in a whole number of
conflicting political ways. As well as merely inverting the relation between
signifier and signified, Hindess and Hirst thus also effect a fatal semiotic
confusion between *signified* and *referent*. For the referent here is the whole
socio-economic situation, the interests contained in which are then signified
in different ways by politics and ideology, but are not simply identical with
them.

Whether 'economics' gives rise to 'politics', or *vice versa* as post-Marxism
would hold, the relationship in both cases is essentially causal. Lurking
behind the post-Marxist view is the Saussurean notion of the signifier as
'producing' the signified. But this semiotic model is in fact quite inadequate
for an understanding of the relation between material situations and ideological discourse. Ideology neither legislates such situations into being, nor is

simply 'caused' by them; rather, ideology offers a set of *reasons* for such material conditions. Hindess and Hirst, in short, overlook the *legitimating* functions of ideology, distracted as they are by a causal model which merely stands vulgar Marxism on its head. The relation between an object and its means of representation is crucially not the same as that between a material practice and its ideological legitimation or mystification. Hindess and Hirst fail to spot this because of the undifferentiated, all-inclusive nature of their concept of discourse. Discourse for them 'produces' real objects; and ideological language is therefore just one way in which these objects get constituted. But this simply fails to identify the specificity of such language, which is not just any way of constituting reality, but one with the more particular functions of explaining, rationalising, concealing, legitimating and so on. Two meanings of discourse are falsely conflated: those which are said to constitute our practices, and those in which we talk about them. Ideology, in short, *goes to work* on the 'real' situation in transformative ways; and it is ironic in one sense that a pair of theorists so eager to stress the activity of the signifier should overlook this. In another sense, it is not ironic at all: for if our discourses are constitutive of our practices, then there would seem no enabling distance between the two in which this transformative labour could occur. And to speak of a transformative labour here implies that something pre-exists this process; some referent, something *worked upon*, which cannot be the case if the signifier simply conjures the 'real' situation into being.

What is being implicitly challenged by Hindess and Hirst is nothing short of the whole concept of representation. For the idea of representation would suggest that the signified exists prior to its signifier, and is then obediently reflected by it; and this, once more, runs against the grain of Saussurean semiotics. But in rightly rejecting an *empiricist* ideology of representation, they mistakenly believe themselves to have disposed of the notion as such. Nobody is much enamoured these days of an idea of representation in which the signified spontaneously puts forth its own signifier; in which some organic bond is imagined to exist between the two, so that the signified can be represented *only* in this way; and in which the signifier in no sense alters the signified, but remains a neutral, transparent medium of expression. Many post-Marxists accordingly abandon the whole term 'representation', while around them the benighted masses continue to speak of a photograph of a chipmunk as 'representing' a chipmunk, or a set of interlinked circles as 'representing' the Olympic games. There is no reason to imagine that the complex conventions involved in associating an image with its referent are adequately explained by the empiricist version of the process, and no need to throw up trying to give an account of the former simply because the latter model has been discredited. The term 'representation' has perfectly valid uses, as the populace, if not some post-Marxists, are well aware; it is just a trickier cultural practice than the empiricists used to think.

The reason why Hindess and Hirst wish to jettison the whole notion of representation is by no means ideologically innocent. They wish to do so because they want to deny the classical Marxist contention that there exists some internal relation between particular socio-economic conditions, and specific kinds of political or ideological positions. They therefore argue either that socio-economic interests are just the product of political and ideological ones, or that the two lie on quite different levels, with no necessary linkage between them. Semiotics, once more, is a kind of politics – since if this is so, then many traditional Marxist theses about the socialist transformation of society being necessarily in the interests of the working class would need to be scrapped. Saussurean linguistics is once more craftily harnessed to the cause of social reformism – a cause rendered more reputable than it might otherwise appear by its glamorous association with 'discourse theory'.

The constructive side of Hindess and Hirst's case is that there are a good many political interests which are by no means necessarily tied to *class* situations, and that classical Marxism has often enough lamentably ignored this truth. Such non-class political movements were gathering force in the 1970s, and the writings of the post-Marxists are among other things a creative theoretical response to this fact. Even so, the move of severing all necessary link between social situations and political interests, intended as a generous opening to these fresh developments, in fact does them a disservice. Consider, for example, the case of the women's movement. It is certainly true that there is no organic relation between feminist politics and social class, *pace* those Marxist reductionists who struggle vainly to funnel the former into the latter. But there is a good case for arguing that there is indeed an internal relation between being a woman (a social situation) and being a feminist (a political position). This is not, needless to say, to claim that all women will spontaneously become feminists; but it is to argue that they *ought* to do so, and that an unmystified understanding of their oppressed social condition would logically lead them in that direction. Just the same is true of the other non-class political currents astir in the 1970s: it seems odd to assert, for example, that there is a purely contingent connection between being part of an oppressed ethnic minority and becoming active in anti-racist politics. The relation between the two is not 'necessary' in the sense of natural, automatic or ineluctable; but it is, in Saussure's terms, a 'motivated' rather than purely arbitrary one even so.

To suggest that someone *ought* to adopt a particular political position may sound peculiarly patronising, dictatorial and elitist. Who am I to presume that I know what is in someone else's interests? Isn't this just the style in which ruling groups and classes have spoken for centuries? The plain fact is that I am in full possession of my own interests, and nobody can tell me what to do. I am entirely transparent to myself, have an utterly unmystified view of my social conditions, and will tolerate no kind of suggestion, however comradely and sympathetic its tone, from anybody else. I do not need telling by some paternal elitist about what is in my 'objective' interests, because as a matter of fact I never behave in a way which violates them. Even though I eat twelve pounds of sausages a day, smoke sixty cigarettes before noon and have just volunteered for a fifty percent wage cut, I resent the idea that I have anything to learn from anyone. Those who tell me that I am 'mystified', just because I spend my weekends gardening free of charge for the local squire, are simply trying to put me down with their pretentious jargon.

As far as the relation between social interests and ideological beliefs goes, [...] they [are] in fact extremely variable. No simple, single homology is at stake here: ideological beliefs may signify material interests, disavow, rationalise or dissemble them, run counter to them, and so on. For the monistic thinking of a Hindess and Hirst, however, there can only ever be one fixed, invariable relation between them: no relation whatsoever. It is true that in their astonishingly repetitive texts the disingenuous word 'necessary' occasionally slides into this formulation: in a whole series of slippages, they glide from arguing that political and ideological forms cannot be conceived of as the *direct* representation of class interests, to claiming that there is no *necessary* relation between the two, to suggesting that there is no connection between them at all. 'There can be no justification', they write, 'for a "reading" of politics and ideology for the class interests they are alleged to represent...political and ideological struggles cannot be conceived as the struggles of economic classes.'[6] The theoretical strategem is plain enough: feminist, ethnic or ecological politics are obviously not internally related to class interests, in which case neither are socialism or Toryism.

Here, as in almost all of their arguments, Hindess and Hirst theatrically overreact to reductionistic forms of Marxism. Their whole discourse is one prolonged bending of the stick in the other direction, recklessly exaggerating what is otherwise a valuably corrective case. If the relations between ideological forms and social interests are not eternally fixed and given, why should one dogmatically rule out the possibility that some types of ideological discourse may be more closely tied to such interests than others? Why limit one's pluralism in this self-denying way? What self-imposed, *a priori* restrictive practice is at work here? If it is true that there is no 'motivated' relation between being, say, a petty-bourgeois intellectual and opposing fascism, does it follow that there is no such relation either between puritan ideology and the early bourgeoisie, anti-imperialist beliefs and the experience of colonialism, or socialism and a lifetime's unemployment? Are all such relations as arbitrary as being an anti-Semite and an abstract expressionist simultaneously? 'Political practice', they comment, 'does not recognise class interests and then represent them: it constitutes the interests which it represents.'[7] If this means that the 'signifier' of political practice is active in respect of the 'signified' of social interests, modifying and transforming them by its interventions, then it is hard to see why one would want to deny such a case. If it means – to return to our example of the galley slave – that this man has no interests whatsoever relevant to his class position before political discourses moved in to articulate them, then it is clearly false. The slave had indeed a whole cluster of interests associated with his material situation – interests in snatching a little rest from time to time, not gratuitously antagonising his superiors, sitting behind a somewhat bulkier slave to win a little protection from the sun, and so on. It is just these sorts of material interests which his political and ideological discourse, when he acquires it, will go to work upon, elaborating, cohering and transforming them in various ways; and in this sense material interests undoubtedly exist prior to and independent of politico-ideological ones. The material situation is the *referent* of the slave's political discourse, not the *signified* of it – if by this we are supposed to believe that it is wholly *produced* by it. Hindess and Hirst fear that to deny that the slave's unenviable condition is the product of a politico-ideological language is to imagine that it is then just a 'brute' fact, independent of discourse altogether. But this apprehension is quite needless. There is no non-discursive way in which the slave can decide not to antagonise his superiors; his 'real' situation is inseparably bound up with linguistic interpretation of one kind or another. It is just a mistake to run together *these* kinds of interpretation, inscribed in everything we do, with those specific forms of discourse which allow us to criticise, rationalise, suppress, explain or transform our conditions of life.

9

'We Anti-Representationalists'

Richard Rorty

Terry Eagleton, *Ideology: An Introduction* (London, 1991). 242 pp. £32.95 hb., £10.95 pb., 0 86091 8 hb., 0 86091 538 7 pb.

The first chapter of this book begins by listing twenty senses of the word 'ideology', many of which are incompatible with one another. Eagleton does not regard this proliferation of inconsistent senses as a reason for dropping the word. 'My own view', he says, 'is that both the wider and narrower senses of ideology have their uses, and that their mutual incompatibility, descending as they do from divergent political and conceptual histories, must be simply acknowledged. This view has the advantage of remaining loyal to the implicit slogan of Bertolt Brecht – "Use what you can!" – and the disadvantage of excessive charity.'

The excess of charity seems to me more obvious than the relevance of Brecht's slogan. But this is probably because I agree with the view which Eagleton goes on to attribute to 'Foucault and his acolytes' – 'that there are no values and beliefs *not* bound up with power' and therefore 'the term ideology threatens to expand to vanishing point'. Eagleton, however, thinks that abandoning 'ideology' in favour of Foucault's term 'discourse' is a bad idea because 'the force of the term ideology lies in its capacity to discriminate between those power struggles which are somehow central to a whole form of social life, and those which are not'.

Granted that 'ideology' may be handy as an abbreviation for 'central and important discourse, discourse whose replacement may be requisite for desirable social change', the utility of the definition of 'ideology' with which Eagleton emerges at the end of his 'What is Ideology?' chapter is another question. In a series of definitions arranged as 'a progressive sharpening of focus', he comes to a fifth: 'ideas and beliefs which help to legitimate the interests of a ruling group or class specifically by distortion and dissimulation'. The sixth and final definition is a gloss on the fifth, specifying that we should 'retain an emphasis on false or deceptive beliefs' but regard such beliefs 'as arising not from the interests of a dominant class but from the material structure of society as a whole'. The 'most celebrated instance of this sense of ideology,' Eagleton says, 'is Marx's theory of the fetishism of commodities.'

This quasi-definition puts a heavy burden on the notion of 'the material structure of society as a whole', a notion which seems to me on a par with 'ideology' in respect to ambiguity and lack of evident utility. But the utility of the former notion is pretty much taken for granted by Eagleton, who has written his book primarily for his fellow-Marxists. This readership gets smaller all the time, because Eagleton's paradigm case of ideology-critique, the theory of the fetishism of commodities, only looked convincing as long as one thought that Marxism offered a feasible proposal for an alternative material structure of society.

Since nobody is clear what socio-economic arrangement Marxists now wish, in the light of the Central European experience, to propose, the Marxist vocabulary is going out of style. The plausibility of that vocabulary depends upon its being used to sketch a concrete political alternative, and that is just what Marxists are no longer offering us. If you have tried Marxist terminology and found it unhelpful, Eagleton's book will do little to reconvert you to it.

The bulk of *Ideology: An Introduction* is history of ideas, interspersed with criticism of various thinkers (from Mannheim to Habermas, from Freud to Bourdieu). But it is not a very exciting or dramatic history of ideas. The organising principles of chapters 3–6 are not perspicuous. Those in search of an 'introduction' to the history of uses of the term 'ideology' might do better to consult a recent 50-page article by Daniel Bell in *The Berkeley Journal of Sociology*. The central chapters of Eagleton's book should be read not as an introduction to that area, but rather as a compendium of Eagleton's evaluations and criticisms – often pointed, and always at least suggestive – of various authors who have recently attracted his attention.

These central chapters are flanked, however, by an 'Introduction' and a concluding chapter called 'Discourse and Ideology'. In those parts of the book, Eagleton takes on 'post-modernism' and offers straight-out philosophy, as opposed to history. They are quite different in aim and in flavour from the central chapters, and I shall focus on them in what follows – not only because I find them of most interest but because, as a philosopher rather than an historian, I am better qualified to comment on them.

In his 'Introduction' Eagleton asks 'Why is it that in a world racked by ideological conflict, the very notion of ideology has evaporated without trace from the writings of postmodernism and poststructuralism?' His answer is that 'three key doctrines of postmodernist thought have conspired to discredit the classical conception of ideology'. These are: (1) 'a rejection of the notion of representation'; (2) 'an epistemological scepticism'; and (3) 'a reformulation of the relations between rationality, interests and power, along roughly neo-Nietzschean lines'.

I am pretty sure that the down-turn in the fortunes of the term 'ideology' owes more to dissatisfaction with Marxist explanations of recent history, and thus with Marxist categories and terminology, than to the prevalence of the philosophical views which Eagleton lists. But, however this may be, his list does zero in on a philosophical standpoint which is common to many recent thinkers (notably Nietzsche and Foucault, and also, I should argue, Davidson and Dewey). It is a standpoint which I have been recommending in my own books.

From this standpoint, the distinction between appearance and reality is one which makes sense within a linguistic practice – within, say, the vocabulary of art dealers, or that of theoretical physicists – but is of no use when applied to linguistic practices as wholes. When we ask 'Is there any such thing as X?' – where 'X' is something like 'micro-structure' (in the case of physics) or 'the material structure of society as a whole' (in the case of Marxism) or 'God' (in the case of religion) or 'art' (in the case of connoisseurship) – neither 'only in appearance' nor 'Yes, there *really and truly* is' is a helpful answer. What is helpful is to be told 'Here is an alternative way of speaking which fulfils the purposes served by talk of X even better than X-talk does', or else to be told 'There is, at present, *no* plausible rival to X-talk'.

Assuming this standpoint makes one an anti-representationalist, in that one stops asking 'Are we representing reality accurately?' and starts asking 'Are there more useful conceptual instruments at our disposal?' But it is hardly clear that it makes one an epistemological sceptic; we anti-representationalists think of ourselves as saying that our knowledge of the world is as much knowledge as it ever was, even when truth is thought of in terms of utility rather than in terms of correspondence to intrinsic features of the world. This sort of pragmatism does indeed, however, bring about 'a reformulation of the relations between rationality, interests and power along roughly neo-Nietzschean lines'. For it entails that a lot of choices between linguistic and other practices boil down to 'utility for what?', and thus to 'utility in serving whose interests?' So, on at least two out of three points, Eagleton gets us right.

Our way of thinking – that common to wet pragmatist liberals like me and dry postmodernist radicals like the Foucauldians – overlaps with a prominent historicist and pragmatist strain in Marx and Marxism. (Think of the eleventh thesis on Feuerbach, of the idea that morality is relative to class interests, and so on.) But it has been stoutly resisted by many Marxists – from Engels, through Lenin's criticisms of Berkeley and Mach in *Materialism and Empirio-Criticism*, to Milton Fisk's *Nature and Necessity* (a pre-Kripkean repudiation of Quinean holism and revivification of Aristotelian essentialism) and Hilary Putnam's politically-driven quest (in his Marxist period) for a physicalist theory of reference. It is as if Marxists were, on the whole, more eager to save the claim that scientific socialism represents the world as it *really* is than to carry through on Hegelian historicism. This eagerness causes them to resist Foucault with the same sort of arguments as they once resisted Dewey and later resisted Wittgenstein. It leads them to say the same sorts of unpleasant things about us neo-Nietzschean (or, as we Americans prefer to say, neo-Emersonian) anti-representationalists as are said about us by people on the political right (sophisticated Straussians in learned journals; simple-minded Blimps propounding 'sound common sense' in letters to newspapers).

The main unpleasant thing said about us is that we have forgotten the difference between ideas and things, or between words and things – that we represent some new-fangled kind of idealism, or perhaps some sort of decadent aestheticism, and so are unable to appreciate the hard, resistant, character of reality. As Johnson thought to refute Berkeley by kicking a stone, so Marxists think to refute pragmatists and postmodernists by emphasising the pre-linguistic character of suffering, and suggesting that anti-representationalists are oblivious to this suffering. So the centrepiece of Eagleton's final chapter is a description of someone who occupies 'an objective location within the social formation known as third galley slave from the front on the starboard side. This location brings along with it certain responsibilities such as rowing non-stop for fifteen hours at a stretch and sending up a feeble chant of praise to the Emperor on the hour.'

The tone of Eagleton's criticism of us anti-representationalists is illustrated by the following passage:

> The galley slave might be instructed by the odd discourse theorists ... that the interests he had now begun to articulate [e.g., an interest in escaping from the galleys] were in no sense a mere passive reflection of social reality, and he would do well to take this point seriously. He would no doubt appreciate the force of it already, recalling the long years during which he held the view that being lashed to ribbons by the emperor's captain was an honour ill-befitting a worm such as himself, and remembering the painful inner struggle which brought him to his current, more enlightened opinions. He might well be brought to understand that 'oppression' is a discursive affair, in the sense that one condition is identifiable as oppressive only by contrast with some other less or non-oppressive state of affairs, and that all this is cognisable only through discourse. ... The galley slave, however, would no doubt be churlishly unimpressed by the suggestion that all this meant that he was not 'really' oppressed at all. He would be unlikely to greet such a judgement with the light-hearted playfulness beloved of some postmodernist theorists. Instead, he would doubtless insist that while what was in question here was certainly an interpretation, and thus always in principle controvertible, what the interpretation enforced was the *fact* that the situation was oppressive.

This last sentence is, I take it, supposed to remind us that, as Eagleton goes on to say, 'The "real" here certainly exists prior to and independent of the slave's discourse, if by the "real" is meant that specific set of practices which provide the reason for what he says, and form the referent of it.' Like Berkeley and Kant, however, contemporary anti-representationalists insist that they do not deny the prior and independent reality of the referents of many beliefs. It is one thing to say, paradoxically and pointlessly (as Foucault, alas, sometimes did), that X did not exist before people used the term 'X'. It is another thing to say that sentences about X are true because they accurately represent, or correspond to, the way the world is in itself. You can drop the idea that true beliefs represent this way, and the idea that there *is* any such a way, while still believing that many referents antedated the discourse which made them cognisable. (E.g., there were electrons before 'electron' came into use, even though there were no bills of lading before 'bill of lading' came into use.) So anti-representationalists see Eagleton's emphatic use of *'fact'* as either smuggling back the view he elsewhere explicitly repudiates – that some objects are somehow 'given' independent of discourse – or as beside the point.

Anti-representationalists can happily agree with Eagleton that when the galley slave thought he was a justly lashed worm, he was wrong, and that he is now right in thinking that his interests consist in escaping the galleys. But they will construe this claim as saying: if the slave tries the discourse of emancipation he will come out with better results than those he achieved with the discourse in which he viewed himself as a worm. Better by whose lights? Ours and Eagleton's. What other lights should we use? (As Putnam puts it: we should use somebody *else's* conceptual scheme? A *worm's*?) So when Eagleton says all women ought to become feminists because 'an unmystified understanding of their oppressed social condition would logically lead them in that direction', we anti-representationalists construe him as saying 'Those non-feminist women will get more of what we think they ought to want if they become feminists'. Analogously, we think that the claim that only 'prejudice and superstition' blinded our eyes to the truth of the Copernican theory is a way of saying that Copernicans get more of what we think astronomers ought to want than Ptolemians. 'Mystification' and 'prejudice', for us anti-representationalists, point to a difference between our wants and interests and somebody else's wants and interests, not a difference between somebody else's wants and the way the world is independent of anybody's wants and anybody's discourse.

A clear difference between this position and Eagleton's emerges only when he stops talking about 'prior and independent existence' and starts talking about the need for an object which will put a stop to argument about what interests are to be served, what needs fulfilled. Consider the following passage:

The thesis that objects are entirely internal to the discourses which constitute them raises the thorny problem of how we could ever judge that a discourse had constructed its object validly. How can anyone, on this theory, ever be wrong? If there can be no meta-language to measure the 'fit' between my language and the object, what is to stop me from constructing the object any way I want?

Anti-representationalists say: nothing stops you except other people, with other wants and interests, construing the object in different ways.

But this reply is not good enough for Eagleton. Like the Straussians and the Blimps, he wants back-up from the intrinsic nature of things. He wants a Way The World Is, and what Putnam calls a 'God's-eye view'. So he continues:

> The pragmatist move here, in other words, simply pushes the question back a step: if what validates my social interpretations are the political ends they serve, how am I to validate these ends? Or am I just forced back here, aggressively and dogmatically, on asserting my interests over yours, as Nietzsche would have urged?

Anti-representationalists say: yes, you *are* so forced. If you cannot find any conversational common ground with your opponents, you may indeed have to be aggressive and dogmatic. Indeed, in the end you may have to fight it out with those opponents. (E.g., in the end the galley slaves may have to stop trying to talk the captain into providing fair wages and hours, and just try to overthrow the imperial system of government by force and violence.)

Anti-representationalists accept the consequence which Eagleton regards as a *reductio ad absurdum*: that 'there can be no way of countering an objectionable political case by an appeal to the way things are with society, for the way things are is just the way you construct them to be'. They do not see the force of 'just' in this last sentence. (Somebody *else* should construct them? The *emperor*, may be?) So when Eagleton protests against the suggestion that 'The working class, or for that matter any other subordinate group, thus becomes clay in the hands of those wishing to coopt it into some political strategy, tugged this way and that between socialists and fascists', we anti-representationalists cannot see the point of the protest. Sometimes subordinated groups *are* clay – happy slaves whom we try to make unhappy as a step toward helping them to become even happier than they were before. (Consider, e.g., feminists trying to convert complacent matrons in Sicily or Utah.) With luck, we happy few, the good and enlightened vanguard, will mould those subordinated groups into an instrument for the purposes we think they ought to have.

When Eagleton asks 'If socialism is not necessarily in the workers' interests, since the workers in fact have no interests outside those they are "constructed" into, why on earth should they bother to become socialists?' I am baffled by the phrase 'not necessarily in the workers' interests'. What does 'necessarily' mean here? Founded upon the way the intrinsic nature of the working class – the one socialists represent accurately and fascists don't?

The reason we anti-representationalists bother to hold the controversial philosophical views we do is that we think that this idea that some descriptions get at the *intrinsic* nature of what is being described brings the whole dreary Cartesian problematic along with it, and that this is a problematic which nobody needs – the result of being held captive by a picture which it was in Descartes' interests to paint, but not in ours. We see the choice as between sticking with this problematic in order to avoid epithets like 'Nietzschean' or 'irrationalist' or 'relativist' and abandoning it in the hope that others will see it as in their interests to abandon it also, and that the epithets will therefore cease to be hurled.

Eagleton, it seems to me, would like to concede enough to Hindess and Hirst, Laclau and Mouffe, Saussure and Foucault, to free himself from imputations of philosophical naïvete, but not so much as to deprive himself of the epithets and sneers which he, like the Straussians and the Blimps, likes to use on the postmodernists. I do not see that he has found a middle ground which permits him to do this.

Despite this strenuous philosophical disagreement, however, I feel considerable sympathy with Eagleton's motives for writing this book – with his hostility to the take-over of leftist politics by people who specialise in 'analysing discourses'. Though, unlike him, I think that Marxism is pretty well finished, I hope that what takes its place on the left will not be postmodernism. For too many postmodernists take philosophy just as seriously as the Marxists did. They thereby drain the left's energy off into unproductive channels – channels which trickle out in the sandy wastes of discussion of, e.g., the difference between 'the signified' and 'the referent'. In my own country, one in which university literature departments think of themselves as (and, God help us, probably *are*) the centres of radical politics, postmodernism has produced a farcically over-theorised left which is not only politically useless but seems proud of being so (because it thereby avoids wetness and what it calls 'complicity').

What we need from left intellectuals is not more of what my fellow-pragmatist Stanley Fish calls 'anti-foundationalist theory hope' (the hope that by seeing things as 'products of discourse' we shall automatically see the oppressed and their needs more clearly) but answers to questions like: what remains of the traditional socialist programme in the light of the results of various experiments in nationalisation and central planning? Just the sort of welfare-statism which Laclau and Mouffe suggest toward the end of *Hegemony and Socialist Strategy*? Or something more radical?

I cannot envisage anything both plausible and more radical myself, but maybe Eagleton can. I wish that he could tell us, rather than delving into the history of Marxist ideas and into anti-anti-representationalist philosophy. *Ideology: An Introduction* will do little to alter the opinions of those who (like some of my left-looking students) would relish the spectacle of the last Marxist being strangled with the entrails of the last postmodernist.

10

Postmodernism and Feminisms

Linda Hutcheon

(A note on the plural 'feminisms' in my title: the designation is as awkward as it is accurate. While there are almost as many feminisms as there are feminists, there is also a very real sense in which there is today no clear cultural consensus in feminist thinking about representation. As Catherine Stimpson has argued, the history of feminist thought on this topic includes the confrontation of dominant representations of women as misrepresentations, the restoration of the past of women's own self-representation, the generation of accurate representations of women, and the acknowledgement of the need to represent differences among women (of sexuality, age, race, class, ethnicity, nationality), including their diverse political orientations.[1] As a verbal sign of difference and plurality, 'feminisms' would appear to be the best term to use to designate, not a consensus, but a multiplicity of points of view which nevertheless do possess at least some common denominators when it comes to the notion of the *politics* of representation.)

POLITICISING DESIRE

If, in the postmodern age, we do live in what has been called a recessionary erotic economy brought about by fear of disease and a fetishisation of fitness, the erotic cannot but be part of that general problematising of the body and its sexuality. And this is one of the sites of the conjunction of interest of both postmodernism and feminisms as they both zero in on the representation of and reference to that body and its subject positions. The body cannot escape representation and these days this means it cannot escape the feminist challenge to the patriarchal and masculinist underpinnings of the cultural practices that subtend those representations. But, without those feminisms, the story would be a rather different one, for I would want to argue for the powerful impact of feminist practices on postmodernism – though not for the conflation of the two.

With the rise of performance and 'body art' in the last decade have come unavoidably gender-specific representations of the body in art. Because of these and other specifically feminist practices, postmodernism's 'de-

101

doxifying' work on the construction of the individual bourgeois subject has had to make room for the consideration of the construction of the *gendered* subject. I say this in full awareness that some of the major theorists of the postmodern have not yet noticed this. While it is certainly demonstrable that both feminisms and postmodernism are part of the same general crisis of cultural authority[2] as well as part of a more specific challenge to the notion of representation and its address, there is a major difference of orientation between the two that cannot be ignored: we have seen that postmodernism is politically ambivalent for it is doubly coded – both complicitous with and contesting of the cultural dominants within which it operates; but on the other side, feminisms have distinct, unambiguous political agendas of resistance. Feminisms are not really either compatible with or even an example of postmodern thought, as a few critics have tried to argue; if anything, together they form the single most powerful force in changing the direction in which (male) postmodernism was heading but, I think, no longer is. It radicalised the postmodern sense of difference and de-naturalised the traditional historiographic separation of the private and the public – and the personal and the political – as the last section of this chapter will investigate.

The reason for the none the less quite common conflation of the feminist and the postmodern may well lie in their common interest in representation, that purportedly neutral process that is now being deconstructed in terms of ideology. In shows like *Difference: On Representation and Sexuality*, held at the New Museum of Contemporary Art in New York in 1985, sexual difference was shown to be something that is continuously reproduced by cultural representations normally taken for granted as natural or given. Few would disagree today that feminisms have transformed art practice: through new forms, new self-consciousness about representation, and new awareness of both contexts and particularities of gendered experience. They have certainly made women artists more aware of themselves as women and as artists; they are even changing men's sense of themselves as gendered artists. They have rendered inseparable feminisms as socio-political movements and feminisms as a (plural) phenomenon of art history. Temporally, it is no accident that they have coincided with the revival of figurative painting and the rise of conceptual art, of what I have called photo-graphy as a high-art form, of video, alternative film practices, performance art – all of which have worked to challenge both the humanist notion of the artist as romantic individual 'genius' (and therefore of art as the expression of universal meaning by a transcendent human subject) and the modernist domination of two particular art forms, painting and sculpture. But feminisms have also refocused attention on the politics of representation and knowledge – and therefore also on power. They have *made* postmodernism think, not just about the body, but about the female body; not just about the female body, but about its desires – and about both as socially and historically constructed through representation.

Whether the medium be linguistic or visual, we are always dealing with systems of meaning operating within certain codes and conventions that are socially produced and historically conditioned. This is the postmodern focus that has replaced the modernist/romantic one of individual expression. And it is not hard to see why suddenly the politics of representation becomes an issue: what systems of power authorise some representations while suppressing others? Or, even more specifically, how is desire instilled through representation by the management of the pleasure of reading or looking? Many feminist theorists have been arguing for the need to de-naturalise our common-sense understanding of the body in art, the need to reveal the semiotic mechanisms of gender positioning which produce both that body image and the desires (male and female) it evokes.

This mixing of the political with the sexual has proved bothersome to some critics, especially to those for whom notions of pleasure and desire are key terms of aesthetic experience. Both feminist and postmodern theory and practice have worked to 'de-doxify' any notion of desire as simply individual fulfilment, somehow independent of the pleasures created *by* and *in* culture. The political impulse of postmodern and feminist art challenges the conditions of desire: desire as satisfaction endlessly deferred, that is, as an anticipatory activity in the future tense; desire as fuelled by the inaccessibility of the object and dissatisfaction with the real. This is the realm of displaced desire – of advertising and pornography – and of Baudrillard's simulacrum. While the very notion of desire would seem to presuppose a coherent subjectivity, we have seen that much feminist and postmodern theory has worked to question and problematise this concept. But such theory has itself been divided, between those for whom desire is something beyond culture and politics, and those who see the desiring subject as inscribed in and by certain ideologically determined subject-positions.

Desire is clearly problematic: is there a difference between desire as textual play, say, and desire as foregrounding the political economy of the image in a patriarchal and capitalist society? Desire is not just a value of poststructuralist ideology; it is also a norm in consumer society, one that Marxist critics have been working to deconstruct. But so too have feminists: Carol Squiers's critical thematic exhibits, such as her 1984 *Design for Living*, bring together magazine images of women with an aim to unmask and challenge, through ordering and positioning, the capitalist and patriarchal politics of mass-media presentations of woman's body and desire.

In her book, *Female Desire*, Rosalind Coward argues from a feminist poststructuralist perspective that women's pleasures are constructed within a range of signifying practices; in other words, they are not natural or innate. Produced by discourses which often sustain male privilege, feminine desire –

its satisfactions, its objects – may need rethinking, especially to consider
what Catherine Stimpson calls its 'herterogeneity'.[3] But first, those male
discourses need confronting, challenging, debunking. This is where the
work of feminist artists is so important. For instance, in a short story called
'Black Venus' by Angela Carter, two discourses meet – and clash: the poetic
language of male sublimated desire for woman (as both muse and object of
erotic fantasy) and the language of the political and contexualising discourses of female experience. This is one of those texts that almost demands
to be read as the site for the discursive construction of the meaning of
gender, but in a problematic sense: there are two conflicting discourses
which work to foreground and contest the history of desire, male desire.

This is the story of Baudelaire and his mulatto mistress, Jeanne Duval. In
his journal, Baudelaire once wrote: 'Eternal Venus, caprice, hysteria, fantasy,
is one of the seductive forms [assumed] by the Devil', a devil he both courted
and despised. His biographers have been rather kind to him, patiently
explaining to us the sublimatory advantages of his preference for desire
over consummation, anticipatory imagination over the actual sexual act –
for us, if not for Duval. We get the poems; she seems to have ended up with
very little. But the same biographers have been considerably less kind to
Duval: as painted by Manet, she is usually described as a sensuous beauty, a
melancholic if exotic shrew, whom Baudelaire treated as a goddess but who
never understood his poetry and who repaid his generosity and kindness with
nagging and ill temper. (What they seem to want to avoid mentioning, by the
way, is that he was also rather generous with his syphilis.) The woman to
whom history denied a voice is the *subject* of Carter's 'Black Venus' – as she
was the *object* of Baudelaire's 'Black Venus' poems.

Carter's text consistently contrasts the language of Baudelairean decadent
male eroticism with the stark social reality of Jeanne Duval's position as a
colonial, a black, and a kept woman. Male erotic iconography of women
seems to have two poles: the romantic/decadent fantasist (like Baudelaire's)
and the realist (the woman as sexual partner), but in neither case is the
woman anything but a mediating sign for the male.[4] Carter's verbal text
attempts to code and then re-code the 'colonised territory' of the female
body; it is coded as erotic masculine fantasy, and then re-coded in terms of
female experience. The text is a complex interweaving of the discourses of
desire and politics, of the erotic and the analytic, of the male and the female.

The story opens with an overt echo of the evening descriptions of Baudelaire's poems, 'Harmonie du soir' and 'Crépuscule du soir'. But the woman
described in Carter's text as a 'forlorn Eve' is represented in a language
different from that of the male poet: she 'never experienced her experience *as*
experience, life never added to the sum of her knowledge; rather subtracted
from it'.[5] In contrast, the male (identified at this point only by the pronoun
'he') offers to her his fantasy, a fantasy that makes him into a parody of 'le

pauvre amoureux des pays chimériques', the Baudelairean inventor of Americas in 'Le Voyage'. The details of his fantasy parody those of the poems 'Voyage à Cythère' and 'La Chevelure' in that they offer the same topoi but vulgarised as bourgeois tourist escapism ('Baby, baby, let me take you back where you belong'). This is mixed with Yeatsian Byzantian parody ('back to your lovely, lazy island where the jewelled parrot rocks on the enamel tree') (p. 10). The woman's reply assaults this fantasy: 'No!...Not the bloody parrot forest! Don't take me on the slavers' route back to the West Indies' (p. 11). Erotic reverie meets political and historical reality, perhaps reminding us that even Cythera, the island of Venus, is no paradise: the Baudelairean poet hangs from its gallows. For the West Indian woman, the island paradise he imagines is one of 'glaring yellow shore and harsh blue skies', of 'fly-blown towns' that are not Paris. Those thousand sonnets that Baudelaire's 'Dame Créole' was to have inspired in the heart of the poet are here used to roll her cheroots. This dream literally goes up in smoke.

Then, the language of male eroticism again takes over. Aroused from her 'féconde paresse', this particular 'Dame Créole' dances naked for him, lets down her fleece-like 'chevelure', clothes herself only in the bangles described in the poem, 'Les Bijoux'. The 'brune enchanteresse' 'grande et svelte' dances, but in Carter's story she does so in 'slumbrous resentment' against her lover, in a room that 'tugged at its moorings, longing to take off on an aerial quest for that Cythera beloved of poets' (p. 12). The text points us directly to Baudelaire here and then makes the intertext problematic. As he dreamily watches, we are told that 'she wondered what the distinction was between dancing naked in front of *one* man who paid and dancing naked in front of a group of men who paid' (p. 12). He dreams erotic dreams; she ponders what is called her 'use value' and her syphilis: 'was pox not the emblematic fate of a creature made for pleasure and the price you paid for the atrocious mixture of corruption and innocence this child of the sun brought with her from the Antilles?' (p. 13). The pox is called America's, 'the raped continent's revenge' against European imperialism, but the revenge has backfired here. The text then returns to the Baudelairean erotic discourse: her hair, the cat. He thinks of her as a 'vase of darkness...not Eve, but herself, the forbidden fruit, and he has eaten her!' (p. 15). We are then offered four lines (in translation) from Baudelaire's poem, 'Sed non satiata' – an ironic intertextual comment on his desire but also on hers, unsatiated as it is.

With a break in the text, what begins (seven and a half pages into the story) is yet another discourse. 'He' is identified as Baudelaire; 'she' as Jeanne Duval, also known as Jeanne Prosper or Lemer 'as if her name were of no consequence' (p. 16). Her origins are equally vague. In parentheses we read: '(Her *pays d'origine* of less importance than it would have been had she been a wine.)' (p. 16). Perhaps she came from the Dominican Republic where, as we are pointedly told, Toussaint L'Ouverture had led a slave revolt. The racial, economic, and gender politics of French colonial imperialism are brought to our attention. Yet the text immediately returns to the Baudelairean erotic discourse to describe Jeanne to us. That it should do so is not surprising. After all, besides a portrait by Manet, today that is all we have to know her by. Through both the literary and the historical references, the text attempts to give back to Jeanne the history of which she was deprived as 'the pure child of the colony' – the 'white, imperious' colony (p. 17). She has also been deprived of her language. We are told that she spoke Créole badly, that she tried to speak 'good' French when she arrived in Paris. But herein lies the true irony of those erotic literary representations by which we know her today:

> you could say, not so much that Jeanne did not understand the lapidary, troubled serenity of her lover's poetry, but that it was a perpetual affront to her. He recited it to her by the hour and she ached, raged and chafed under it because his eloquence denied her language. (p. 18).

She cannot hear his tributes to herself outside of her colonial – racial and linguistic – context.

The text then adds yet another context, the obvious one of gender: 'The goddess of his heart, the ideal of the poet, lay resplendently on the bed ... ; he liked to have her make a spectacle of herself, to provide a sumptuous feast for his bright eyes that were always bigger than his belly. Venus lies on the bed, waiting for a wind to rise: the sooty albatross hankers for the storm' (p. 18). But, for the reader of Baudelaire's poetry, there is a curious reversal here – not only of colour ('sooty albatross'), but of roles. In the poem called 'L'Albatros', it is the poet who flies on the wings of poesy, though clumsy on earth. In Carter's parodic version, the woman is the graceful albatross; the poet is instead that great dandy of birds (from Poe's *Adventures of Arthur Gordon Pym*), the one who always builds its nest near that of the albatross: the penguin – flightless, bourgeois, inescapably comic. We are told: 'Wind is the element of the albatross just as domesticity is that of the penguin' (p. 19). The poet is demystified, as is the lover.

The erotic encounters of these two strange birds are carefully and sharply coded and the text situates the code historically and culturally for us:

> It is essential to their connection that, if she should put on the private garments of nudity, its non-sartorial regalia of jewellery and rouge, then he himself must retain the public nineteenth-century masculine impedimenta of frock coat (exquisitely cut); white shirt (pure silk, London tailored); oxblood cravat; and impeccable trousers. (p. 19)

That Manet's work might come to mind here is no accident:

There's more to 'Le Déjeuner sur l'Herbe' than meets the eye. (Manet, another friend of his.) Man does and is dressed to do so; his skin is his own business. He is artful, the creation of culture. Woman is; and is, therefore, fully dressed in no clothes at all, her skin is common property. (p. 20)

Together Baudelaire and Duval untangle 'the history of transgression' (p. 21) but his customary erotic rhetoric keeps giving way to her reality. The statement that 'Jeanne stoically laboured over her lover's pleasure, as if he were her vineyard' (p. 21) recalls (though ironically) his poem 'Les Bijoux' where her breasts are the 'grappes de ma vigne' – that is, the poet's. In that revisionist version, she does not have to labour over his pleasure; she is passive: 'elle se laissait aimer.'

The text breaks here. He dies 'deaf, dumb and paralysed'; she loses her beauty and then her life. But Carter offers a second fate for her Jeanne Duval. She buys new teeth, a wig, and restores some of her ravaged beauty. She returns to the Caribbean using the money from the sale of Baudelaire's manuscripts and from what he could sneak to her before his death. ('She was surprised to find out how much she was worth.') She reverses the associations of this trip's direction – it is the 'slavers' route', after all. She dies, in extreme old age, after a life as a madam. The text then betrays its fantasy status through its future tense: from her grave, 'she will continue to dispense, to the most privileged of the colonial administration, at a not excessive price, the veritable, the authentic, the true Baudelairean syphilis' (p. 23). This is Angela Carter's parodic voicing of a doubled discourse of complicity and challenge, of the feminist politicisation of desire.

But I said earlier that it was the *postmodern* that was characterised by complicity and critique, not the feminist. Yet perhaps this is another point of overlap that might be theorised: in other words, it is not just a matter of feminisms having had a major impact on postmodernism, but perhaps postmodern strategies can be deployed by feminist artists to deconstructive ends – that is, in order to *begin* the move towards change (a move that is not, in itself, part of the postmodern). Carter's text is not alone in suggesting that the erotic is an apt focus for this kind of critique, since it raises the question of desire and its gendered politics and also the issue of representation and its politics. The exploring of the role of our cultural and social discourses in constructing both pleasure and sexual representations is what results from the clash of two discursive practices across which conflicting notions of gender and sexual identity are produced in Carter's story. A similar, even more direct politicising of male desire can be seen in Margaret Harrison's collage/painting *Rape*. In this work, a frieze across the top presents reproductions of high-art male erotic images of women as available, passive, offering themselves to the male gaze: familiar canonical paintings by Ingres, Rubens, Rossetti, Manet, and so on. Underneath is a strip of press cuttings about rape trials where the legal profession is shown to condone violence against women. Beneath that is a series of painted representations of instruments of rape: knives, scissors, broken bottles. Like Carter's text, *Rape* presents a parodic clashing of discourses: high-art nudes, judicial reports, representations of violence. Yet what all the discourses are shown to share is the objectification of the female body.

The parodic use (even if also abuse) of male representations of women in both Carter's and Harrison's work is a postmodernist strategy at least in so far as it implies a paradoxically complicitous critique. But even the more generally accepted articulations of specifically female and feminist contestation, such as Mary Kelly's *Post-Partum Document*, could be seen as an implicitly parodic challenge to the patriarchal madonna and child tradition of western high art: as I suggested earlier, it politicises and de-naturalises what has been seen as the most 'natural' of relationships by articulating it through the everyday discourse of the actual female experience of mothering. But it is this change of discourse that makes Kelly's work less problematic as a feminist work than that of some others. When artists like Cindy Sherman or Hannah Wilke parodically use the female nude tradition, for example, different issues arise, for the femaleness of the nude tradition – like that of the Baudelairean erotic – makes it an art form in which the male viewer is explicit and the notion of masculine desire is constitutive. Yet, this very femaleness is what has been ignored in art historical accounts of the nude genre.
[...]

FEMINIST POSTMODERNIST PARODY

[...]

There is, then, a two-way involvement of the postmodern with the feminist: on the one hand, feminisms have successfully urged postmodernism to reconsider – in terms of gender – its challenges to that humanist universal called 'Man' and have supported and reinforced its de-naturalisation of the separation between the private and the public, the personal and the political; on the other hand, postmodern parodic representational strategies have offered feminist artists an effective way of working within and yet challenging dominant patriarchal discourses. That said, there is still no way in which the feminist and the postmodern – as cultural enterprises – can be conflated. The differences are clear, and none so clear as the political one. Chris Weedon opens her book on feminist practice with the words: 'Feminism is a politics.'[6] Postmodernism is not; it is certainly political, but it is politically ambivalent, doubly encoded as both complicity and critique, so that it can be (and has been) recuperated by both the left and the right, each ignoring half of that double coding.

Feminisms will continue to resist incorporation into postmodernism, largely because of their revolutionary force as political movements working for real social change. They go beyond making ideology explicit and deconstructing it to argue a need to change that ideology, to effect a real transformation of art that can only come with a transformation of patriarchal social practices. Postmodernism has not theorised agency; it has no strategies of resistance that would correspond to the feminist ones. Postmodernism manipulates, but does not transform signification; it disperses but does not (re)construct the structures of subjectivity.[7] Feminisms must. Feminist artists may use postmodern strategies of parodic inscription and subversion in order to initiate the deconstructive first step but they do not stop there. While useful (especially in the visual arts where the insistence of the male gaze seems hard to avoid), such internalised subversion does not automatically lead to the production of the new, not even new representations of female desire. As one critic asks: 'is it possible to create new erotic codes – and I assume that is what feminism is striving for – without in some ways reusing the old?'[8] Perhaps postmodern strategies do, however, offer ways for women artists at least to contest the old – the representations of both their bodies and their desires – without denying them the right to re-colonise, to reclaim both as sites of meaning and value. Such practices also remind us all that every representation always has its politics.

11

Gender Trouble: From Parody to Politics

Judith Butler

I began with the speculative question of whether feminist politics could do without a 'subject' in the category of women. At stake is not whether it still makes sense, strategically or transitionally, to refer to women in order to make representational claims in their behalf. The feminist 'we' is always and only a phantasmatic construction, one that has its purposes, but which denies the internal complexity and indeterminacy of the term and constitutes itself only through the exclusion of some part of the constituency that it simultaneously seeks to represent. The tenuous or phantasmatic status of the 'we', however, is not cause for despair or, at least, it is not *only* cause for despair. The radical instability of the category sets into question the *foundational* restrictions on feminist political theorising and opens up other configurations, not only of genders and bodies, but of politics itself.

The foundationalist reasoning of identity politics tends to assume that an identity must first be in place in order for political interests to be elaborated and, subsequently, political action to be taken. My argument is that there need not be a 'doer behind the deed', but that the 'doer' is variably constructed in and through the deed. This is not a return to an existential theory of the self as constituted through its acts, for the existential theory maintains a prediscursive structure for both the self and its acts. It is precisely the discursively variable construction of each in and through the other that has interested me here.

The question of locating 'agency' is usually associated with the viability of the 'subject', where the 'subject' is understood to have some stable existence prior to the cultural field that it negotiates. Or, if the subject is culturally constructed, it is nevertheless vested with an agency, usually figured as the capacity for reflexive mediation, that remains intact regardless of its cultural embeddedness. On such a model, 'culture' and 'discourse' *mire* the subject, but do not constitute that subject. This move to qualify and enmire the pre-existing subject has appeared necessary to establish a point of agency that is not fully *determined* by that culture and discourse. And yet, this kind of reasoning falsely presumes (a) agency can only be established through

110

recourse to a prediscursive 'I', even if that 'I' is found in the midst of a discursive convergence, and (b) that to be *constituted* by discourse is to be *determined* by discourse, where determination forecloses the possibility of agency.

Even within the theories that maintain a highly qualified or situated subject, the subject still encounters its discursively constituted environment in an oppositional epistemological frame. The culturally enmired subject negotiates its constructions, even when those constructions are the very predicates of its own identity. In Beauvoir, for example, there is an 'I' that does its gender, that becomes its gender, but that 'I', invariably associated with its gender, is nevertheless a point of agency never fully identifiable with its gender. That *cogito* is never fully *of* the cultural world that it negotiates, no matter the narrowness of the ontological distance that separates that subject from its cultural predicates. The theories of feminist identity that elaborate predicates of colour, sexuality, ethnicity, class, and able-bodiedness invariably close with an embarrassed 'etc.' at the end of the list. Through this horizontal trajectory of adjectives, these positions strive to encompass a situated subject, but invariably fail to be complete. This failure, however, is instructive: what political impetus is to be derived from the exasperated 'etc.' that so often occurs at the end of such lines? This is a sign of exhaustion as well as of the illimitable process of signification itself. It is the *supplément*, the excess that necessarily accompanies any effort to posit identity once and for all. This illimitable *et cetera*, however, offers itself as a new departure for feminist political theorising.

If identity is asserted through a process of signification, if identity is always already signified, and yet continues to signify as it circulates within various interlocking discourses, then the question of agency is not to be answered through recourse to an 'I' that pre-exists signification. In other words, the enabling conditions for an assertion of 'I' are provided by the structure of signification, the rules that regulate the legitimate and illegitimate invocation of that pronoun, the practices that establish the terms of intelligibility by which that pronoun can circulate. Language is not an *exterior medium or instrument* into which I pour a self and from which I glean a reflection of that self. The Hegelian model of self-recognition that has been appropriated by Marx, Lukács, and a variety of contemporary liberatory discourses presupposes a potential adequation between the 'I' that confronts its world, including its language, as an object, and the 'I' that finds itself as an object in that world. But the subject/object dichotomy, which here belongs to the tradition of Western epistemology, conditions the very problematic of identity that it seeks to solve.

What discursive tradition establishes the 'I' and its 'Other' in an epistemological confrontation that subsequently decides where and how questions of knowability and agency are to be determined? What kinds of agency are foreclosed through the positing of an epistemological subject precisely because the rules and practices that govern the invocation of that subject and regulate its agency in advance are ruled out as sites of analysis and critical intervention? That the epistemological point of departure is in no sense inevitable is naïvely and pervasively confirmed by the mundane operations of ordinary language – widely documented within anthropology – that regard the subject/object dichotomy as a strange and contingent, if not violent, philosophical imposition. The language of appropriation, instrumentality, and distanciation germane to the epistemological mode also belong to a strategy of domination that pits the 'I' against an 'Other' and, once that separation is effected, creates an artificial set of questions about the knowability and recoverability of that Other.

As part of the epistemological inheritance of contemporary political discourses of identity, this binary opposition is a strategic move within a given set of signifying practices, one that establishes the 'I' in and through this opposition and which reifies that opposition as a necessity, concealing the discursive apparatus by which the binary itself is constituted. The shift from an *epistemological* account of identity to one which locates the problematic within practices of *signification* permits an analysis that takes the epistemological mode itself as one possible and contingent signifying practice. Further, the question of *agency* is reformulated as a question of how signification and resignification work. In other words, what is signified as an identity is not signified at a given point in time after which it is simply there as an inert piece of entitative language. Clearly, identities *can* appear as so many inert substantives; indeed, epistemological models tend to take this appearance as their point of theoretical departure. However, the substantive 'I' only appears as such through a signifying practice that seeks to conceal its own workings and to naturalise its effects. Further, to qualify as a substantive identity is an arduous task, for such appearances are rule-generated identities, ones which rely on the consistent and repeated invocation of rules that condition and restrict culturally intelligible practices of identity. Indeed, to understand identity as a *practice*, and as a signifying practice, is to understand culturally intelligible subjects as the resulting effects of a rulebound discourse that inserts itself in the pervasive and mundane signifying acts of linguistic life. Abstractly considered, language refers to an open system of signs by which intelligibility is insistently created and contested. As historically specific organisations of language, discourses present themselves in the plural, coexisting within temporal frames, and instituting unpredictable and inadvertent convergences from which specific modalities of discursive possibilities are engendered.

As a process, signification harbours within itself what the epistemological discourse refers to as 'agency'. The rules that govern intelligible identity, i.e., that enable and restrict the intelligible assertion of an 'I', rules that are partially structured along matrices of gender hierarchy and compulsory heterosexuality, operate through *repetition*. Indeed, when the subject is said to be constituted, that means simply that the subject is a consequence of certain rule-governed discourses that govern the intelligible invocation of identity. The subject is not *determined* by the rules through which it is generated because signification is *not a founding act, but rather a regulated process of repetition* that both conceals itself and enforces its rules precisely through the production of substantialising effects. In a sense, all signification takes place within the orbit of the compulsion to repeat; 'agency', then, is to be located within the possibility of a variation on that repetition. If the rules governing signification not only restrict, but enable the assertion of alternative domains of cultural intelligibility, i.e., new possibilities for gender that contest the rigid codes of hierarchical binarisms, then it is only *within* the practices of repetitive signifying that a subversion of identity becomes possible. The injunction *to be* a given gender produces necessary failures, a variety of incoherent configurations that in their multiplicity exceed and defy the injunction by which they are generated. Further, the very injunction to be a given gender takes place through discursive routes: to be a good mother, to be a heterosexually desirable object, to be a fit worker, in sum, to signify a multiplicity of guarantees in response to a variety of different demands all at once. The coexistence or convergence of such discursive injunctions produces the possibility of a complex reconfiguration and redeployment; it is not a transcendental subject who enables action in the midst of such a convergence. There is no self that is prior to the convergence or who maintains 'integrity' prior to its entrance into this conflicted cultural field. There is only a taking up of the tools where they lie, where the very 'taking up' is enabled by the tool lying there.

What constitutes a subversive repetition within signifying practices of gender? I have argued ('I' deploy the grammar that governs the genre of the philosophical conclusion, but note that it is the grammar itself that deploys and enables this 'I', even as the 'I' that insists itself here repeats, redeploys, and – as the critics will determine – contests the philosophical grammar by which it is both enabled and restricted) that, for instance, within the sex/gender distinction, sex poses as 'the real' and the 'factic', the material or corporeal ground upon which gender operates as an act of cultural *inscription*. And yet gender is not written on the body as the torturing instrument of writing in Kafka's 'In the Penal Colony' inscribes itself unintelligibly on the flesh of the accused. The question is not: what meaning does that inscription carry within it, but what cultural apparatus arranges this meeting between instrument and body, what interventions into this ritualistic repetition are possible? The 'real' and the 'sexually factic' are phantasmatic constructions – illusions of substance – that bodies are compelled to approximate, but never can. What, then, enables the exposure of the rift between the phantasmatic and the real whereby the real admits itself as phantasmatic? Does this offer the possibility for a repetition that is not fully constrained by the injunction to reconsolidate naturalised identities? Just as bodily surfaces are enacted *as* the natural, so these surfaces can become the site of a dissonant and denaturalised performance that reveals the performative status of the natural itself.

Practices of parody can serve to re-engage and reconsolidate the very distinction between a privileged and naturalised gender configuration and one that appears as derived, phantasmatic, and mimetic – a failed copy, as it were. And surely parody has been used to further a politics of despair, one which affirms a seemingly inevitable exclusion of marginal genders from the territory of the natural and the real. And yet this failure to become 'real' and to embody 'the natural' is, I would argue, a constitutive failure of all gender enactments for the very reason that these ontological locales are fundamentally uninhabitable. Hence, there is a subversive laughter in the pastiche-effect of parodic practices in which the original, the authentic, and the real are themselves constituted as effects. The loss of gender norms would have the effect of proliferating gender configurations, destabilising substantive identity, and depriving the naturalising narratives of compulsory heterosexuality of their central protagonists: 'man' and 'woman'. The parodic repetition of gender exposes as well the illusion of gender identity as an intractable depth and inner substance. As the effects of a subtle and politically enforced performativity, gender is an 'act', as it were, that is open to splittings, self-parody, self-criticism, and those hyperbolic exhibitions of 'the natural' that, in their very exaggeration, reveal its fundamentally phantasmatic status.

I have tried to suggest that the identity categories often presumed to be foundational to feminist politics, that is, deemed necessary in order to mobilise feminism as an identity politics, simultaneously work to limit and constrain in advance the very cultural possibilities that feminism is supposed to open up. The tacit constraints that produce culturally intelligible 'sex' ought to be understood as generative political structures rather than naturalised foundations. Paradoxically, the reconceptualisation of identity as an *effect*, that is, as *produced* or *generated*, opens up possibilities of 'agency' that are insidiously foreclosed by positions that take identity categories as foundational and fixed. For an identity to be an effect means that it is neither fatally determined nor fully artificial and arbitrary. That the *constituted* status of identity is misconstrued along these two conflicting lines suggests the ways in which the feminist discourse on cultural construction remains trapped within the unnecessary binarism of free will and determinism. Construction is not opposed to agency; it is the necessary scene of agency, the very terms in which agency is articulated and becomes culturally intelligible. The critical task for feminism is not to establish a point of view outside of constructed identities; that conceit is the construction of an epistemological model that would disavow its own cultural location and, hence, promote itself as a global subject, a position that deploys precisely the imperialist strategies that feminism ought to criticise. The critical task is, rather, to locate strategies of subversive repetition enabled by those constructions, to affirm the local possibilities of intervention through participating in precisely those practices of repetition that constitute identity and, therefore, present the immanent possibility of contesting them.

This theoretical inquiry has attempted to locate the political in the very signifying practices that establish, regulate, and deregulate identity. This effort, however, can only be accomplished through the introduction of a set of questions that extend the very notion of the political. How to disrupt the foundations that cover over alternative cultural configurations of gender? How to destabilise and render in their phantasmatic dimension the 'premises' of identity politics?

This task has required a critical genealogy of the naturalisation of sex and of bodies in general. It has also demanded a reconsideration of the figure of the body as mute, prior to culture, awaiting signification, a figure that cross-checks with the figure of the feminine, awaiting the inscription-as-incision of the masculine signifier for entrance into language and culture. From a political analysis of compulsory heterosexuality, it has been necessary to question the construction of sex as binary, as a hierarchical binary. From the point of view of gender as enacted, questions have emerged over the fixity of gender identity as an interior depth that is said to be externalised in various forms of 'expression'. The implicit construction of the primary heterosexual construction of desire is shown to persist even as it appears in the mode of primary bisexuality. Strategies of exclusion and hierarchy are also shown to persist in the formulation of the sex/gender distinction and its recourse to 'sex' as the prediscursive as well as the priority of sexuality to culture and, in particular, the cultural construction of sexuality as the prediscursive. Finally, the epistemological paradigm that presumes the priority of the doer to the deed establishes a global and globalising subject who disavows its own locality as well as the conditions for local intervention.

If taken as the grounds of feminist theory or politics, these 'effects' of gender hierarchy and compulsory heterosexuality are not only misdescribed as foundations, but the signifying practices that enable this metaleptic misdescription remain outside the purview of a feminist critique of gender relations. To enter into the repetitive practices of this terrain of signification is not a choice, for the 'I' that might enter is always already inside: there is no possibility of agency or reality outside of the discursive practices that give those terms the intelligibility that they have. The task is not whether to repeat, but how to repeat or, indeed, to repeat and, through a radical proliferation of gender, *to displace* the very gender norms that enable the repetition itself. There is no ontology of gender on which we might construct a politics, for gender ontologies always operate within established political contexts as normative injunctions, determining what qualifies as intelligible sex, invoking and consolidating the reproductive constraints on sexuality, setting the prescriptive requirements whereby sexed or gendered bodies come into cultural intelligibility. Ontology is, thus, not a foundation, but a normative injunction that operates insidiously by installing itself into political discourse as its necessary ground.

The deconstruction of identity is not the deconstruction of politics; rather, it establishes as political the very terms through which identity is articulated. This kind of critique brings into question the foundationalist frame in which feminism as an identity politics has been articulated. The internal paradox of this foundationalism is that it presumes, fixes, and constrains the very 'subjects' that it hopes to represent and liberate. The task here is not to celebrate each and every new possibility *qua* possibility, but to redescribe those possibilities that *already* exist, but which exist within cultural domains designated as culturally unintelligible and impossible. If identities were no longer fixed as the premises of a political syllogism, and politics no longer understood as a set of practices derived from the alleged interests that belong to a set of ready-made subjects, a new configuration of politics would surely emerge from the ruins of the old. Cultural configurations of sex and gender might then proliferate or, rather, their present proliferation might then become articulable within the discourses that establish intelligible cultural life, confounding the very binarism of sex, and exposing its fundamental unnaturalness. What other local strategies for engaging the 'unnatural' might lead to the denaturalisation of gender as such?

12

Crises in Legitimation: Crossing the Great Voids

Alice A. Jardine

The legitimate renunciation of a certain style of causality perhaps does not give one the right to renounce all aetiological demands.

(Jacques Derrida)

In *The Postmodern Condition*, Jean-François Lyotard defines the postmodern as 'incredulity with regard to the master narratives'.[1] He goes on to say that this lack of belief, this suspicion in the West, is no doubt due to scientific progress, but that – on the other hand – our accelerating scientific progress has already presupposed a lack of belief. According to Lyotard, we cannot possibly know the origin or the historical why of this incredulity, we can only *describe* its present manifestations, the places where it appears most consistently: 'to the obsolescence of the master narrative device of legitimation corresponds notably the crisis of metaphysical philosophy, and that of the institution of the university which depends upon it. The narrative function loses its foundations, the great hero, the great perils, the great quests, and the great goal.'[2] Lyotard here emphasises two such places, one literal, the other figurative, each dependent upon the other: the university and the narratives of a certain philosophy. The crisis in legitimation in the West is necessarily a crisis in the status of *knowledge* – traditionally, the ability to decide what is true and just – functions that have remained inseparable up to the present. According to Lyotard, any attempt to attribute this crisis in legitimation to specific causes (Technology? Capitalism?) would be caught in the same impossibility of knowing. We can only talk about the seeds of this crisis. They were buried, for example, in two of the major kinds of narratives of the nineteenth century: those of speculation (for example, Freud) and emancipation (Marx).

Lyotard emphasises that this crisis in legitimation is, first and foremost, a crisis in governing, in the validity of the social contract itself, rather than in that of any one particular ideology, within patriarchal culture. Although paternity *per se* is not a major topic in Lyotard's text, he makes it clear that the crisis is not sexually neutral. He does this primarily through his

117

descriptions of the only viable source and place he sees for legitimacy in postmodern culture: 'para-logic'. This kind of logic is dependent upon and valorises the kinds of incomplete 'short stories' historically embedded, hidden, within so-called 'scientific' or 'objective' discourse: the kinds of short narratives that this discourse attempts to evacuate in order to shore up its 'Truths'.[3] These short narratives are described as antisystematic, antimethodical; their proponents would be in favour of 'temporary pacts' rather than 'universal social contracts'.[4] They are the components of what Lyotard will call, in a later article, a new kind of 'pseudotheory': 'a feminine relation of ductility and ductibility, polymorphism'.[5] Lyotard argues in favour of establishing a 'philosophy of fairies [sic] and women' whose primary characteristics would be anonymity, passivity, and a theatrics of faceless masks. But his rather timid insights into how the crises in question are crises in the fables, systems, and theories imagined by men become bolder and more explicit elsewhere; for example, in his 'One of the Things at Stake in Women's Struggles': 'Deceitful like Eubulides and like realities, women are discovering something that could cause the greatest revolution in the West, something that (masculine) domination has never ceased to stifle: there is no signifier; or else, the class above all classes is just one among many; or again, we Westerners must rework our space-time and all our logic on the basis of non-centricism, non-finality, non-truth'.[6]

The slippage in male theoretical discourse from the *feminine* (anonymity, passivity, and so on) to women (as metaphysically opposed to men) and, finally, to 'we' ('we Westerners') will be of concern throughout this study. What is important here is simply the recognition that delegitimation, experienced as crisis, is the loss of the paternal fiction, the West's heritage and guarantee, and that *one* of the responses to that loss on the part of those engaged by modernity has been to look to the future, to *affirm* and *assume* that loss.

Other reactions to this disinheritance are most often tainted by nostalgia. This nostalgia tends to take the form of a critique of what is called conformity or mass culture: of 'the society without a father' where (male) authority is no longer internalised and (female) 'primary instinctual wishes' are no longer controlled.[7] From the critical theory of the Frankfurt School to the pop-critique of Christopher Lasch, the discussion of loss of authority inevitably comes around to women, who return, empirically, as among those principally to blame for this loss.[8] Other forms of sociological nostalgia are more complex and sophisticated; for example, nostalgia is itself considered as a topic, as an inevitable symptom of something being 'wrong': 'the nostalgia for a sociality of more uncertain pacts and rituals, the nostalgia for a more cruel but more fascinating destiny of exchange, is more profound than the rational demands of the social with which we have been rocked to sleep.'[9] The only recognition that can help us return to this ritual state, according to

Baudrillard, is that of 'femininity as the principle of uncertainty' – femininity as *seduction*. And, according to him, it is women who are blindest to this fact; it is women who are working against the possibilities for true cultural renewal. For women to demand autonomy or recognition of sexual difference is for them to desire power, to act as men, to lose the female power of seduction regarded by Baudrillard as the best way to master the symbolic universe.[10]

It may be true that social hysteria on a large scale – signalled by both men's and women's confusion about their own gender – entails a loss of seduction. But once again, only *women* are seen as responsible for, indeed guilty of, blocking the flow of desire. Curiously, Baudrillard's modern code of conduct for young ladies echoes a form of traditional maternal discourse, the 'secret wisdom' mothers have historically shared with their daughters: how they must awaken the desire of men, but never respond to or initiate it, for that is the secret of women's power.

Another variant of nostalgia, in another mode and, here, from another culture, is that for 'inner speech', for that which is 'secret', 'quiet' and 'private'. As George Steiner puts it, 'at the present juncture it would appear that "total emancipation" has in fact brought a new servitude'. The rendering explicit of sexuality has brought about a 'drastic reapportionment', according to Steiner. And once again, as we might expect: 'This would be most dramatically so in the case of middle class women, many of whom will have passed within a generation from zones of near-silence or total inwardness in respect of sexual language to a milieu of permissiveness and, indeed, of competitive display.' Women who speak are men and, therefore, threaten the very *humanity* of Man: 'Because it lies at the heart of consciousness, sexual experience offers both a denial and challenge to the genius of language...and it is through this genius that *men* have, *at least until now*, principally defined their humanity.'[11]

Loss of legitimation, loss of authority, loss of seduction, loss of genius – *loss*. I thread my way quickly through the narratives of these few somewhat randomly chosen theoretical fictions to emphasise only a small corner of the contemporary network that articulates this loss by speaking of woman – and women. It extends, of course, beyond theory, from politics to journalism to fiction. It may be that men always feel as if they have 'lost something' whenever they speak of woman or women. In any case, within the network of the Cartesian orphans of the twentieth century, those who are nostalgic are certainly the least interesting: faced with this loss, we can only return to the family (Adorno, Horkheimer, Lasch), to the sacred (Baudrillard), or to the 'aesthetic' (Steiner). If I have emphasised that nostalgia here, it is because my interest from this point forward will not be with that melancholic search for a recognisable solution, but, rather, with those discourses of modernity which have *assumed, internalised,* and *affirmed* the loss – that is, the difference – of modernity, even if only temporarily, even if all they can ultimately suggest for the future is that everyone have access to his or her own computer terminal (Lyotard).

The state of crisis endemic to modernity is experienced primarily as a loss, or at least a breakdown, of *narrative*. The two figures placed, at least conceptually, at the inceptions of narrative – metaphor and metonymy – have thus become the obsession of those human sciences in-formed by modernity.[12] The intensive analysis of their forms and functions, across so-called disciplinary boundaries, attests to a wide-ranging reorganisation of figurability; one that began to take shape at the end of the nineteenth century, but that has only today touched enough fields of knowledge to be recognised as entailing a major repositioning of conceptual boundaries in the West, a reimagining of the status of the image itself. The analogical link and mimesis of metaphor – the possibilities for difference and resemblance – and the contiguity and syntax of metonymy – the possibilities for continuity and desire – have themselves become primary objects of modernity's passionate rethinking.

Now, if 'what created humanity is narration',[13] then it may be that Humanity itself has been a myth that has outlived its time; or perhaps the West's momentarily delinquent narratives will soon fall back into their legitimate places; or perhaps we are talking here about something else, about another kind of question altogether:

> Here there is a kind of question, let us still call it historical, whose *conception, formation, gestation*, and *labour* we are only catching a glimpse of today. I employ these words, I admit, with a glance toward the operations of child-bearing – but also with a glance toward those who, in a society from which I do not exclude myself, turn their eyes away when faced by the as yet unnameable which is proclaiming itself and which can do so, as is necessary whenever a birth is in the offing, only under the species of the nonspecies, in the formless, mute, infant, and terrifying form of monstrosity.[14]

In any case, those writing modernity as a crisis-in-narrative, and thus in legitimation, are exploring newly contoured fictional spaces, hypothetical and unmeasurable, spaces freely coded as *feminine*. Gynesis, designating the process of internalising these feminine spaces while accounting for those crises, is either static or dynamic depending upon the narrative in which it is embedded. Let us now look briefly at three of those narratives, traditionally called 'disciplines', or 'fields of knowledge': philosophy, religion, history. We shall look there for threads of gynesis while exploring the fabric of several discourses in France that are *in the process of* describing themselves as experiencing a crisis in legitimation: a set of theoretical fictions presented here without privilege and without hierarchy – a kind of story with little or no history. (I shall come back to that problem later.)

PHILOSOPHY, RELIGION, HISTORY: BOUNDARIES, SPACES, CONNOTATIONS

I was unable to avoid expressing my thinking in a philosophical mode. But I am not addressing philosophers.

(Georges Bataille, *Méthode de méditation*)

In describing what she sees as a typical fantasy of the adult male, Michèle Montrelay focuses on the following image:

First, a central tube which cannot be the closed and satisfying container of an interior. It's not that the plan of the container is non-existent. Intestine, pipe, image of cavern, of dark, deep, inner spaces, all that exists, but submitted to forces of suction that empty them in the most painful fashion. Or else, the void is already established ... Or else, the fullness is such a tremendous threat it must be parried at all costs ... Inside, either it's the void, or else a superfluidity that must be jettisoned as soon as possible. A kind of vague and terrifying suction. A permanent state of blurring. On the surface – and isn't that characteristic of male sexuality – there's an eye.[15]

As Montrelay goes on to say, we do not need to wonder about this fantasy: 'You have all read Sade, Bataille, Klossowski, Lacan'... It would not be difficult to add numerous other names to her list. This orifice, penis, mouth, anus, egg, eye, vagina seems to incorporate that which has fascinated male philosophers and male artists in dialogue with philosophy from the beginning of Western time: boundaries and spaces. The suction, the breath, of space is a movement which must be *contained* ... or *thought* ... for we are talking about the very definition of the world.[16]

In fact, one is tempted to see the exploration of boundaries and spaces as the very essence of philosophy.[17] This becomes clear when one examines the 'exemplary images' used by philosophers since antiquity to define the world: for example, Plato's 'cavern', Descartes' 'closed room', Kant's 'island', or, in another register, Kierkegaard's 'finger in the mud'. One of the most familiar examples, very close to our own time, is Alexandre Kojève's illustration of his ontology through the use of *the* Sartrean image: the gold ring whose hole is as essential to its existence as is its gold.[18] The mutual interdependency of the parts of any such structure has had infinite variations, but those variations, now historicised, are no longer sufficient for modernity, according to the philosophers: the crisis in the discursive itineraries of Western philosophy and the human sciences isomorphic to it involves first and foremost a problematisation of the boundaries and spaces necessary to their existence, and this, in turn, involves a disruption of the male and female connotations upon which the latter depend.

In his early essay, 'Structure, Sign, and Play in the Discourse of the Human Sciences',[19] Jacques Derrida shows that both the concept and the word *structure* are as old as the West and that that structure has always assumed a centre, a presence, an origin – one with different names according to the historical moment. At some point, however, there was an event, a disruption, and as Derrida puts it, one began to suspect there was no centre; the centre was decentred; the structure began to collapse.[20] Like Lyotard, he insists that trying to name the event or time that brought about this decentring would be naïve. We can only name the work that opened the way to this decentring: the Nietzschean critique of metaphysics, the Freudian critique of self-presence, and the Heideggerian destruction of metaphysics, of onto-theology, of the determination of being as presence.[21]

What was disrupted, decentred, put into question, particularly by these writers, was the 'Big Dichotomies',[22] those that had allowed Western philosophers to think about boundaries and spaces, about structures – most especially about Culture and Nature – up until the nineteenth century. Since then, the major concern of philosophy, the human sciences, and the natural sciences seems to have been the same: as Lévi-Strauss says in reference to anthropology, 'It would not be enough to reabsorb particular humanities into a general one. This first enterprise opens the way for others ... which are incumbent on the exact natural sciences: the reintegration of culture in nature and finally of life within the whole of its physico-chemical conditions.'[23]

This collapsing of both human and natural structures back into their so-called sources involves an exceedingly complex destructuring, disintegration, of the founding structures in the West through the exploration of the spaces that have defined them. From biology to nuclear physics, from the plastic arts to telecommunications and computer sciences, from architecture to mathematics, from modern theatre and music to contemporary fiction, the collapsing of certain structures into, within, and through new spaces is what is at stake: modernity as a *re*definition of the world.

The dichotomies defining boundaries and spaces up until 'the event' that is evidently so difficult to define are the dichotomies of metaphysics: the possibility of Man giving form to content, a certain conception of conception, how to create something different from the same, how to build a structure. As Hélène Cixous and others have abundantly shown, the dichotomies necessary to those structures have never been sexually neuter; they are the classically heterosexual couples of Western philosophy. For example:[24]

Male		*Female*
Mind	vs	Body
Culture	vs	Nature
Technē	vs	Physis
Intelligible	vs	Sensible
Activity	vs	Passivity
Sun	vs	Moon
Day	vs	Night
Father	vs	Mother
Intellect	vs	Sentiment
Logos	vs	Pathos
Form	vs	Matter
Same	vs	Other

The list is endless. But when the structures based in these dichotomies began to vacillate, there also began, necessarily, an intensive exploration of those terms not attributable to *Man*: the spaces of the *en-soi*, Other, without history – the feminine. Most important, through those explorations, the male philosophers found that those spaces have a certain force that *might be useful to Man if they were to be given a new language.*

Here we are at the heart of gynesis. To give a new language to these other spaces is a project filled with both promise and fear, however, for these spaces have hitherto remained unknown, terrifying, monstrous: they are made, unconscious, improper, unclean, non-sensical, oriental, profane. If philosophy is truly to question those spaces, it must move away from all that has defined them, held them in place: Man, the Subject, History, Meaning. It must offer itself over to them, embrace them. But this is also a dangerous and frightening task, for, as Walter Benjamin put it: 'It is a metaphysical truth [which we cannot lose sight of] that all of nature would begin to lament if it were endowed with language. (Though to "endow with language" is more than to "make able to speak".)'[25]

Throughout the history of metaphysics, the only way to give a language to Nature, to Space, has been through the *technē* – through technique.[26] The technē has been seen as the active, masculine aspect of 'creation'; it either accomplishes what female, passive *physis* is incapable of doing, or else it imitates her. In either case, it is active, transitive, programmatic, and operative, giving a narrative to physis through the art(s) of mimesis; its origin and telos is to make nature speak, to give her a narrative.[27]

Modern definitions of technique and technology demonstrate their semantic and ontological origins in the Greek and Roman *technē*.[28] Scientific and technological knowledge may have replaced more traditional ways of knowing, but the process has remained the same – as well as the *subject* of that process. The subject of technique and its technologies is the *ego cogito* – Man in history, Man of progress. This process, closer to our own time, becomes *praxis*, but the subject does not change: 'What Marx calls *praxis* is the meaning which works itself out spontaneously in the intercrossing of those activities by which man organises his relations with nature and with other men.'[29] It is important to point out here that technique and its derivations should not be confused with experience as productive of meaning. According to the philosophers and founders of rhetoric, experience is as mute and passive as are the fragments of the real that remain *beyond the technē*, outside of the creative process. Experience can be brought to *expression* (idealism) or turned into a *practice* (dialectical thought), but in and of itself, without mediation, it remains passive.

The space or *Topic* acted upon by the technē, the one from which Man may extract his arguments or within which he is forced to base his actions – most especially when this space becomes internalised as his soul or his thoughts – has undergone astounding semantic transformations throughout Western history. But it is always some kind of place, space, reserve, or region. Most often, before the nineteenth century, it was called Nature or Matter – to which Man could give form and from which he could then produce culture. Even in the nineteenth and twentieth centuries, the names for this space have continued to multiply: among its modern equivalents are *force* (Hegel), *hylē* (Husserl), and *pratico-inerte* (Sartre). These spaces remain, as in the past, nothing more than material multiplicities, purely sensorial and without intentionality.

At the end of the nineteenth century the possible relationships between technique and its spaces began to change radically, however, at the same time as the radical upheavals in familial, religious, and political structures seemed to accelerate. Suddenly, technique was engulfed by the very spaces that until that time had remained its passive sources, its objects. Technique itself became an object of both fear and wonder; space and matter were beginning to speak a language that Man did not want to hear. Although technique had always been an ambiguous instrument, one of both death and civilisation, by the early twentieth century, its potentials for destruction as well as new forms of life began to overwhelm Man.

For instance, the invention of photography was an event of exemplary importance for philosophers thinking about these new relationships, these new kinds of spaces with new potentials. This particular technique actually turned Man into an object, it 'froze' him, and, as Walter Benjamin would say many years later, destroyed the 'aura' of the work of art. In the photograph, there is no more physis, but only a new kind of space, what Benjamin called a new nature: 'another nature speaks to the camera in as much as it speaks to the eye; and, especially, it speaks in another mode because a space consciously elaborated by man is replaced by one where he operates unconsciously.'[30] A new space, which was suddenly larger (or smaller) than Man, found a language, began to objectify Man, to turn him into an image.

The anguish of Man – faced with this particular technique – has not diminished; it was, for example, described with passion by Roland Barthes just before his death: 'In front of the lens, I am at the same time: he who I believe myself to be, he who I hope to be seen as; he who the photographer believes me to be; and he whom he uses to exhibit his art...'[31] Barthes evokes the violent experience of becoming and then being an object ('a micro-experience of death'), of being turned into an Image, nothing but a source for others' use.[32] And beyond a solely existential anguish, the instantaneous slippage between subject and object – the oscillation between the two – as he describes it, sounds remarkably similar to how *women* have described the process they undergo in patriarchal systems of representation.[33] It is almost as if technique, as concept and practice, has turned Man into an Object-Woman.[34]

In the twentieth century, these new spaces for and of technology, these new 'natures with a language', capable of, at least potentially, objectifying Man – from the Freudian unconscious to atomic physics – forced themselves upon the philosophers. But how to think this new energy, this new force, this thought, this language, organised in space, in matter?

Jean-Paul Sartre once glimpsed the possibility of a 'speaking matter', but, as Vincent Descombes has pointed out, he rapidly withdrew his suggestion. The notion that the female connoted (natural) *en-soi* could ever *modify itself* with the male connoted (human) *pour-soi*[35] in order to attain the dignity of a being created in, of, by, and for itself is rejected by Sartre because this Being-conscious-of-itself would be the *ens causa sui*, that is, God...and '[with Sartre] the passage from *human* subjectivity ("I speak of the world.") to absolute subjectivity ("The world speaks of itself.") is prohibited'.[36] Sartre's conclusion is that all Man can do in the twentieth century is proceed 'as if': 'Everything happens as if the world, man, and man-in-the-world succeeded in realising only a missing God [*un Dieu manqué*].'[37]

Almost but not quite a God...Could it be that the end result of the history of technique, here incarnated by Man's *pour-soi*, is the creation of an *automaton*, a kind of 'spirit-in-matter'? Could this be the phantasmatic, utopian end point not only of all technical progress but of philosophy itself? A kind of sacred materiality that can communicate nothing detached from itself? A kind of 'pregnant matter', as Derrida might put it? So closely associated with Western notions of God, this 'spirit-in-matter' is terrifying, *unnameable*; it can engender itself; it has no need of a mother or father. It is beyond the representation that Man has always presented himself with and controlled. It is, in its essence, an indistinctness between the inside and the outside, between original boundaries and spaces. To think this indistinctness in the twentieth century has been to think a crisis of indescribable propor-tions, to throw all of the Big Dichotomies into question: for if the exterior is interior, then the interior is also exterior; Man's soul is outside of him-self; history is but the exterior of his own no longer interior imagination.

An exploration of this crisis, as an exploration of the figural, has been experienced as a necessity by those philosophers attuned to the violence of technique and its technologies in the twentieth century. Either Nature, for modern Man, can become nothing more than a complex 'data bank', a source from which he will extract what he needs until it is empty, or she can become more plastic, she can be assumed and affirmed – saved from her own violence? Instead of *making* physis speak, perhaps Man should let her speak. But to do this, to conceptualise this confusion of borderlines, the Philosopher-Man cannot remain at the centre as in the past. He has modelled himself, rather, after Orpheus, '[who] did not descend into night in order to put himself in the position of being able to produce a harmonious song, to bring about the reconciliation between night and day and to have himself crowned for his art. He went to seek the figural instance, the other of his *very work*, to see the invisible, to see death.'[38] Like the 'artist', the Philosopher-Man in the late twentieth century must descend, then find and embrace that *figure*, figurative device, which has no *visage*, no recognisable traits. And that figure, Eurydice, is *woman*.[39]

It is no accident that Lyotard has here chosen the Orpheus myth to exemplify the problem of the figural, of the imagistic, for modern Man. Already a central myth for many philosophers, especially since the nine-teenth century, this myth has taken on special significance in contemporary French thought (most notably, in echo to the work of Maurice Blanchot).[40] Orpheus is the poet who descends into Hades to search for Eurydice; but if he wants to rescue her and bring her out into the daylight, he must not, above all, turn and look at her. But, of course, he does look (in French, *il la dévisage*) and thus *loses* her and, at the same time, *finds* his poetry and his song. That is, in order to find the poetic *figure*, the *visage* must not be seen: 'La figure est ce qui n'a pas de visage' (the figure is that which has no face).[41] Like literature, philosophy will have to put aside its fear of moving beyond what is merely human and male (the *visage*); it must accelerate its search for Eurydice, for what is female, for the *figure*, if it wishes to invent new songs.

In fact, modernity has increasingly been qualified as what Gilles Deleuze calls the process of *dévisagification*, a kind of de-individualisation.[42] For him, the visage, the identifiable face, is 'black holes on a white wall', an abstract, European, white male machine that has a definite social function: 'to be identified, catalogued, recognised'.[43] For Jacques Derrida (reading

Emmanuel Levinas), the visage is: 'expression and [...] speech. Not only as glance, but as the original unity of glance and speech, eyes and mouth [...].'[44] Citing Aristotle, Ludwig Feuerbach, Hegel, Kierkegaard, and Levinas (among others), Derrida shows that the visage – (Man's) identity and (Man's) humanity – is that which has always commanded: 'The face is presence, *ousia*. The face is not a metaphor, not a figure.'[45]

Following the directions of Derrida's own footnote at this point, we find the following statement, still in reference to Levinas: 'It would be useless to attempt, here, to enter into the descriptions devoted to interiority, economy, enjoyment, habitation, femininity, Eros, to everything suggested under the title *Beyond the Face*, matters that would doubtless deserve many questions.'[46] I would respond 'Most certainly', but would argue that the ways in which those questions are tied to gender deserve more attention: why is it Eurydice who must incarnate the almost monstrously duplicitous role of visage/figure? Or else, when not Eurydice, why is it Christ (as pointed out in different ways by other writers like Eugénie Lemoine-Luccioni and Deleuze)?[47] Or God, as written by Edmond Jabès?[48]

These questions remain open, but the genderisation of the visage as male (hence to be rejected) and of the figure as female (hence to be embraced) is one of contemporary philosophy's own peculiar modes for gynesis. It is not a terribly original one. First of all, the indistinctness and distortion of the visage, the descent into the uncharted space of night, has everything to do with the infantile exploration of the *mother's face* – the first point of reference mapped by the infant in search of the breast.[49] But second and most important, it has always been the woman's figure, her lack of visage, of individual traits, of identity and humanity, that has saved the male artist.

> I no longer look into the eyes of the woman I hold in my arms but I swim through, head and arms and legs, and I see that behind the sockets of the eyes there is a region unexplored, the world of futurity, and here there is no logic whatever.

This passage from Henry Miller's *Tropic of Capricorn* is cited by Deleuze and Félix Guattari as a perfect example of the road to be taken by modern thought: 'Yes, the *visage* has a great future, provided it is destroyed, undone. En route toward the asignifiant, toward the asubjective. But we still have explained nothing about what we feel.'[50]

But then neither has the feminist critic.

13

Postmodern Blackness

bell hooks

Postmodernist discourses are often exclusionary even as they call attention to, appropriate even, the experience of 'difference' and 'Otherness' to provide oppositional political meaning, legitimacy, and immediacy when they are accused of lacking concrete relevance. Very few African-American intellectuals have talked or written about postmodernism. At a dinner party I talked about trying to grapple with the significance of postmodernism for contemporary black experience. It was one of those social gatherings where only one other black person was present. The setting quickly became a field of contestation. I was told by the other black person that I was wasting my time, that 'this stuff does not relate in any way to what's happening with black people'. Speaking in the presence of a group of white onlookers, staring at us as though this encounter were staged for their benefit, we engaged in a passionate discussion about black experience. Apparently, no one sympathised with my insistence that racism is perpetuated when blackness is associated solely with concrete gut level experience conceived as either opposing or having no connection to abstract thinking and the production of critical theory. The idea that there is no meaningful connection between black experience and critical thinking about aesthetics or culture must be continually interrogated.

My defence of postmodernism and its relevance to black folks sounded good, but I worried that I lacked conviction, largely because I approach the subject cautiously and with suspicion.

Disturbed not so much by the 'sense' of postmodernism but by the conventional language used when it is written or talked about and by those who speak it, I find myself on the outside of the discourse looking in. As a discursive practice it is dominated primarily by the voices of white male intellectuals and/or academic elites who speak to and about one another with coded familiarity. Reading and studying their writing to understand postmodernism in its multiple manifestations, I appreciate it but feel little inclination to ally myself with the academic hierarchy and exclusivity pervasive in the movement today.

Critical of most writing on postmodernism, I perhaps am more conscious of the way in which the focus on 'Otherness and difference' that is often alluded to in these works seems to have little concrete impact as an analysis or standpoint that might change the nature and direction of postmodernist theory. Since much of this theory has been constructed in reaction to and against high modernism, there is seldom any mention of black experience or writings by black people in this work, specifically black women (though in more recent work one may see a reference to Cornel West, the black male scholar who has most engaged postmodernist discourse). Even if an aspect of black culture is the subject of postmodern critical writing, the works cited will usually be those of black men. A work that comes immediately to mind is Andrew Ross's chapter 'Hip, and the Long Front of Color' in *No Respect: Intellectuals and Popular Culture;* while it is an interesting reading, it constructs black culture as though black women have had no role in black cultural production. At the end of Meaghan Morris' discussion of postmodernism in her collection of essays *The Pirate's Fiancée: Feminism and Postmodernism,* she provides a bibliography of works by women, identifying them as important contributions to a discourse on postmodernism that offer new insight as well as challenging male theoretical hegemony. Even though many of the works do not directly address postmodernism, they address similar concerns. There are no references to works by black women.

The failure to recognise a critical black presence in the culture and in most scholarship and writing on postmodernism compels a black reader, particularly a black female reader, to interrogate her interest in a subject where those who discuss and write about it seem not to know black women exist or even to consider the possibility that we might be somewhere writing or saying something that should be listened to, or producing art that should be seen, heard, approached with intellectual seriousness. This is especially the case with works that go on and on about the way in which postmodernist discourse has opened up a theoretical terrain where 'difference and Otherness' can be considered legitimate issues in the academy. Confronting both the absence of recognition of black female presence that much postmodernist theory re-inscribes and the resistance on the part of most black folks to hearing about real connection between postmodernism and black experience, I enter a discourse, a practice, where there may be no ready audience for my words, no clear listener, uncertain then, that my voice can or will be heard.

During the sixties, black power movement was influenced by perspectives that could easily be labelled modernist. Certainly many of the ways black folks addressed issues of identity conformed to a modernist universalising agenda. There was little critique of patriarchy as a master narrative among black militants. Despite the fact that black power ideology reflected a modernist sensibility, these elements were soon rendered irrelevant as militant protest was stifled by a powerful, repressive postmodern state. The period directly after the black power movement was a time when major news magazines carried articles with cocky headlines like 'Whatever

Happened to Black America?' This response was an ironic reply to the aggressive, unmet demand by decentred, marginalised black subjects who had at least momentarily successfully demanded a hearing, who had made it possible for black liberation to be on the national political agenda. In the wake of the black power movement, after so many rebels were slaughtered and lost, many of these voices were silenced by a repressive state; others became inarticulate. It has become necessary to find new avenues to transmit the messages of black liberation struggle, new ways to talk about racism and other politics of domination. Radical postmodernist practice, most powerfully conceptualised as a 'politics of difference', should incorporate the voices of displaced, marginalised, exploited, and oppressed black people. It is sadly ironic that the contemporary discourse which talks the most about heterogeneity, the decentred subject, declaring breakthroughs that allow recognition of Otherness, still directs its critical voice primarily to a specialised audience that shares a common language rooted in the very master narratives it claims to challenge. If radical postmodernist thinking is to have a transformative impact, then a critical break with the notion of 'authority' as 'mastery over' must not simply be a rhetorical device. It must be reflected in habits of being, including styles of writing as well as chosen subject matter. Third world nationals, elites, and white critics who passively absorb white supremacist thinking, and therefore never notice or look at black people on the streets or at their jobs, who render us invisible with their gaze in all areas of daily life, are not likely to produce liberatory theory that will challenge racist domination, or promote a breakdown in traditional ways of seeing and thinking about reality, ways of constructing aesthetic theory and practice. From a different standpoint, Robert Storr makes a similar critique in the global issue of *Art in America* when he asserts:

> To be sure, much postmodernist critical inquiry has centred precisely on the issues of 'difference' and 'Otherness'. On the purely theoretical plane the exploration of these concepts has produced some important results, but in the absence of any sustained research into what artists of colour and others outside the mainstream might be up to, such discussions become rootless instead of radical. Endless second guessing about the latent imperialism of intruding upon other cultures only compounded matters, preventing or excusing these theorists from investigating what black, Hispanic, Asian and Native American artists were actually doing.

Without adequate concrete knowledge of and contact with the non-white 'Other', white theorists may move in discursive theoretical directions that are threatening and potentially disruptive of that critical practice which would support radical liberation struggle.

The postmodern critique of 'identity', though relevant for renewed black liberation struggle, is often posed in ways that are problematic. Given a pervasive politic of white supremacy which seeks to prevent the formation of radical black subjectivity, we cannot cavalierly dismiss a concern with identity politics. Any critic exploring the radical potential of postmodernism as it relates to racial difference and racial domination would need to consider the implications of a critique of identity for oppressed groups. Many of us are struggling to find new strategies of resistance. We must engage decolonisation as a critical practice if we are to have meaningful chances of survival even as we must simultaneously cope with the loss of political grounding which made radical activism more possible. I am thinking here about the postmodernist critique of essentialism as it pertains to the construction of 'identity' as one example.

Postmodern theory that is not seeking to simply appropriate the experience of 'Otherness' to enhance the discourse or to be radically chic should not separate the 'politics of difference' from the politics of racism. To take racism seriously one must consider the plight of underclass people of colour, a vast majority of whom are black. For African-Americans our collective condition prior to the advent of postmodernism and perhaps more tragically expressed under current postmodern conditions has been and is characterised by continued displacement, profound alienation, and despair. Writing about blacks and postmodernism, Cornel West describes our collective plight:

> There is increasing class division and differentiation, creating on the one hand a significant black middle-class, highly anxiety-ridden, insecure, willing to be co-opted and incorporated into the powers that be, concerned with racism to the degree that it poses constraints on upward social mobility; and, on the other, a vast and growing black underclass, an underclass that embodies a kind of walking nihilism of pervasive homicide, and an exponential rise in suicide. Now because of the deindustrialisation, we also have a devastated black industrial working class. We are talking here about tremendous hopelessness.

This hopelessness creates longing for insight and strategies for change that can renew spirits and reconstruct grounds for collective black liberation struggle. The overall impact of postmodernism is that many other groups now share with black folks a sense of deep alienation, despair, uncertainty, loss of a sense of grounding even if it is not informed by shared circumstance. Radical postmodernism calls attention to those shared sensibilities which cross the boundaries of class, gender, race, etc., that could be fertile ground for the construction of empathy – ties that would promote recognition of common commitments, and serve as a base for solidarity and coalition.

Yearning is the word that best describes a common psychological state
shared by many of us, cutting across boundaries of race, class, gender, and
sexual practice. Specifically, in relation to the postmodernist deconstruction
of 'master' narratives, the yearning that wells in the hearts and minds of
those whom such narratives have silenced is the longing for critical voice. It
is no accident that 'rap' has usurped the primary position of rhythm and
blues music among young black folks as the most desired sound or that it
began as a form of 'testimony' for the underclass. It has enabled underclass
black youth to develop a critical voice, as a group of young black men told
me, a 'common literacy'. Rap projects a critical voice, explaining, demand-
ing, urging. Working with this insight in his essay 'Putting the Pop Back into
Postmodernism', Lawrence Grossberg comments:

> The postmodern sensibility appropriates practices as boasts that announce
> their own – and consequently our own – existence, like a rap song boasting
> of the imaginary (or real – it makes no difference) accomplishments of the
> rapper. They offer forms of empowerment not only in the face of nihilism
> but precisely through the forms of nihilism itself: an empowering nihilism,
> a moment of positivity through the production and structuring of affective
> relations.

Considering that it is as subject one comes to voice, then the postmodernist focus on the critique of identity appears at first glance to threaten and
close down the possibility that this discourse and practice will allow those
who have suffered the crippling effects of colonisation and domination to
gain or regain a hearing. Even if this sense of threat and the fear it evokes are
based on a misunderstanding of the postmodernist political project, they
nevertheless shape responses. It never surprises me when black folks respond
to the critique of essentialism, especially when it denies the validity of
identity politics by saying, 'Yeah, it's easy to give up identity, when you
got one'. Should we not be suspicious of postmodern critiques of the 'subject'
when they surface at a historical moment when many subjugated people feel
themselves coming to voice for the first time. Though an apt and oftentimes
appropriate comeback, it does not really intervene in the discourse in a way
that alters and transforms.

Criticisms of directions in postmodern thinking should not obscure
insights it may offer that open up our understanding of African-American
experience. The critique of essentialism encouraged by postmodernist
thought is useful for African-Americans concerned with reformulating outmoded notions of identity. We have too long had imposed upon us from
both the outside and the inside a narrow, constricting notion of blackness.
Postmodern critiques of essentialism which challenge notions of universality
and static over-determined identity within mass culture and mass conscious-

ness can open up new possibilities for the construction of self and the assertion of agency.

Employing a critique of essentialism allows African-Americans to acknowledge the way in which class mobility has altered collective black experience so that racism does not necessarily have the same impact on our lives. Such a critique allows us to affirm multiple black identities, varied black experience. It also challenges colonial imperialist paradigms of black identity which represent blackness one-dimensionally in ways that reinforce and sustain white supremacy. This discourse created the idea of the 'primitive' and promoted the notion of an 'authentic' experience, seeing as 'natural' those expressions of black life which conformed to a pre-existing pattern or stereotype. Abandoning essentialist notions would be a serious challenge to racism. Contemporary African-American resistance struggle must be rooted in a process of decolonisation that continually opposes re-inscribing notions of 'authentic' black identity. This critique should not be made synonymous with a dismissal of the struggle of oppressed and exploited peoples to make ourselves subjects. Nor should it deny that in certain circumstances this experience affords us a privileged critical location from which to speak. This is not a re-inscription of modernist master narratives of authority which privilege some voices by denying voice to others. Part of our struggle for radical black subjectivity is the quest to find ways to construct self and identity that are oppositional and liberatory. The unwillingness to critique essentialism on the part of many African-Americans is rooted in the fear that it will cause folks to lose sight of the specific history and experience of African-Americans and the unique sensibilities and culture that arise from that experience. An adequate response to this concern is to critique essentialism while emphasising the significance of 'the authority of experience'. There is a radical difference between a repudiation of the idea that there is a black 'essence' and recognition of the way black identity has been specifically constituted in the experience of exile and struggle.

When black folks critique essentialism, we are empowered to recognise multiple experiences of black identity that are the lived conditions which make diverse cultural productions possible. When this diversity is ignored, it is easy to see black folks as falling into two categories: nationalist or assimilationist, black-identified or white-identified. Coming to terms with the impact of postmodernism for black experience, particularly as it changes our sense of identity, means that we must and can rearticulate the basis for collective bonding. Given the various crises facing African-Americans (economic, spiritual, escalating racial violence, etc.), we are compelled by circumstance to reassess our relationship to popular culture and resistance struggle. Many of us are as reluctant to face this task as many non-black postmodern thinkers who focus theoretically on the issue of 'difference' are to confront the issue of race and racism.

Music is the cultural product created by African-Americans that has most attracted postmodern theorists. It is rarely acknowledged that there is far greater censorship and restriction of other forms of cultural production by black folks – literary, critical writing, etc. Attempts on the part of editors and publishing houses to control and manipulate the representation of black culture, as well as the desire to promote the creation of products that will attract the widest audience, limit in a crippling and stifling way the kind of work many black folks feel we can do and still receive recognition. Using myself as an example, that creative writing I do which I consider to be most reflective of a postmodern oppositional sensibility, work that is abstract, fragmented, non-linear narrative, is constantly rejected by editors and publishers. It does not conform to the type of writing they think black women should be doing or the type of writing they believe will sell. Certainly I do not think I am the only black person engaged in forms of cultural production, especially experimental ones, who is constrained by the lack of an audience for certain kinds of work. It is important for postmodern thinkers and theorists to constitute themselves as an audience for such work. To do this they must assert power and privilege within the space of critical writing to open up the field so that it will be more inclusive. To change the exclusionary practice of postmodern critical discourse is to enact a postmodernism of resistance. Part of this intervention entails black intellectual participation in the discourse.

In his essay 'Postmodernism and Black America', Cornel West suggests that black intellectuals 'are marginal – usually languishing at the interface of Black and white cultures or thoroughly ensconced in Euro-American settings'. He cannot see this group as potential producers of radical postmodernist thought. While I generally agree with this assessment, black intellectuals must proceed with the understanding that we are not condemned to the margins. The way we work and what we do can determine whether or not what we produce will be meaningful to a wider audience, one that includes all classes of black people. West suggests that black intellectuals lack 'any organic link with most of Black life' and that this 'diminishes their value to Black resistance'. This statement bears traces of essentialism. Perhaps we need to focus more on those black intellectuals, however rare our presence, who do not feel this lack and whose work is primarily directed towards the enhancement of black critical consciousness and the strengthening of our collective capacity to engage in meaningful resistance struggle. Theoretical ideas and critical thinking need not be transmitted solely in written work or solely in the academy. While I work in a predominantly white institution, I remain intimately and passionately engaged with black community. It's not like I'm going to talk about writing and thinking about postmodernism with other academics and/or intellectuals and not discuss these ideas with underclass non-academic black folks who are family, friends, and comrades. Since I have not broken the ties that bind me to underclass poor black community, I have seen that knowledge, especially that which enhances daily life and strengthens our capacity to survive, can be shared. It means that critics, writers, and academics have to give the same critical attention to nurturing and cultivating our ties to black community that we give to writing articles, teaching, and lecturing. Here again I am really talking about cultivating habits of being that reinforce awareness that knowledge can be disseminated and shared on a number of fronts. The extent to which knowledge is made available, accessible, etc. depends on the nature of one's political commitments.

Postmodern culture with its decentred subject can be the space where ties are severed or it can provide the occasion for new and varied forms of bonding. To some extent, ruptures, surfaces, contextuality, and a host of other happenings create gaps that make space for oppositional practices which no longer require intellectuals to be confined by narrow separate spheres with no meaningful connection to the world of the everyday. Much postmodern engagement with culture emerges from the yearning to do intellectual work that connects with habits of being, forms of artistic expression, and aesthetics that inform the daily life of writers and scholars as well as a mass population. On the terrain of culture, one can participate in critical dialogue with the uneducated poor, the black underclass who are thinking about aesthetics. One can talk about what we are seeing, thinking, or listening to; a space is there for critical exchange. It's exciting to think, write, talk about, and create art that reflects passionate engagement with popular culture, because this may very well be 'the' central future location of resistance struggle, a meeting place where new and radical happenings can occur.

14

Locations of Culture: the Post-colonial and the Postmodern

Homi K. Bhabha

A boundary is not that at which something stops but, as the Greeks recognised, the boundary is that from which *something begins its presencing*.

(Martin Heidegger, 'Building, dwelling, thinking')

BORDER LIVES: THE ART OF THE PRESENT

It is the trope of our times to locate the question of culture in the realm of the *beyond*. At the century's edge, we are less exercised by annihilation – the death of the author – or epiphany – the birth of the 'subject'. Our existence today is marked by a tenebrous sense of survival, living on the borderlines of the 'present', for which there seems to be no proper name other than the current and controversial shiftiness of the prefix 'post': *postmodernism, postcolonialism, postfeminism.* ...

The 'beyond' is neither a new horizon, nor a leaving behind of the past. ... Beginnings and endings may be the sustaining myths of the middle years; but in the *fin de siècle*, we find ourselves in the moment of transit where space and time cross to produce complex figures of difference and identity, past and present, inside and outside, inclusion and exclusion. For there is a sense of disorientation, a disturbance of direction, in the 'beyond': an exploratory, restless movement caught so well in the French rendition of the words *au-delà* – here and there, on all sides, *fort/da*, hither and thither, back and forth.[1]

The move away from the singularities of 'class' or 'gender' as primary conceptual and organisational categories, has resulted in an awareness of the subject positions – of race, gender, generation, institutional location, geo-political locale, sexual orientation – that inhabit any claim to identity in the modern world. What is theoretically innovative, and politically crucial, is the need to think beyond narratives of originary and initial subjectivities and to focus on those moments or processes that are produced in the articulation of cultural differences. These 'in-between' spaces provide the terrain for elabor-

136

ating strategies of selfhood – singular or communal – that initiate new signs of identity, and innovative sites of collaboration, and contestation, in the act of defining the idea of society itself.

It is in the emergence of the interstices – the overlap and displacement of domains of difference – that the intersubjective and collective experiences of *nationness*, community interest, or cultural value are negotiated. How are subjects formed 'in-between', or in excess of, the sum of the 'parts' of difference (usually intoned as race / class / gender, etc.)? How do strategies of representation or empowerment come to be formulated in the competing claims of communities where, despite shared histories of deprivation and discrimination, the exchange of values, meanings and priorities may not always be collaborative and dialogical, but may be profoundly antagonistic, conflictual and even incommensurable?

The force of these questions is borne out by the 'language' of recent social crises sparked off by histories of cultural difference. Conflicts in South Central Los Angeles between Koreans, Mexican-Americans and African-Americans focus on the concept of 'disrespect' – a term forged on the borderlines of ethnic deprivation that is, at once, the sign of racialised violence and the symptom of social victimage. In the aftermath of the *The Satanic Verses* affair in Great Britain, Black and Irish feminists, despite their different constituencies, have made common cause against the 'racialisation of religion' as the dominant discourse through which the State represents their conflicts and struggles, however secular or even 'sexual' they may be.

Terms of cultural engagement, whether antagonistic or affiliative, are produced performatively. The representation of difference must not be hastily read as the reflection of *pre-given* ethnic or cultural traits set in the fixed tablet of tradition. The social articulation of difference, from the minority perspective, is a complex, on-going negotiation that seeks to authorise cultural hybridities that emerge in moments of historical transformation. The 'right' to signify from the periphery of authorised power and privilege does not depend on the persistence of tradition; it is resourced by the power of tradition to be reinscribed through the conditions of contingency and contradictoriness that attend upon the lives of those who are 'in the minority'. The recognition that tradition bestows is a partial form of identification. In restaging the past it introduces other, incommensurable cultural temporalities into the invention of tradition. This process estranges any immediate access to an originary identity or a 'received' tradition. The borderline engagements of cultural difference may as often be consensual as conflictual; they may confound our definitions of tradition and modernity; realign the customary boundaries between the private and the public, high and low; and challenge normative expectations of development and progress.

> I wanted to make shapes or set up situations that are kind of open. ... My
> work has a lot to do with a kind of fluidity, a movement back and forth,
> not making a claim to any specific or essential way of being.[2]

Thus writes Renée Green, the African-American artist. She reflects on the
need to understand cultural difference as the production of minority identities that 'split' – are estranged unto themselves – in the act of being
articulated into a collective body:

> Multiculturalism doesn't reflect the complexity of the situation as I face it
> daily. ... It requires a person to step outside of him/herself to actually see
> what he/she is doing. I don't want to condemn well-meaning people and
> say (like those T-shirts you can buy on the street) 'It's a black thing, you
> wouldn't understand'. To me that's essentialising blackness.[3]

Political empowerment, and the enlargement of the multiculturalist cause,
come from posing questions of solidarity and community from the interstitial perspective. Social differences are not simply given to experience
through an already authenticated cultural tradition; they are the signs of
the emergence of community envisaged as a project – at once a vision and a
construction – that takes you 'beyond' yourself in order to return, in a spirit
of revision and reconstruction, to the political *conditions* of the present:

> Even then, it's still a struggle for power between various groups within
> ethnic groups about what's being said and who's saying what, who's
> representing who? What is a community anyway? What is a black com-
> munity? What is a Latino community? I have trouble with thinking of all
> these things as monolithic fixed categories.[4]

If Renée Green's questions open up an interrogatory, interstitial space
between the act of representation – who? what? where? – and the presence of
community itself, then consider her own creative intervention within this in-
between moment. Green's 'architectural' site-specific work, *Sites of Genealogy*
(Out of Site, The Institute of Contemporary Art, Long Island City, New York),
displays and displaces the binary logic through which identities of difference
are often constructed – Black/White, Self/Other. Green makes a metaphor of
the museum building itself, rather than simply using the gallery space:

> I used architecture literally as a reference, using the attic, the boiler room,
> and the stairwell to make associations between certain binary divisions
> such as higher and lower and heaven and hell. The stairwell became a
> liminal space, a pathway between the upper and lower areas, each of which
> was annotated with plaques referring to blackness and whiteness.[5]

The stairwell as liminal space, in-between the designations of identity, becomes the process of symbolic interaction, the connective tissue that constructs the difference between upper and lower, black and white. The hither and thither of the stairwell, the temporal movement and passage that it allows, prevents identities at either end of it from settling into primordial polarities. This interstitial passage between fixed identifications opens up the possibility of a cultural hybridity that entertains difference without an assumed or imposed hierarchy:

> I always went back and forth between racial designations and designations from physics or other symbolic designations. All these things blur in some way. ... To develop a genealogy of the way colours and noncolours function is interesting to me.[6]

'Beyond' signifies spatial distance, marks progress, promises the future; but our intimations of exceeding the barrier or boundary – the very act of going *beyond* – are unknowable, unrepresentable, without a return to the 'present' which, in the process of repetition, becomes disjunct and displaced. The imaginary of spatial distance – to live somehow beyond the border of our times – throws into relief the temporal, social differences that interrupt our collusive sense of cultural contemporaneity. The present can no longer be simply envisaged as a break or a bonding with the past and the future, no longer a synchronic presence: our proximate self-presence, our public image, comes to be revealed for its discontinuities, its inequalities, its minorities. Unlike the dead hand of history that tells the beads of sequential time like a rosary, seeking to establish serial, causal connections, we are now confronted with what Walter Benjamin describes as the blasting of a monadic moment from the homogenous course of history, 'establishing a conception of the present as the "time of the now" '.[7]

If the jargon of our times – postmodernity, postcoloniality, postfeminism – has any meaning at all, it does not lie in the popular use of the 'post' to indicate sequentiality – *after*-feminism; or polarity – *anti*-modernism. These terms that insistently gesture to the beyond, only embody its restless and revisionary energy if they transform the present into an expanded and ex-centric site of experience and empowerment. For instance, if the interest in postmodernism is limited to a celebration of the fragmentation of the 'grand narratives' of postenlightenment rationalism then, for all its intellectual excitement, it remains a profoundly parochial enterprise.

The wider significance of the postmodern condition lies in the awareness that the epistemological 'limits' of those ethnocentric ideas are also the enunciative boundaries of a range of other dissonant, even dissident histories and voices – women, the colonised, minority groups, the bearers of policed sexualities. For the demography of the new internationalism is the history of postcolonial migration, the narratives of cultural and political diaspora, the major social displacements of peasant and aboriginal communities, the poetics of exile, the grim prose of political and economic refugees. It is in this sense that the boundary becomes the place from which *something begins its presencing* in a movement not dissimilar to the ambulant, ambivalent articulation of the beyond that I have drawn out: 'Always and ever differently the bridge escorts the lingering and hastening ways of men to and fro, so that they may get to other banks. . . . The bridge *gathers* as a passage that crosses.'[8]

The very concepts of homogeneous national cultures, the consensual or contiguous transmission of historical traditions, or 'organic' ethnic communities – *as the grounds of cultural comparativism* – are in a profound process of redefinition. The hideous extremity of Serbian nationalism proves that the very idea of a pure, 'ethnically cleansed' national identity can only be achieved through the death, literal and figurative, of the complex interweavings of history, and the culturally contingent borderlines of modern nationhood. This side of the psychosis of patriotic fervour, I like to think, there is overwhelming evidence of a more transnational and translational sense of the hybridity of imagined communities. Contemporary Sri Lankan theatre represents the deadly conflict between the Tamils and the Sinhalese through allegorical references to State brutality in South Africa and Latin America; the Anglo-Celtic canon of Australian literature and cinema is being rewritten from the perspective of Aboriginal political and cultural imperatives; the South African novels of Richard Rive, Bessie Head, Nadine Gordimer, John Coetzee, are documents of a society divided by the effects of apartheid that enjoin the international intellectual community to mediate on the unequal, assymetrical worlds that exist elsewhere; Salman Rushdie writes the fabulist historiography of post-Independence India and Pakistan in *Midnight's Children* and *Shame*, only to remind us in *The Satanic Verses* that the truest eye may now belong to the migrant's double vision; Toni Morrison's *Beloved* revives the past of slavery and its murderous rituals of possession and self-possession, in order to project a contemporary fable of a woman's history that is at the same time the narrative of an affective, historic memory of an emergent public sphere of men and women alike.

What is striking about the 'new' internationalism is that the move from the specific to the general, from the material to the metaphoric, is not a smooth passage of transition and transcendence. The 'middle passage' of contemporary culture, as with slavery itself, is a process of displacement and disjunction that does not totalise experience. Increasingly, 'national' cultures are being produced from the perspective of disenfranchised minorities. The most significant effect of this process is not the proliferation of 'alternative histories of the excluded' producing, as some would have it, a pluralist anarchy. What my examples show is the changed basis for making international connections. The currency of critical comparativism, or aesthetic judgement, is no longer the sovereignty of the national culture conceived as Benedict Anderson proposes as an 'imagined community' rooted in a 'homogeneous empty time' of modernity and progress. The great connective narratives of capitalism and class drive the engines of social reproduction, but do not, in themselves, provide a foundational frame for those modes of cultural identification and political affect that form around issues of sexuality, race, feminism, the lifeworld of refugees or migrants, or the deathly social destiny of AIDS.

The testimony of my examples represents a radical revision in the concept of human community itself. What this geopolitical space may be, as a local or transnational reality, is being both interrogated and reinitiated. Feminism, in the 1990s, finds its solidarity as much in liberatory narratives as in the painful ethical position of a slavewoman, Morrison's Sethe, in *Beloved*, who is pushed to infanticide. The body politic can no longer contemplate the nation's health as simply a civic virtue; it must rethink the question of rights for the entire national, and international, community, from the AIDS perspective. The Western metropole must confront its postcolonial history, told by its influx of postwar migrants and refugees, as an indigenous or native narrative *internal to its national identity*; and the reason for this is made clear in the stammering, drunken words of Mr 'Whisky' Sisodia from *The Satanic Verses*: 'The trouble with the Engenglish is that their hiss hiss history happened overseas, so they dodo don't know what it means.'[9]

Postcoloniality, for its part, is a salutary reminder of the persistent 'neocolonial' relations within the 'new' world order and the multinational division of labour. Such a perspective enables the authentication of histories of exploitation and the evolution of strategies of resistance. Beyond this, however, postcolonial critique bears witness to those countries and communities – in the North and the South, urban and rural – constituted, if I may coin a phrase, 'otherwise than modernity'. Such cultures of a postcolonial *contramodernity* may be contingent to modernity, discontinuous or in contention with it, resistant to its oppressive, assimilationist technologies; but they also deploy the cultural hybridity of their borderline conditions to 'translate', and therefore reinscribe, the social imaginary of both metropolis and modernity. Listen to Guillermo Gomez-Peña, the performance artist who lives, amongst other times and places, on the Mexico/US border:

hello America
this is the voice of *Gran Vato Charollero*
broadcasting from the hot deserts of Nogales, Arizona
zona de libre cogercio
2000 megaherz en todas direciones

you are celebrating Labor Day in Seattle
while the Klan demonstrates
against Mexicans in Georgia
ironia, 100% ironia[10]

Being in the 'beyond', then, is to inhabit an intervening space, as any
dictionary will tell you. But to dwell 'in the beyond' is also, as I have shown,
to be part of a revisionary time, a return to the present to redescribe our
cultural contemporaneity; to reinscribe our human, historic commonality; *to
touch the future on its hither side*. In that sense, then, the intervening space
'beyond', becomes a space of intervention in the here and now. To engage with
such invention, and intervention, as Green and Gomez-Peña enact in their
distinctive work, requires a sense of the new that resonates with the hybrid
chicano aesthetic of *'rasquachismo'* as Tomas Ybarra-Frausto describes it:

> the utilisation of available resources for syncretism, juxtaposition, and
> integration. *Rasquachismo* is a sensibility attuned to mixtures and con-
> fluence... a delight in texture and sensuous surfaces... self-conscious
> manipulation of materials or iconography... the combination of found
> material and satiric wit... the manipulation of *rasquache* artifacts, code
> and sensibilities from both sides of the border.[11]

The borderline work of culture demands an encounter with 'newness' that
is not part of the continuum of past and present. It creates a sense of the new
as an insurgent act of cultural translation. Such art does not merely recall the
past as social cause or aesthetic precedent; it renews the past, refiguring it as
a contingent 'in-between' space, that innovates and interrupts the performance of the present. The 'past-present' becomes part of the necessity,
not the nostalgia, of living.

Pepon Osorio's *objets trouvés* of the Nuyorican (New York/Puerto Rican)
community – the statistics of infant mortality, or the silent (and silenced)
spread of AIDS in the Hispanic community – are elaborated into baroque
allegories of social alienation. But it is not the high drama of birth and death
that captures Osorio's spectacular imagination. He is the great celebrant of
the migrant act of survival, using his mixed-media works to make a hybrid
cultural space that forms contingently, disjunctively, in the inscription
of signs of cultural memory and sites of political agency. *La Cama (The
Bed)* turns the highly decorated four poster into the primal scene of lost-
and-found childhood memories, the memorial to a dead nanny Juana, the
mise-en-scène of the eroticism of the 'emigrant' everyday. Survival, for
Osorio, is working in the interstices of a range of practices: the 'space' of
installation, the spectacle of the social statistic, the transitive time of the
body in performance.

Finally, it is the photographic art of Alan Sekula that takes the borderline condition of cultural translation to its global limit in *Fish Story*, his photographic project on harbours: 'the harbour is the site in which material goods appear in bulk, in the very flux of exchange'.[12] The harbour and the stockmarket become the *paysage moralisé* of a containerised, computerised world of global trade. Yet, the non-synchronous time–space of transnational 'exchange', and exploitation, is embodied in a navigational allegory:

> Things are more confused now. A scratchy recording of the Norwegian national anthem blares out from a loudspeaker at the Sailor's Home on the bluff above the channel. The container ship being greeted flies a Bahamian flag of convenience. It was built by Koreans working long hours in the giant shipyards of Ulsan. The underpaid and the understaffed crew could be Salvadorean or Filipino. Only the Captain hears a familiar melody.[13]

Norway's nationalist nostalgia cannot drown out the babel on the bluff. Transnational capitalism and the impoverishment of the Third World certainly create the chains of circumstance that incarcerate the Salvadorean or the Filipino/a. In their cultural passage, hither and thither, as migrant workers, part of the massive economic and political diaspora of the modern world, they embody the Benjaminian 'present': that moment blasted out of the continuum of history. Such conditions of cultural displacement and social discrimination – where political survivors become the best historical witnesses – are the grounds on which Frantz Fanon, the Martinican psychoanalyst and participant in the Algerian revolution, locates an agency of empowerment:

> As soon as I *desire* I am asking to be considered. I am not merely here-and-now, sealed into thingness. I am for somewhere else and for something else. I demand that notice be taken of my *negating activity* [my emphasis] insofar as I pursue something other than life; insofar as I do battle for the creation of a human world – that is a world of reciprocal recognitions.
>
> I should constantly remind myself that the real *leap* consists in introducing invention into existence.
> In the world in which I travel, I am endlessly creating myself. And it is by going beyond the historical, instrumental hypothesis that I will initiate my cycle of freedom.[14]

Once more it is the desire for recognition, 'for somewhere else and for something else' that takes the experience of history *beyond* the instrumental hypothesis. Once again, it is the space of intervention emerging in the cultural interstices that introduces creative invention into existence. And one last time, there is a return to the performance of identity as iteration, the re-creation of the self in the world of travel, the resettlement of the borderline community of migration. Fanon's desire for the recognition of cultural presence as 'negating activity' resonates with my breaking of the time-barrier of a culturally collusive 'present'.

15

Politics and the Limits of Modernity

Ernesto Laclau

The theme of postmodernity, which first appeared within aesthetics, has been displaced to ever wider areas until it has become the new horizon of our cultural, philosophical, and political experience. In the latter realm, to which I shall here limit my analysis, postmodernity has advanced by means of two converging intellectual operations whose complex interweavings and juxtapositions have, however, also contributed to a large extent to obscuring the problems at hand. Both operations share, without doubt, one characteristic: the attempt to establish *boundaries*, that is to say, to separate an ensemble of historical features and phenomena (postmodern) from others also appertaining to the past and that can be grouped under the rubric of modernity. In both cases the boundaries of modernity are established in radically different ways. The first announces a weakening of the metaphysical and rationalist pretensions of modernity, by way of challenging the *foundational* status of certain narratives. The second challenges not the ontological status of narrative as such, but rather the current validity of *certain* narratives: those that Lyotard has called metanarratives (*meta-recits*), which unified the totality of the historical experience of modernity (including science as one of its essential elements) within the project of global, human emancipation.

In what follows, I shall consider the status of metanarratives and offer as basic theses: 1) that there has been a radical change in the thought and culture of the past few decades (concerning which there would be no inconvenience in considering it as the entry to a sort of postmodernity), which, however, passes neither through a crisis nor, much less, to an abandonment of metanarratives; 2) that the very idea of the abandonment of metanarratives is logically contradictory for it reproduces within postmodern discourse the 'logic of foundations' that supposedly characterised modernity; and 3) that the decisive change relates to the new status of the discursive and the new language games practised around narratives – of all sorts, metanarratives included. The very idea of a boundary between modernity and postmodernity marked by the outmodedness of metanarratives presupposes a theoretical discourse in which the *end* of something is thinkable, which is to say, transparent and intellectually graspable. What does it mean for something to 'end'? It may be conceived, in a teleological sense, as the attainment of its highest form; in a dialectical sense, as its transformation into its contrary; in the movement of the eternal return, as a moment in the periodic becoming of forms; or as an annihilation that manifests its radical contingency. This is to say that a discourse is required that can conceive and construct the separation – even temporal separation – of two entities. To merely proclaim the end of something is an empty gesture.

Even worse, the uncritical introduction of the category *end* into a discourse, to substitute an effective 'making an end' for the voluntarist transparency of a simply announced and postulated end, means to smuggle back in what was to have been jettisoned. This can happen in two ways. First, insofar as something ends, something radically different must commence. In such a case, it is impossible to avoid the category of the 'new' and the idea of an innovative vanguard, which is precisely what the discourse of postmodernity purports to have left behind. On the other hand, to postulate the outmodedness of metanarratives (without taking into consideration what happens to other narrative species) is to achieve rather modest intellectual gains in comparison with the objectives sought. The logic of identity, of full presence, is simply displaced, fully intact, from the field of totality to the field of multiplicity of atomised narratives.

If there is a sense of postmodernity, that is, an ensemble of pre-theoretical references that establish certain 'family resemblances' among its diverse manifestations, this is suggested by the process of erosion and disintegration of such categories as 'foundation', 'new', 'identity', 'vanguard', and so on. What the 'situation of postmodernity' challenges is not so much the discrimination and choice between social and cultural identities but the status and logic of the construction of those identities. Consequently, drawing up the limits of modernity involves a more complex and evolving operation than merely setting boundaries. Postmodernity cannot be a simple *rejection* of modernity; rather, it involves a different modulation of its themes and categories, a greater proliferation of its language games.

Some of these games, which avoid conceiving the tradition with which they play in terms of rejection or affirmation of the radical novelty of the present, have long been inscribed in the intellectual history of this century. What Heidegger has called the 'de-struction of the history of ontology' is an example:

> The answer (to the question of Being) is not properly conceived if what it asserts propositionally is just passed along, especially if it gets circulated as a free-floating result, so that we merely get informed about a 'stand point' which may perhaps differ from the way this has hitherto been treated. Whether the answer is a 'new' one remains quite a superficial problem and

is of no importance. Its positive character must lie in its being *ancient* enough for us to learn to conceive the possibilities which the 'ancients' have made ready for us.[1]

This excludes the possibility of a simple rejection. Instead, it attempts to trace the genealogy of the present, dissolve the apparent obviousness of certain categories that are the trivialised and hardened sedimentations of tradition, and in this way bring to view the original problem to which they constitute a response. So, too, in Heidegger:

If the question of Being is to have its own history made transparent, then this hardened tradition must be loosened up, and the concealments which it has brought about by taking the question of Being as our clue, we are to destroy the traditional content of ancient ontology until we arrive at those primordial experiences in which we achieved our first ways of determining the nature of Being – the ways which have guided us ever since.[2]

This same argument can be extended to the most diverse theoretical discourses. Consider, for example, the category of 'class' within marxism. Central to the series of recent exchanges are the following questions: Is it classes or social movements that constitute the fundamental agents of historical change in advanced industrial societies? Or, is the working class in the process of disappearing? But these questions are quite secondary because, whatever answers they elicit, they *presuppose* what is fundamental: the obviousness and transparency of the category 'class'. The 'de-struction' of the history of marxism, in Heidegger's sense, involves showing that a category such as 'class', far from being obvious, is already a synthesis of determinations, a particular response to a more primary question of social agency. Because the contemporary situation poses this problem again in much more complex terms than were available to Marx, it is necessary to understand his response as a partial and limited synthesis, while appreciating more clearly the original sense of his questions. The sense of an intellectual intervention emerges only when it is possible to reconstitute the system of questions that it seeks to answer. On the other hand, when these questions are taken as simply obvious, their sense is obscured if not entirely lost. It is precisely the limitation of the responses that keeps alive the sense of a question.

In sketching out the limits of modernity, we must be agreed on what, in modernity, is being put to the test. If we question the specific values of the social/political/intellectual project that began globally with the Enlightenment, the narrative of its crisis requires the affirmation of *other* values; this, however, does not change the ontological status of the category of *value* as such. In this regard, it is important to point out that the critics of modernity have not even tried to introduce different values. When the theorists of the eighteenth century are presented as the initiators of a project of 'mastery' that would eventually lead to Auschwitz, it is forgotten that Auschwitz was repudiated by a set of values that, in large part, also stem from the eighteenth century. So, too, when criticism is directed at the category of totality implicit in metanarratives, only the possibility of reuniting the partial narratives into a global emancipatory narrative comes under fire; the category of 'narrative' itself is left completely unchallenged. I would like to argue that it is precisely the *ontological status* of the central categories of the discourses of modernity, and not their *content*, that is at stake; that the erosion of this status is expressed through the 'postmodern' sensibility; and that this erosion, far from being a negative phenomenon, represents an enormous amplification of the content and operability of the values of modernity, making it possible to ground them on foundations much more solid than those of the Enlightenment project (and its various positivist or Hegelian-Marxist reformulations).

LANGUAGE AND REALITY

Postmodernity does not imply a *change* in the values of Enlightenment modernity but rather a particular weakening of their absolutist character. It is therefore necessary to delimit an analytic terrain from whose standpoint this weakening is thinkable and definable. This terrain is neither arbitrary nor freely accessible to the imagination, but on the contrary it is the historical sedimentation of a set of traditions whose common denominator is the collapse of the immediacy of the *given*. We may thus propose that the intellectual history of the twentieth century was constituted on the basis of three illusions of immediacy (the referent, the phenomenon, and the sign) that gave rise to the three intellectual traditions of analytical philosophy, phenomenology, and structuralism. The crisis of that illusion of immediacy did not, however, result solely from the abandonment of those categories but rather from a weakening of their aspirations to constitute full presences and from the ensuing proliferation of language games which it was possible to develop around them. This crisis of the absolutist pretensions of 'the immediate' is a fitting starting point for engaging those intellectual operations that characterise the specific 'weakening' we call postmodernity. Each of these three intellectual traditions might serve as an equally valid point of departure for our analysis; in what follows, however, I shall base my argument on the crisis in structuralism.

As is well known, structuralism was constituted around the new centrality it accorded to the linguistic model. If we want to concentrate on the crisis of 'immediacy', which originally pretended to characterise the notion of the sign, we should concentrate not so much on the invasion of new ontic areas by the linguistic model but on the internal transformation of the linguistic model itself. The crisis consisted precisely in the increasing difficulty of defining the limits of language, or, more accurately, of defining the specific identity of the linguistic object.

In this respect, I could mention three fundamental stages in the structuralist tradition. The first is associated with Saussure, who, as it is well known, tried to locate the specific object of linguistics in what he called *langue*, an abstraction from the ensemble of language phenomena based on a set of oppositions and definitions, the most important of which are: langue/parole, signifier/signified, syntagm/paradigm. The two basic principles that oversaw the constitution of the linguistic object were the propositions that there are no positive terms in language, only differences, and that language is form not substance. Both principles were central to the category of *value*, which acquired increasing importance vis-à-vis *signification* in the subsequent evolution of the structuralist tradition.

The increasing refinement of linguistic formalism soon led, however, to an understanding that Saussurean theory was based on a set of ambiguities that could only be covered over by recourse to principles that contradicted its basic postulates. Take the distinction between signifier and signified: if language is all form and not substance, and if there is a perfect isomorphism between the order of the signifier and that of the signified, how is it possible to establish the difference between the two? Saussure could only do so by recourse to the idea of substance, phonic in one case, conceptual in the other. As for the distinction between *langue* and *parole* – between language as collective 'treasure' and its use by each individual speaker – this distinction can be maintained *only* if one assumes a subject exterior to the linguistic system. Consequently, one of the fundamental oppositions of this system was required to be externally defined, thus confining linguistic formalism within a new limit. Beyond this point it was impossible to posit a 'linguistics of discourse', if by discourse we mean a linguistic unit greater than the sentence. Saussure had spoken of semiology as a general science of signs in social life, but so long as *langue* remained anchored in the materiality of the *linguistic* sign, such a project could not proceed beyond a vaguely metaphorical and programmatic level.

From this point on, post-Saussurean structuralism emphasised linguistic formalism in its bid to transcend the ambiguities and inconsistencies of Saussure's own work. This, then, is the second phase, in which Hjelmslev, for example, broke with the strict isomorphism between the order of the signifier and the order of the signified by defining units smaller than the sign, whose distinctive features are no longer isomorphic. In this manner, he was able to establish the difference between the two orders on purely formal grounds. Furthermore, the critique that had been taking place, of the Cartesianism inherent in the category of the subject, made it possible to progressively show that the linguistic interventions of individual speakers reveal patterns and regularities conceivable only as *systems of differences*. This enabled the linguistic model to be expanded to the field of discourse.

There was, however, one further development. Once linguistic formalism had radically eradicated substance, there was no way of distinguishing between those systems of differential positions proper to speech and the 'extralinguistic' or 'extradiscursive' actions to which they are linked, for both speech and actions are differential positions within operations of much larger scope. But if this development expanded the value range of the 'linguistic model', the linguistic *object* tended to lose its specificity. In this second moment of the radicalisation of structuralism, the stable character of the relation between signifier and signified had not, however, been questioned; only the structural isomorphism between the two had been broken. The boundaries of linguistics had been expanded, but the immediacy and the characteristic of full presence of its objects were only reaffirmed.

When the presence and self-evidence of these objects have faded, we can detect the transition to a third moment, which, following a certain tradition, we can denominate poststructuralism. At issue now was the fixed link between signifier and signified. The quasi-Cartesian transparency that structural formalism had established between the purely relational identities of the linguistic system served only to make them more *vulnerable* to any new system of relations. In other words, as the ideal conditions of closure were defined more precisely, it was increasingly more difficult to hold to the *closed* character of the system. From this point the radical questioning of the immediacy and transparency of the sign takes place, the sundry variants of which are well known: the critique of the denotation/connotation distinction in the later Barthes, the affirmation of the primacy of the signifier and the increasing centrality of the 'real' vis-à-vis the symbolic in Lacan, the emphasis on the constitutive character of *difference*, and the critique of the metaphysics of presence in Derrida.

The crisis of the immediacy of the sign appears to be dominated by a double movement: while the signified was ever less closed within itself and could be defined only in relation to a specific context, the limits of that context were increasingly less well defined. In effect, the very logic of limit was increasingly more difficult to define. For Hegel, for example, the perception of a limit was the perception of what is beyond it; the limit, then, lies within the conceivable. Structuralism's radical relationalism would thus be subsumable under the category of the infinite regress. This point could be generalised: the most diverse forms of contemporary thought are permeated by the relational character of identities in conjunction with the impossibility of intellectual mastery over the context. Consider the various contortions of Husserl's ego/splits, and his efforts to affirm the transcendental constitutivity of the subject: the weakening of the distinction between semantics and pragmatics in Wittgensteinian and post-Wittgensteinian philosophy; the character of Kuhn's paradigms; the unresolved problems in the transition from *epistemes* to *dispositifs* in Foucault; the pragmatic turn of dogmaless empiricism in Quine. Some of these examples, especially Husserl's, are attempts to break the impasse by means of an essentialist reaffirmation of closure. However, in the majority of cases, the realisation of the openness of context has been the point of departure for a radical antiessentialist critique.

Let us turn our attention, at this point, to the various dimensions opened up by the unfixed character of the signifier/signified relation, that is, of all identity. In the first place, its effect is polysemic: if a plurality of signifieds is joined in an unstable fashion to certain signifiers, the necessary result is the introduction of equivocality (in the Aristotelian sense). But if one can affirm that this instability does not depend entirely on the equivocality of the signifier but on the contexts in which the signifier is used, it is no longer a question of *equivocality* but of *ambiguity* and *unfixity*, in the strict sense of the terms. For example, when I say 'down the hill' or 'the soft down on his cheek'[3] the term *down* is equivocal: its meaning varies in relation to different contexts, although in each context its meaning is perfectly clear. On the other hand, if I speak about 'democracy' in the political context of Western Europe during the cold war years, the ambiguity of the term proceeds from the context itself, which is constituted to some extent by the simultaneous presence of communist and anticommunist discourses. The term, therefore, is radically ambiguous and not simply polysemous. It is not a matter of its meaning one thing in communist discourse and another in anticommunist discourse; this, of course, may happen, but if that were the sole distinguishing circumstance, we would be left with a plurality of perfectly well-defined contexts and, consequently, with a case of simple equivocalness. Something very different, however, takes place: since both discourses are antagonistic and yet operate largely in the same argumentative context, there is a loosening of the relational systems that constitute the identity of the term. Thus, the term becomes a floating signifier. This radical ambiguity, which subverts the fixity of the sign, is precisely what gives the context its openness.

Three consequences follow from the above. First, that the concept of discourse is not linguistic but prior to the distinction between the linguistic and the extralinguistic. If I am building a wall and I tell someone 'hand me a brick' and then place it on the wall, my first act is linguistic and the second is behavioural, but it is easy to perceive that they are both connected as part of a total operation, namely, the construction of the wall. This relational moment within the total operation is neither linguistic nor extralinguistic, for it includes both types of actions. If, on the other hand, we think about it positively, the concepts that apprehend it must be prior to the linguistic/extralinguistic distinction. This instance of ground is called discourse and is therefore coterminous with the 'social'. Because every social action has a *meaning*, it is constituted in the form of discursive sequences that articulate linguistic and extralinguistic elements.[4]

A second consequence is that the relational character of discourse is precisely what permits the generalisation of the linguistic model within the ensemble of social relations. It is not that reality is language, but that the increasing formalisation of the linguistic system brought about the definition of a set of relational logics that embrace more than the linguistic narrowly defined. The act of placing a brick on a wall is not linguistic, but *its relation* to the linguistic act of previously asking for the brick is a particular discursive relation: a syntagmatic combination of the two acts. The relational logics of the social widen considerably, which opens up the path toward a new conceptualisation of objectivity.

The third consequence clearly derives from the two previous ones. The radical relationalism of social identities increases their vulnerability to new relations and introduces within them the effects of ambiguity to which we referred above.

These three consequences give us a framework that makes possible an approximation to the postmodern experience. If something has characterised the discourses of modernity, it is their pretension to intellectually dominate the foundation of the social, to give a rational context to the notion of the totality of history, and to base in the latter the project of a global human emancipation. As such, they have been discourses about essences and fully present identities based in one way or another upon the myth of a transparent society. Postmodernity, on the contrary, begins when this fully present identity is threatened by an ungraspable exterior that introduces a dimension of opacity and pragmatism into the pretended immediacy and transparency of its categories. This gives rise to an unbreachable abyss between the real (in the Lacanian sense) and concepts, thus weakening the absolutist pretensions of the latter. It should be stressed that this 'weakening' does not in any way negate the contents of the project of modernity; it shows only the radical vulnerability of those contents to a plurality of contexts that redefine them in an unpredictable way. Once this vulnerability is accepted in all its radicality, what does not necessarily follow is either the abandonment of the emancipatory values or a generalised scepticism concerning them, but rather, on the contrary, the awareness of the complex strategic-discursive operations implied by their affirmation and defence.

The narration of the beginnings of postmodernity – as with all beginnings – involves a multiple genealogy. In the next section, I shall attempt to trace this in relation to a particular tradition – marxism – which constituted both one of the highest points of the emancipatory narratives of modernity and one of their first crises. Whence the emergence of a post-marxism or a postmodern marxism resulting from the new relational contexts in which the categories of classical marxism were involved. Subject to increasing tensions, these categories became involved in newer and ever more complex language games.

CAPITALISM, UNEVEN DEVELOPMENT, AND HEGEMONY

Let us clarify the sense of our genealogical question; the narrative that is being sought does not attempt to establish the *causes* of a certain process, if by causes we mean that which possesses all the internal virtualities that bring about an effect. If that were the case, we would have simply inscribed the past anew onto the rationalistic transparency of a conceptually graspable foundation. On the contrary, it is rather a question of narrating the *dissolution* of a foundation, thus revealing the radical contingency of the categories linked to that foundation. My intention is *revelatory* rather than *explanatory*.

I shall begin with a central tenet of marxism: that capitalism exists only by dint of the constant transformation of the means of production and the increasing dissolution of pre-existing social relations. The history of capitalism, therefore, is, on the one hand, the history of the progressive destruction of the social relations generated by it and, on the other, the history of its border with social forms exterior to it. Actually, it is a question of two borders that the very logic of capitalism must constantly recreate and re-define. Such a situation engenders two conceptual alternatives: either the movement of these borders is a process of contingent struggle whose outcome is largely indeterminate, or it is History brought to a predetermined and predeterminable end by a cunning Reason, which works on the contradictions of that History. It is clear that a philosophy of history can *only* be formulated along the lines of the second alternative. And there is little doubt that classical marxism followed those lines. Suffice it to mention the preface to *A Contribution to the Critique of Political Economy*.[5]

Let us consider this latter alternative in relation to the radically relational character of identity discussed above. If the limits of the system can be subverted by a reality exterior to it, then, insofar as every identity is relational, the new relations of exteriority cannot but transform the identities. Identities can remain stable only in a closed system. Is there any compatibility, then, between the idea of historical agents – particularly the working class – as identities defined within the capitalist system, and the fact that the system always acts upon a reality exterior to it? Yes, if one accepts the solution put forth by classical marxism: that the relation of exteriority can be *internally* defined, since every exterior relation is destined *a priori* to succumb as a result of capitalist expansion. The internal logic of capital thus comes to constitute the rational substrate of History and the advent of socialism is thought to be made possible only by the results of the *internal* contradictions of capitalism.

If this were all, little would be left to say and the attempts to trace within marxist discourses the genealogy of a post-marxism would be doomed to failure. But this is not the whole story. In fact, emergent within marxism are diverse discourses in which the relation between the 'internal' and the 'external' has become increasingly complex and has begun to deconstruct the categories of classical marxism. The language games played around these categories became ever more difficult and risky: 'classes', for example, were conceived as constituted by relational complexes quite removed from those originally attributed to them.

The history of marxism has met with several such nodal moments of ambiguity and discursive proliferation. However, those phenomena grouped under the rubric of 'uneven and combined development' must be singled out for special consideration because of the variety and centrality of the effects they have produced. In a recently published book,[6] I have described the basic lines of the emergence and expansion of this concept of uneven and combined development, and so I shall only summarise its distinctive features here. At the beginning, this concept attempted only to characterise an exceptional context. The Russian bourgeoisie, having entered history belatedly and consequently having been rendered incapable of taking on the democratic tasks of overthrowing czarist absolutism, gave way to the working class who assumed these tasks. But the tasks 'proper' to the working class are socialist and not democratic. Therefore, how does one define the 'exceptionality' of one class taking over another class's tasks? The *name* given to this taking over was 'hegemony', but the *nature* of the relation it implied was far from being clear. Was the relation between the working class and the democratic tasks it took on *internal* or *external* to its nature as class? And what do we make of the fact that this uneven development soon ceased to have an exceptional character? The social upheavals proper to the age of imperialism necessitated ever more complex articulatory practices as a result of their operation in ever less orthodox historical contexts. Trotsky came to understand uneven and combined development as the historical law of our era. But what, then, is *normal* development supposed to be?

At this point I can return to some of the points made earlier. Every (social or other type of) identity is relational and vulnerable to the subversion of any exteriority. This implies that the combination of tasks proper to uneven development cannot but modify the nature of the social agents that enact them. Such was clearly the case in the emergence, during the era of popular fronts, of such entities as 'the masses', the 'national', the 'popular', etc., excluded from marxist discourse in the heyday of the Second International. But this also implied, necessarily, that the suturing, foundational, and metaphysical value of classist categories had been radically questioned. That is, if classist identities are subverted by an exteriority, by new relational and articulatory contexts, they cannot be the *foundation* of History. The pragmatism and the contingency pass from the task to the agents, and the ground of possibility of a philosophy of History is dissolved.

This radical questioning of the logic of foundations is precisely the weakening effect that I and my colleague Chantal Mouffe found to be intrinsic to postmodern experience. And by exploring those points in the marxist tradition in which the weakening effect operates, we can trace the genealogy of a post-marxism. Let's look at two examples: Sorel and Gramsci. Sorel was clear on two issues: that the logic of capitalist development did not move in the direction that Marx predicated, and that the participation of the working class in the democratic political system led to its integration within that system. The first process weakened the logic of capital as the foundation of History; the second produced the same effect of weakening by showing that the social identity of the working class was vulnerable to the new system of relations by virtue of that class's very political participation. Sorel's response to this is well known: on the one hand, he posited a theory of myth that implied a radical relationalism, for only violence and the total severance of relations between the working class and the political system permitted a proletarian identity, and on the other, the absolute rejection of the underlying rationality of History, insofar as social relations assume structural coherence only when patterned by myth.

Gramsci presents us with an identical relationalism that leads, however, to the opposite solution. Sorel rejected all relations of exteriority and proposed a pristine proletarian identity. Gramsci, on the contrary, fully explored the multiplicity of relational ensembles which developed in the Italy of his time, thus systematically expanding the field of hegemonic relations, but as a result of that he had to acknowledge that the political subjects were not the classes but what he denominated as collective wills. Where Sorel saw all participation within the political system as a loss of identity, Gramsci conceived of hegemonic articulations as a process of creating identities. Both, however, posited the same relational, and ultimately ungrounded, character of identities.

If we situate these two examples in a broader historical perspective, the direction our genealogical exploration should take is more easily discerned. The systematic discovery of discursive areas in the marxist tradition saw the emergence of new entities and categories that, rather than prolong the basic concepts of classical marxism through their cumulative enrichment, added a logically unintegratable *supplement* to them, in the manner of what Derrida has called the 'logic of supplementarity' – that hingelike discursive play that renders opposition ambiguous. I do not think it is an exaggeration to argue that the fundamental terminological additions to marxism, from Lenin to Gramsci, constitute supplements in this very sense. The genealogy of marxism, then, coincides with the deconstruction of its myth of origins.

This myth is continually nourished by a multitude of operations that tend to conceal its fissures. These operations find their crudest form in the glorious and invincible marxism-Leninism à la Soviet, but it at least has the virtue of being visible, in the conspicuous clumsiness of the bureaucrat; the *trahison des clercs* shows a greater sophistication, which operates, however, in the service of concealment. All of Lukács's sophistication is reduced to mediations that make the highest forms of 'bourgeois' culture compatible with a transparent notion of class not much different from that held by a member of the Soviet Academy of Science. More recently, a highly capable group of German theorists wasted a great deal of their time, as well as that of their readers, in the alchemistic quest of trying to derive the concept of the State from the concept of Capital. When it comes to *the last instance*, the convictions of the 'refined' materialist are not much different from those of the vulgar materialist. What all this means is that the history of marxism loses its plurality; the language games within that history and its relation to our period are defined and codified beforehand. Marxism is accepted or rejected *in toto*; Marx's texts are not read as one reads texts by Freud, Hegel, or Plato, that is, by questioning them from the perspective of our own problems and present situation.

Rather, a final revelation is awaited that will allow us to distance ourselves from the reality we live and to inhabit a different history, an illusory one to be sure. But when we take up our current problems, our engagement with them is merely impressionistic and pragmatic. Most frequently, the ultimate act of servility and faith in the unity of marxism is to abandon it completely; but this serves only to maintain the myth of its coherence and unity.

This attitude has become so generalised that the preceding arguments probably sound a bit outdated. This indifference to the marxist tradition, however, leads to an important loss as regards the constitution of a radical politics. In the first place, there is an impoverishment of the tradition. If the isolated struggles cannot be inserted within a wider horizon that 'totalises' an ensemble of an experience, the result is the impossibility of constructing a radical imaginary. Furthermore, an abstract, nondeconstructive rejection of a tradition in no way implies going beyond it. This brings us back to our original problem: to affirm the end of something means nothing unless we specify the form in which it ends. Both Spinoza's philosophy and Hitlerism have historically come to an *end* in some sense, but the different forms in which we conceive their end and closure impinge upon us, with respect to not only how we determine our relation to the past but also how we define our present.

Let us return to our arguments concerning the destruction of a tradition, in the Heideggerian sense. To set the limits of an answer is to re-create the original meaning of the question. To set the historical limits of marxism is to re-establish a living dialogue with that tradition, to endow it with a certain contemporaneity against the *timelessness* that its orthodox defenders attribute to it. In this sense, 'post-marxism' is not an 'ex-marxism', for it entails an active involvement in its history and in the discussion of its categories. But this involvement does not imply a dogmatic affirmation of its unity and coherence; rather, it requires specification of its plurality. By tracing our current problems within the marxist tradition – in the writings of Luxemburg, Bauer, Sorel, or Gramsci, in which many violently repressed intuitions brought about deconstructive effects – it becomes possible to construct a discourse that can creatively appropriate the past. Historical amnesia is a recipe for parochialism at best. At worst, it leads to the appropriation of one's struggles by antagonistic discourses.

Here, however, it is necessary to be more precise: if we are to *reconstruct* radical tradition (because this is precisely what this is about), not as a necessary departure from a point of origin, but as the genealogy of the present, it is clear that marxism cannot be its only point of reference. The plurality of current social struggles, emerging in a radically different and more complex world than could have been conceived in the nineteenth century, entails the necessity of breaking with the provincial myth of the 'universal class'. If one can talk about universality, it is only in the sense of the relative centralities constructed hegemonically and pragmatically. The struggles of the working class, of women, gays, marginal populations, third-world masses, must result in the construction of their own reappropriations of tradition through their specific genealogical efforts. This means, of course, that there is no *a priori* centrality determined at the level of structure, simply because there is no rational foundation of History. The only 'rationality' that History might possess is the relative rationality given to it by the struggles and the concrete pragmatic-hegemonic constructions. Sorel's and Gramsci's basic intuitions ought to be radically developed with this in mind. Only thus, by lowering the ontological pretensions of marxist categories and treating them not as the ground of History but as pragmatic and limited syntheses of a historical reality that subverts and surpasses them, will it be possible to entertain their current validity. This puts us squarely within the discussion around postmodernity from the point of view of marxism. Two central problems are at stake. The first is that of the consequences of the collapse of the discourse of foundation from the point of view of a radical political discourse: does not this collapse lead to political nihilism, to the impossibility of giving a foundation to the political practice and critique? The second refers to the unity of the emancipatory project as conceived by the Enlightenment: does not the plurality and dispersion of the current social struggles imply its necessary abandonment as a global project?

THE PROCESS OF ARGUING AND COMMON SENSE

The collapse of the myth of foundations deprives History and society of an ultimate meaning, of an absolute point of departure for political reasoning in the sense of a Cartesian cogito. In classical ontological terms, this means that the social is groundless; if we accept the relational character of all identity, the ideal conditions of closure for a system are never achieved and therefore all identity is more or less a floating signifier. This lack of closure modifies the nature and importance of political argument in two important senses. In the first place, if an ultimate ground is posited, political argument would consist in *discovering* the action of a reality external to the argument itself. If, however, there is no ultimate ground, political argument increases in importance because, through the conviction that it can contribute, it itself *constructs*, to a certain extent, the social reality. Society can then be understood as a vast argumentative texture through which people construct their own reality.[7]

However, in a second sense, this transition from argument as discovery to argument as social construction entails a necessary modification of the *type of argument*. On the one hand, if we could take as a point of departure a foundation of the social operating as *cogito*, the argument would be of a logical or algorithmic type insofar as it would constitute a forum of judgement beyond appeal. Without such a forum, however, the argument would have the tendency to prove the *verisimilitude* of an argument rather than its truth, thus becoming pragmatic and open-ended. This brings us back to the Aristotelian notion of *phronesis*. Let us suppose that we are trying to determine if an enemy is to attack by land or by sea. Recourse to an algorithm would be to no avail; we could, however, reason that one possibility is *more likely* than the other. This greater likelihood is, in turn, determined by other arguments used on other occasions. The ensemble of arguments constitutes the texture of a group's *common sense*. And this common sense, extended in time, is what constitutes a *tradition* (of struggle, of exercise of power, etc.). Now, since this tradition is by definition open-ended – that is, ungrounded in any ultimate algorithmic certainty – it is responsive to the diverse argumentative practices that take place in society. One argument answers another, but in this process of counterargumentation, the argument itself, that is, its own identity, is itself modified in one way or another.

Here is the basis for our answer to the first question. Abandonment of the myth of foundations does not lead to nihilism, just as uncertainty as to how an enemy will attack does not lead to passivity. It leads, rather, to a proliferation of discursive interventions and arguments that are necessary, because there is no extradiscursive reality that discourse might simply reflect. Inasmuch as argument and discourse constitute the social, their open-ended character becomes the source of a greater activism and a more radical libertarianism. Humankind, having always bowed to external forces – God, Nature, the necessary laws of History – can now, at the threshold of postmodernity, consider itself for the first time the creator and constructor of its own history. The dissolution of the myth of foundations – and the concomitant dissolution of the category 'subject' – further radicalises the emancipatory possibilities offered by the Enlightenment and marxism.

Another objection could be raised to this withdrawal of foundations: wouldn't this eliminate any motivation for action? Are we not then in the situation, evoked by Sartre, of a chooser with no motive to choose? This, however, is not a valid objection, for the lack of foundations leads only to the affirmation that 'human' as such is an empty entity, but social agents are never 'humans' in general. On the contrary, social agents appear in concrete situations and are constituted by precise and limited discursive networks. In this sense, lack of grounding does not abolish the meaning of their acts; it only affirms their limits, their finitude, and their historicity.

GLOBAL EMANCIPATION AND EMPTY SIGNIFIERS

I shall now take up the second problem of whether the dispersion and plurality of social struggles dissolve the global character of the emancipatory project. To be sure, one cannot smuggle in the unity and totality of a project once one has rejected its foundation. But is unity of foundation the only form of totalising practice in society? Are there not also totalising effects on the level of what we have called pragmatic hegemonic practices? Remember that any identity is ambiguous insofar as it is unable to constitute itself as a precise difference within a closed totality. As such, it becomes a floating signifier whose degree of emptiness depends on the distance that separates it from its fixedness to a specific signified. (Earlier, we used 'democracy' as an example of such a signifier.) This degree of fixity of a signifier varies in inverse proportion to the extent of its circulation in a given discursive formation. The ambiguity of the signifier 'democracy' is a direct consequence of its discursive centrality; only those signifiers around which important social practices take place are subject to this systematic effect of ambiguity. (The same argument could be made for the 'imprecision' of populist symbols.)

In reality, effective ambiguity does not arise only from the attempts to fix signifiers to antagonistic discourses, although this latter case is more interesting to us. It may have a multiplicity of sources, and it can be ascribed to the phenomenon of symbolic representation. A signifier is emptied when it is disengaged from a particular signified and comes to symbolise a long chain of equivalent signifieds. This displacement and expansion of the signifying function constitute the symbol.

The relationship between a foundation and what it founds is quite different from a symbolic representation and that which is symbolised. In foundational logic there is a necessary, determining relation between the founding agency and the founded entity; in symbolic representation, on the other hand, no such internal motivation exists and the chain of equivalent signifieds can be extended indefinitely. The former is a relation of delimitation and determination, i.e., fixation. The latter is an open-ended horizon.

It is the contraposition between foundation and horizon that I think enables us to understand the change in the ontological status of emancipatory discourses and, in general, of metanarratives, in the transition from modernity to postmodernity. A formation that is unified or totalised in relation to a horizon is a formation without foundation; it constitutes itself as a unity only as it delimits itself from that which it negates. The discourses of equality and rights, for example, need not rely on a common human essence as their foundation; it suffices to posit an egalitarian logic whose limits of operation are given by the concrete argumentative practices existing in a society. A horizon, then, is an empty locus, a point in which society symbolises its very groundlessness, in which concrete argumentative practices operate over a backdrop of radical freedom, of radical contingency. The dissolution of the myth of foundations does not dissolve the phantom of its own absence. This absence is – at least in the last third of the nineteenth century – the condition of possibility for affirming the historical validity of our projects and their radical metaphysical contingency. This double insertion constitutes the horizon of postmodern freedom, as well as the specific metanarrative of our age.

Summaries and Notes

1. SIMON MALPAS, INTRODUCTION

1. This is not to say that writers who discuss postmodernism as an outgrowth of modernism are simply wrong. This is certainly an aspect of the postmodern, but it is only one aspect. For an extremely informative and rigorous account of this sort of postmodernism that links it with other notions of postmodernity, see Linda Hutcheon, *A Poetics of Postmodernism: History, Theory, Fiction* (London, 1988); and Hutcheon, *The Politics of Postmodernism* (London, 1989).
2. The range of problems linked with this idea of 'Man' are discussed in detail by in the debates about gender (chapters 10, 11 and 12) and race (chapters 13 and 14).
3. Fredric Jameson, 'Postmodernism and Consumer Society', in Hal Foster (ed.), *Postmodern Culture* (London, 1983), p. 113; reprinted here as chapter 3.
4. These descriptions are presented in this book in the essays by Jean-François Lyotard (chapters 2 and 5), Fredric Jameson (chapter 3) and Ernesto Laclau (chapter 15), respectively.
5. Jean-François Lyotard, *The Postmodern Condition: A Report on Knowledge*, trans. Geoff Bennington and Brian Massumi (Manchester, 1984), p. xxiv.
6. For a more detailed discussion of the politics of genre and narrative in postmodern theory than there is room for here, see Jean-François Lyotard, *The Differend: Phrases in Dispute*, trans. Georges Van Den Abeele (Manchester, 1988), pp. 128–150. Another highly pertinent discussion is Jacques Derrida's 'The Law of Genre', in *Acts of Literature*, ed. Derek Attridge (London, 1992), pp. 221–52.
7. Aristotle, 'On the Art of Poetry', in *Aristotle, Horace, Longinus, Classical Literary Criticism*, trans. T. S. Dorsch (Harmondsworth, 1965), p. 43.
8. Lyotard, *The Postmodern Condition*, p. 42.
9. Lyotard, 'Rewriting Modernity', in *The Inhuman: Reflections on Time*, trans. Geoffrey Bennington and Rachel Bowlby (Cambridge, 1991), p. 25.
10. Jürgen Habermas, *The Philosophical Discourse of Modernity: Twelve Lectures*, trans. Frederick Lawrence (Cambridge, 1987), p. 5.
11. Immanuel Kant, 'Idea for a Universal History from a Cosmopolitan Point of View', in Kant, *On History*, ed. Lewis White Beck (London, 1963), p. 12.
12. Lyotard, *The Postmodern Condition*, p. xxiii. The examples Lyotard gives at the end of this quotation refer to Hegel's philosophy in which reason guides progress, Wilhelm Dilthey's discussion of the development of meaning in history, Marxism and capitalism (particularly Adam Smith's *The Wealth of Nations*), respectively.
13. Of course, this description of the Bible as a grand narrative is far too reductive of the complexities of Christian theology. For a more detailed analysis of the relationship between theology and postmodern critical theory, see Mark C. Taylor, *Altarities* (Chicago, 1987).

14. An example of this idea of modernity can be found in G. W. F. Hegel, *The Philosophy of History*, trans. J. Sibree (New York, 1991).
15. See Martin Heidegger, 'The Age of the World Picture', in *The Question Concerning Technology and Other Essays*, trans. William Lovitt (London, 1977).
16. For an extended discussion of this form of modernity, see Habermas, *The Philosophical Discourse of Modernity*, and his essay in this book (chapter 4).
17. Jean-Luc Nancy, *The Birth to Presence*, trans. Brian Holmes and others (Stanford, CA, 1993), pp. 144–5.
18. Diane Elam, *Romancing the Postmodern* (London, 1992), pp. 9–10.
19. See, for example, Alex Callinicos, *Against Postmodernism: A Marxist Critique* (Cambridge, 1989). This problem is explored in essays in this book by Fredric Jameson (chapter 3), Terry Eagleton (chapter 8) and, from a position that is more positive about the postmodern, Ernesto Laclau (chapter 15).

2.   JEAN-FRANÇOIS LYOTARD, 'A POSTMODERN FABLE'

(From *Postmodern Fables*, trans. Georges Van Den Abeele [Minneapolis and London, 1997], pp. 83–101. *Postmodern Fables* was originally published as *Moralités Postmodernes* [Paris, 1993].)

Summary

By writing and then critically discussing a fable about the end of the world, Lyotard presents a series of key descriptions about the ways in which postmodernity distinguishes itself from the grand narratives of modernity. To this end, it questions the centrality of the human, it disrupts straightforwardly chronological ideas of time, and it challenges the notion that historical progress is directed towards emancipation and freedom.

Note

This essay was originally a talk, portions of which were presented as a Whitney Museum Lecture in fall, 1982; it is published here essentially unrevised.

3.   FREDRIC JAMESON, 'POSTMODERNISM AND CONSUMER SOCIETY'

(From Hal Foster [ed.], *Postmodern Culture* [London, 1985], pp. 111–25; this volume was first published in the US as Hal Foster [ed.], *The Anti-Aesthetic* [Port Townsend, WA, 1983].)

Summary

Fredric Jameson argues that postmodernism emerges as a reaction to high modernism and that, because modernism was never a unified movement, there are therefore a multiplicity of different postmodernisms. He also states that postmodernism marks the erosion of the distinction between high and low culture, as well as the different artistic genres. However, postmodernism is not just a particular style; rather, Jameson sees it as intrinsically tied up with the emergence of a post-industrial consumer society.

The essay proceeds to set out two key features of postmodernism. The first is the replacement of parody's critical stance towards its targets by the politically neutral mimicry of pastiche. Jameson argues that, in postmodern film and literature, history is replaced by pastiche simulations of the past that disguise any meaningful relationship between it and the present, thereby replacing historical knowledge with nostalgia for misunderstood past ages. This breakdown of historical understanding leads to the second feature of postmodernism, which Jameson calls schizophrenia. He describes schizophrenia in terms of the inability to make sense of temporal continuity so that all that remains are images and signifiers that refer only to other images and signifiers, thereby losing touch with reality.

The essay ends by asking whether postmodernism has any radical or oppositional potential, or if it simply replicates and reproduces the market forces that underlie contemporary consumer society.

Notes

1. Renee Sechehaye, *Autobiography of a Schizophrenic Girl* (London, 1951).
2. Jean-Paul Sartre, *What is Literature?* (London, 1967).

4. JÜRGEN HABERMAS, 'MODERNITY: AN UNFINISHED PROJECT'

(From Maurizio Passerin d'Entrèves and Seyla Benhabib [eds], *Habermas and the Unfinished Project of Modernity* [Cambridge, 1996], pp. 38–55; trans. Nicholas Walker.)

Summary

This essay sets out to defend modernity against critiques levelled at it by postmodernists. It traces the history of the different concepts of modernity back to the fifth century, and discusses its relationship with the classical age. For Habermas, artistic modernism consists of various attempts by the avant-gardes to disrupt the chronological certainty of history by forging new links with the past to redefine contemporary culture. He argues that these attempts have been overcome by a new conservatism which seeks to impose new disciplines and restraints on both artistic culture and society itself.

The essay then describes a broader discourse of modernity that arises from the separation of scientific knowledge, morality and aesthetics into different 'value spheres' (areas with different sets of rules and criteria for judging the success or failure of a particular event or work), and the development of expert cultures whose task is to police them. Habermas claims that this has led to a fragmentation of modern social existence. But this fragmentation can be positive, as it allows room for the possibility of emancipation. Conservative attempts to eliminate the differences between the spheres or privilege one sphere over the others lead only to a totalitarian culture. For this reason, Habermas argues that it is vital that we continue to work within modernity instead of rejecting its problems and possibilities. Taking a series of examples from modern art, he illustrates the potential for political progress that emerges from the fragmented relation between science, morality and art. The essay ends with an explanation of the problems of conservative postmodernism.

Notes

This is the first complete English translation of the original version of a speech given by Habermas in September 1980, when he was awarded the Adorno Prize by the City of Frankfurt. The German text was published in Habermas's *Kleine Politische Schriften I–IV* (Frankfurt, 1981). Translated by Nicholas Walker.

1. W. Pehnt, 'Die Postmoderne als Lunapark', *Frankfurter Allgemeine Zeitung*, 18 Aug. 1980, p. 17.
2. 'Literarische Tradition und gegenwärtiges Bewusstsein der Moderne', in H. R. Jauss, *Literaturgeschichte als Provokation* (Frankfurt, 1970), pp. 11ff.
3. T. W. Adorno, 'Ästhetische Theorie', in *Gesammelte Werke*, vol. 7 (Frankfurt, 1970), p. 45.
4. Octavio Paz, *Essays* (Austin, TX and London, 1976).
5. Adorno, 'Ästhetische Theorie', p. 41.
6. Walter Benjamin, *Gesammelte Schriften* (Frankfurt, 1974), vol. 1.2, pp. 701f. In English see 'Theses on the Philosophy of History', in *Illuminations*, trans. H. Zohn (New York, 1969), pp. 261, 263.
7. Paz, *Essays*.
8. Daniel Bell, *The Cultural Contradictions of Capitalism* (London, 1979).
9. Peter Steinfels, *The Neoconservatives* (New York, 1979), p. 65.
10. Bell, *The Cultural Contradictions of Capitalism*, p. 17.
11. Immanuel Kant, *The Critique of Judgement* (Oxford, 1952), para. 7.
12. Ibid., para. 49.
13. Adorno, 'Ästhetische Theorie', p. 52.
14. D. Wellershoff, *Die Auflösung des Kunstbegriffs* (Frankfurt, 1976).
15. Peter Weiss, *Ästhetik des Widerstands* (Frankfurt, 1978), vol. 1, p. 54.

5. JEAN-FRANÇOIS LYOTARD, 'ANSWERING THE QUESTION: WHAT IS POSTMODERNISM?'

(From *The Postmodern Condition: A Report on Knowledge*, trans. Geoff Bennington and Brian Massumi [Manchester 1984], pp. 71–82. *The Postmodern Condition* was originally published as *La Condition Postmoderne: Rapport sur le Savoir* [Paris, 1979.])

Summary

This essay identifies a slackening in avant-garde experimentation and radical critique as it is put under pressure by thinkers like Habermas, who want to usher in a new, unified order for culture and society. It goes on to discuss the differences between realism, modernism and postmodernism as ways of representing the world that either uphold or challenge this order. Realism aims to make the world appear stable, secure and immediately available to the subject. This is manifest not only in the conservative ideas of classical beauty, but also in the cultural eclecticism of modern capitalist society.

Against realism, Lyotard sets the modern and postmodern sublime. Based on an incompatibility between what can be conceived and what can be presented, the sublime disrupts the comforts of realism by presenting the fact that, within realism, certain issues, events, problems and possibilities must remain unpresentable. Rather than being distinct historical modes, for Lyotard the modern and the postmodern are different sublime responses to realism. Modernism employs a nostalgic sublime in which the unpresentable is alluded to as gaps in the content of a work that retains a predominantly realist form. In postmodernism, on the other hand, the work's formal structure is itself sublime: it is a work that breaks the established rules of representation as it sets off in search of new ways to testify to the existence of the unpresentable. On this basis, Lyotard argues that the postmodern is the most effective way to combat the slackening of critique and challenge the terror of realist totalitarianism.

6. JEAN BAUDRILLARD, 'THE GULF WAR: IS IT REALLY TAKING PLACE?'

(From *The Gulf War did not Take Place*, trans. Paul Patton [Bloomington and Indianapolis, 1995], pp. 31–2, 40–59. *The Gulf War did not Take Place* was originally published as *La Guerre de Golfe n'a pas eu lieu* [Paris, 1991].)

Summary

This essay argues that the proliferation of spectacular images in the media's representation of the Gulf War, instead of providing information about its reality, presents a masquerade of contradictory signs that transform it into a virtual conflict. The 'reality' of war and suffering thereby becomes an object of endless speculation and evaluation that results only in total uncertainty about what is actually happening. Tying this proliferation of images to the promotional marketing strategies of modern capitalism, Baudrillard reads the war as a global advertising campaign for Western military and communications technology. He claims that the politicians and intellectuals who argue the rights and wrongs of the war are dupes of the advertiser's images. Instead, Baudrillard urges us sceptically to resist the rottenness of the war's simulations.

7. JACQUES DERRIDA, 'DECONSTRUCTION AND ACTUALITY'

(From 'The Deconstruction of Actuality: An Interview with Jacques Derrida', *Radical Philosophy*, (Autumn 1994), 28–30. This interview took place in Paris in August 1993, and was originally published in French in *Passages* in September 1993.)

Summary

In this interview, Derrida questions the possibility of maintaining a stable opposition between actuality and artificiality in modern culture, and explores the ways in which the two terms are inextricably interlinked. He coins two compound words to describe their relation: 'artifactuality' and 'actuvirtuality'. The first term insists that actuality is produced by fictional and artificial narratives that come into play when we attempt to interpret the world. The second term indicates that the virtual is not simply a second-hand reproduction of the actual, but that it penetrates right to the heart of contemporary reality. For Derrida, the task of the critic is not simply to deny the reality of the actual and focus on the virtual, but rather to examine the social and political effects and implications of the ways in which these apparently opposed terms have become intimately related.

8. TERRY EAGLETON, 'IDEOLOGY, DISCOURSE AND THE PROBLEMS OF "POST-MARXISM"'

(From *Ideology: An Introduction* [London, 1991], pp. xi–xii, 199–213.)

Summary

This essay sets out to argue that a concept of ideology is crucial for a critical under-standing of the modern world, and that this concept is absent from the linguistic orientation of postmodern theory. Eagleton condemns critics such as Roland Barthes and Paul de Man for their equation of ideology with language, because they stretch the concept of ideology to its breaking point and force it to collapse into mean-inglessness. He argues that uses of language are not all equally ideological and that important opportunities for political critique are lost if one follows this mode of analysis.

The essay then discusses the 'Post-Marxist' position of those critics who discuss the world in terms of 'discourse'. For Eagleton, they refuse a separation between objects and language, claiming that the difference between them is only a function of discourse; that reality is produced through the ways in which we act and experience the world. Eagleton raises the question how, if this really is the case, any statement about the world can be wrong. He argues that the consequences of this position are that no political system can objectively be judged better or worse than any other, and that the traditional Marxist focus on the emancipation of the working class can have no final justification. The essay concludes by asserting that a person's material interests cannot simply be reduced to language or discourse, and that one way to avoid this is to retain a Marxist notion of ideological critique.

Notes

1. V. N. Voloshinov, *Marxism and the Philosophy of Language* (New York, 1973), p. 9.
2. Roland Barthes, *Mythologies* (London, 1972), p. 143.
3. Christopher Norris, *Paul de Man: Deconstruction and the Critique of Aesthetic Ideology* (London, 1988), pp. 48–9.
4. Paul de Man, *The Resistance to Theory* (Minneapolis, 1986), p. 11.
5. See in particular Barry Hindess and Paul Hirst, *Pre-Capitalist Modes of Production* (London, 1975), and *Mode of Production and Social Formation* (London, 1977), John Frow promotes a similar 'semiotic' theory of ideology in his *Marxism and Literary History* (Oxford, 1986), pp. 55–8.
6. A. Cutler, B. Hindess, P. Hirst and A. Hussain, *Marx's 'Capital' and Capitalism Today*, vol. 1 (London, 1977), pp. 222, 236.
7. Ibid., p. 237.

9. RICHARD RORTY, 'WE ANTI-REPRESENTATIONALISTS'

(From *Radical Philosophy*, 60 (Spring 1992), 40–2.)

Summary

In his review of Eagleton's *Ideology: an Introduction,* Rorty takes issue with the importance of a Marxist notion of ideology for modern thought. He argues that the ambiguities of the term 'ideology', and also the imprecise ideas of how it distorts what is really at stake in the material structures of society, are of negligble value for critical analysis. Rorty argues that a pragmatic approach to politics based on judgements about the practical utility of conflicting claims is more important than questions about whether those claims accurately represent the way the world 'really is' for the simple reason that one can never be certain about what 'really is'. For Rorty, politics must thus become a process of negotiation about the utility of different actions in different circumstances.

10. LINDA HUTCHEON, 'POSTMODERNISM AND FEMINISMS'

(From *The Politics of Postmodernism* [London, 1989], pp. 141–150, 167–8.)

Summary

This essay describes how the interests of postmodernism and different forms of feminism converge around a problematisation of the body and sexuality. However, it argues against the conflation of the two discourses as, while feminisms present explicitly political sets of interventions, postmodernism is frequently politically ambivalent. For Hutcheon, feminisms have drawn out the political implications of postmodern theories of representation. On the other hand, postmodernism's parodic representations can provide feminisms with useful means of challenging ideas of natural gender identity, as Hutcheon illustrates through readings of Angela Carter and Margaret Harrison. The essay concludes with a discussion of the ways in which postmodern strategies might support feminist politics.

Notes

1. Catherine R. Stimpson, 'Nancy Reagan Wears a Hat: Feminism and its Cultural Consensus', *Critical Inquiry*, 14:2 (1988), 223–43, 223.
2. Craig Owens, 'The Discourse of Others: Feminists and Postmodernism', in Hal Foster, *The Anti-Aesthetic: Essays on Postmodern Culture* Port Townsend, WA, 1983), pp. 57–82, p. 57.
3. Stimpson, 'Nancy Reagan Wears a Hat', p. 241.
4. Lisa Tickner, 'The Body Politic: Female Artists and the Body Politic since 1970', in Roziska Parker and Griselda Pollock (eds), *Framing Feminism: Art and the Women's Movement 1970–85* (London and New York, 1987), pp. 263–276, p. 264.
5. Angela Carter, *Black Venus* (London, 1985), p. 9. Subsequent references cited by page numbers in the text.
6. Chris Weedon, *Feminist Practice and Poststructuralist Theory* (Oxford, 1987).

7. Hal Foster, *Recodings: Art, Spectacle, Cultural Politics* (Port Townsend, WA, 1985), p. 6.
8. Janice Winship, ' "A Girl Needs to Get Streetwise": Magazines for the 1980s', in Rosemary Betterton (ed.), *Looking On: Images of Femininity in the Visual Arts and Media* (London and New York, 1987), pp. 127–41, p. 127.

11. JUDITH BUTLER, 'GENDER TROUBLE: FROM PARODY TO POLITICS'

(From *Gender Trouble: Feminism and the Subversion of Identity* [London, 1990], pp. 142–9.)

Summary

Appearing at the end of *Gender Trouble*, the argument of this extract develops from the premise that modern feminism can retain a political force despite the loss of foundational ideas of gender and identity in postmodernity. It sets out to challenge the notion of a subject that is distinct from discourse, that there is an 'I' that pre-exists signification. Instead, Butler argues, gender and identity are functions of signifying practices in a culture, and subjectivity is thereby regulated by the discourses and social practices in which it appears. She concludes that the task of modern feminism is parodically to subvert and displace those discourses that produce the restrictive norms of gender identity.

12. ALICE A. JARDINE, 'CRISES IN LEGITIMATION: CROSSING THE GREAT VOIDS'

(From *Gynesis: Configurations of Woman and Modernity* [Ithaca and London, 1985], pp. 65–79.)

Summary

This essay traces the implications of the postmodern crises in metanarratives for questions of gender. It argues that these crises result in the loss of the paternal fiction that disguises gender difference under the universal name, 'Man'. There are two forms of response to these crises: nostalgia and affirmation. After illustrating how the nostalgic response seeks to return women to their traditional roles, the essay explores the potential of what might be at stake if 'Man' were to internalise these postmodern crises affirmatively.

Jardine argues that the crises facing modernity have been figured as feminine, and describes the process of internalising them as 'gynesis'. The essay then discusses the ways in which gynesis might occur in philosophy, religion and history. In these disciplines, the disruption of traditional structures of thought has opened the way for writers such as Derrida and Hélène Cixous to question the relation between Man and the feminine principle that is traditionally projected as his Other. Relating Man to *technē* (active technology) and the feminine to *physis* (passive nature), Jardine traces the development of technological thought up to a point where it threatens to destroy Man by turning him into a passive, feminised object. In response to this, Jardine argues that criticism must work through these crises of Man to rediscover the figurality of the feminine.

Notes

1. Lyotard, *La condition postmoderne: Rapport sur le Savoir* (Paris, 1979), p. 7.
2. Ibid., pp. 7–8.
3. On scientific discourse and gender, see Evelyn Fox Keller, 'Feminism and Science', *Signs*, 7 (Spring 1982).
4. Lyotard, *La condition*, p.98.
5. Jean-François Lyotard, 'For a Pseudo-Theory', *Yale French Studies*, 52 (1975), 126.
6. Lyotard, 'One of the Things at Stake in Women's Struggles', *Substance*, 20 (1978), 16.
7. See Jessica Benjamin, 'Authority and the Family Revisited', *New German Critique*, 13 (1977).
8. See, for example, Alexander Mitscherlich, *Society without the Father: A Contribution to Social Psychology*, trans. Eric Mosbacher (London, 1969); and Christopher Lasch, *The Culture of Narcissim: American Life in an Age of Diminishing Expectations* (New York, 1980).
9. Jean Baudrillard, *De la séduction* (Paris, 1979), p. 208.
10. Ibid., pp. 19–22.
11. George Steiner, 'The Distribution of Discourse' and 'Eros and Idiom', in *On Difficulty* (Oxford, 1978), pp. 80, 135–6 (my emphases).
12. On these two figures and narrative, see, for example: Brooks, 'Freud's Masterplot', *Yale French Studies*, 55/56 (1977), 280. Cf., in particular, Roman Jakobson's famous essay, 'Two Types of Language and Two Types of Aphasic Disturbances', in Jakobson and Halle, *Fundamentals of Language* (The Hague, 1956); Jacques Lacan's 'The Agency of the Letter in the Unconscious', in *Ecrits: A Selection*, trans. Alan Sheridan (New York, 1977); as well as Le Guern, *Sémantique de la métaphore et de la métonymie* (Paris, 1973). On metaphor, see especially Derrida's 'White Mythology: Metaphor in the Text of Philosophy' in *Margins of Philosophy*, trans. Alan Bass (Brighton, Sussex, 1982), pp. 207–73.
13. Pierre Janet, *L'évolution de la mémoire et la notion du temps* (Paris, 1928), p. 261.
14. Derrida, *Writing and Difference* (London, 1978), p. 293.
15. Michèle Montrelay, 'Toward the Other Body' (unpublished paper).
16. One of the most audacious of contemporary philosophers in this realm is Gilles Deleuze.
17. See especially Michelle Le Doeuff, *L'imaginaier philosophique* (Paris, 1980). See also Luce Irigaray's *Speculum de l'autre femme* (Paris, 1974).
18. Alexander Kojève, *Introduction to the Reading of Hegel*, trans. James H. Nichols, Jr (New York, 1969), p. 214.
19. Jacques Derrida, 'Structure, Sign, and Play in the Discourse of the Human Sciences', in *Writing and Difference*, p. 278.
20. Ibid., p. 280.
21. Ibid.
22. I borrow this expression from Meaghan Morris. See 'French Feminist Criticism'.
23. Claude Lévi-Strauss, *The Savage Mind* (London, 1972), p. 247.
24. See, for example, Hélène Cixous, 'Sorties', in *La jeune née* (Paris, 10/18, 1975), pp. 115–246.

25. Walter Benjamin, 'On Language as Such and on the Language of Man', in *One Way Street*, trans. Edmund Jephcott and Kingsley Shorter (London, 1979), p. 121.

26. For a thorough discussion of the *technē* in the context of the history of rhetoric, see Roland Barthes, 'L'ancienne rhétorique', *Communications*, 6 (1970), 173. The present schematic overview cannot, of course, substitute for close analysis of 'sources' – but that is another project.

27. See, especially, Barthes on *inventio* in 'L'ancienne rhétorique', p. 197.

28. Cf. Martin Heidegger, *'The Question concerning Technology' and Other Essays*, trans. William Lovitt (New York, 1977); and Lyotard, *La condition*, esp. p. 73.

29. Maurice Merleau-Ponty, *In Praise of Philosophy*, trans. John Wild and James M. Edie (Evanston, IL, Maurice 1963), p. 50.

30. Walter Benjamin, 'La photographie', in *Poésie et révolution* (Paris, 1971), p. 19.

31. R. Barthes, *La chambre claire* (Paris, 1980), p. 29.

32. Ibid., esp. pp. 30–1.

33. The experience of becoming and being an object has been central to feminist theory since Simone de Beauvoir's *The Second Sex*. On woman as specular object, see especially Irigaray's *Speculum*.

34. Full discussion of this highly self-conscious speculative leap cannot be undertaken here, but a note sketching the grounds for it is certainly in order.

    One of the most promising and fertile areas of feminist criticism is that of photographic and cinematic theory – where male scopophilia, fetishism, and voyeurism are analysed, often in relation to the Lacanian pre-mirror stage and its attendant lack of sexual differentiation. (See, for example, Laura Mulvey, 'Visual Pleasure and Narrative Cinema', *Screen*, 16:3 [Fall 1975]. Other journals devoting extensive space to the image and sexual difference include *Camera Obscura* and *M/F*. Parallel developments may be found in psychoanalytically oriented feminist analyses of pornography: e.g., Claire Pajaczkowska, 'Imagistic Representation and the Status of the Image in Pornography', paper presented at the International Film Conference, University of Wisconsin, March 1980.)

    Julia Kristeva, among others, has analysed the specificities of specular pleasure within contemporary culture. Of particular relevance here is the following remark in reference to the dream as cinema deprived of a public: 'Let us note the lack of dissociation between the object as waste, itself not yet separated from the body proper, and the paternal eye [the Subject], which represents the first instance of visual and/or symbolic representation. The indistinction object-waste/eye-symbolic instance is inevitably accompanied by another: the hesitation around sexual difference: active or passive, seeing or seen, my eye or his eye, "man" or the erotic object of the Father's sadism ("woman").' (Julia Kristeva, 'Ellipse sur la frayeur et la séduction spéculaire', in *Polylogue*, p. 378.) Other articles of immediate interest include: Roland Barthes, 'The Rhetoric of the Image', in *Image-Music-Text* (London, 1977); Janet Bergstrom, 'Alternation, Segmentation, Hypnosis: Interview with Raymond Bellour', *Camera Obscura*, 3/4 (Summer 1979); and Umberto Eco, 'L'analyse des images', *Communications*, 15 (1970).

35. These connotations are now widely recognised in feminist criticism; for an introduction, see, for example, Dorothy Kaufmann McCall, 'Simone de Beauvoir, *The Second Sex*, and Jean-Paul Sartre', *Signs*, 5:2 (Winter 1979).

36. Vincent Descombes, *Modern French Philosophy* (translation of *Le même et l'autre: Quarante-cinq ans de philosophie française*), trans. L. Scott-Fox and J. M. Harding (Cambridge, 1980), pp. 52–3.

37. Jean-Paul Sartre, *Being and Nothingness*, trans. Hazel E. Barnes (New York, 1956), p. 623.

38. Jean-François Lyotard, *Dérive à partir de Marx et Freud* (Paris, 1973), pp. 59–60.
39. *Figure*, in French, is both a generic term for the face and a rhetorical term (as in English). *Visage* refers to that aspect of the human face which renders it recognisable, representable.
40. E.g., Maurice Blanchot, *The Space of Literature: A Translation of L'espace littéraire*, trans. Ann Smock (Lincoln, NA, 1982).
41. Lyotard, *Dérive*, p. 59.
42. For an extended discussion of the *visage* versus *figure* problematic in the context of modernity, see Gilles Deleuze and Félix Guattari, 'Année zéro: Visagéité', in *Mille plateaux* (Paris, 1980), pp. 205–34.
43. Deleuze and Parnet, *Dialogues* (Paris, 1977), p. 25.
44. Jacques Derrida, 'Violence and Metaphysics', in *Writing and Difference*, p. 100.
45. Ibid., p. 101.
46. Ibid., note 40, p. 315.
47. See: Eugénie Lemoine-Luccioni, 'Beauté', in *Partage des femmes* (Paris, 1976), pp. 160, 162, 170; and Deleuze and Guattari, 'Visagéité', esp. pp. 216–23.
48. 'Tous les visages sont le Sien; c'est pourquoi Il n'a pas de visage.' ('All faces are His; this is why He has no face.') Quoted by Derrida in 'Violence and Metaphysics', p. 109.
49. See, for example, René Spitz, *De la naissance à la parole* (Paris, 1968), pp. 57–63.
50. Deleuze and Guattari, 'Visagéité', pp. 209–10. Also see Henry Miller, *Tropic of Capricorn* (New York, 1961), p. 121.

13.   BELL HOOKS, 'POSTMODERN BLACKNESS'

(From *Yearning: Race, Gender and Cultural Politics* [Boston, MA, 1990], pp. 23–31.)

Summary

This essay raises a series of questions about the applicability of postmodern theories to black experience. Starting from the proposition that postmodernism is dominated by white male writers, the essay challenges the abstract nature of many postmodern accounts of difference and otherness. It argues that contemporary critiques of identity, although sometimes relevant to black experience, are too frequently posed in ways that are problematic for oppressed groups, for whom notions of class, race or gender identity are important unifying structures. On the other hand, it claims that the critique of essentialism challenges processes of racial stereotyping, and opens possibilities of new forms of racial or cultural identity. The essay ends by calling for a postmodernity that can contribute to the day-to-day struggle of hitherto excluded communities.

14.   HOMI K. BHABHA, 'LOCATIONS OF CULTURE: THE POSTCOLONIAL AND THE POSTMODERN'

(From *The Locations of Culture* [London, 1994], pp. 1–9.)

Summary

This essay describes postmodernity as a culture of borders (whether spatial, temporal, or of race, gender or class) across which contemporary thought travels to produce complex accounts of identity and difference. It is at these borderlines between hitherto discrete identities that new possibilities of defining culture arise. The essay argues that political empowerment occurs from the continual renegotiation of identities rather than essentialist ideas of traditional community. For Bhabha, the 'post' of postmodernism and postcolonialism does not simply mark a new age but, rather, points towards a 'beyond' that disrupts fixed ideas of the self-identity of the present and makes space for political renegotiations to occur. He argues that postcolonial theory presents a contra-modernity in which cultural hybridity is reinscribed in the universalist discourses of modernity that attempt to exclude difference in the name of identity.

Notes

1. For an interesting discussion of gender boundaries in the *fin de siècle*, see E. Showalter, *Sexual Anarchy: Gender and Culture in the Fin de Siècle* (London, 1990), especially 'Borderlines', pp. 1–18.
2. Renée Green interviewed by Elizabeth Brown, from catalogue published by Allen Memorial Art Museum, Oberlin College, Ohio.
3. Interview conducted by Miwon Kwon for the exhibition 'Emerging New York Artists', Sala Mendonza, Caracas, Venezuela (xeroxed manuscript copy).
4. Ibid., p. 6.
5. Renée Green in conversation with Donna Harkavy, Curator of Contemporary Art at the Worcester Museum.
6. Ibid.
7. W. Benjamin, 'Theses on the philosophy of history', in his *Illuminations* (London, 1970), p. 265.
8. M. Heidegger, 'Building, dwelling, thinking', in *Poetry, Language, Thought* (New York, 1971), pp. 152–3.
9. S. Rushdie, *The Satanic Verses* (London, 1988), p. 343.
10. G. Gomez-Pena, *American Theatre* (October 1991), 8:7.
11. T. Ybarra-Frausto, 'Chicano movement/chicano art' in I. Karp and S.D. Lavine (eds) (Washington and London, 1991), pp. 133–4.
12. A. Sekula, *Fish Story*, manuscript, p. 2.
13. Ibid., p. 3.
14. F. Fanon, *Black Skin, White Masks*, Introduction by H. K. Bhabha (London, 1986), pp. 218, 229, 231.

15.   ERNESTO LACLAU, 'POLITICS AND THE LIMITS OF MODERNITY'

(From Andrew Ross (ed.), *Universal Abandon? The Politics of Postmodernism* [Edinburgh, 1988], pp. 63–82.)

Summary

This essay discusses the political implications of postmodernity's challenge to foundational metanarrative forms. It begins by questioning any radical historical distinction between modernity and postmodernity, and argues instead that the postmodern engages in a disruption of modernity's central categories and a problematisation of its traditional assumptions while still retaining its emancipatory aspirations. Postmodernity is thus not a break with modernity, but a dissolution of its foundations.

The first disruption of modernity that the essay investigates is structuralism's challenge to the idea of an immediate relationship between language and reality. After tracing the development from structural linguistics to poststructuralism, Laclau argues that the political consequences of the deconstruction of immediacy uncover a series of problems in the global projects of modernity. For Laclau, postmodernity must therefore engage with this new range of problems in order to continue modernity's project of human emancipation.

The next section of the essay traces postmodernity's relation to Marxism, which is both the central emancipatory project of modernity and the site of some of its most conspicuous crises. Laclau traces the development of a series of Marx's categories (history, class and hegemony) through their transformations in response to the crises they encounter, and argues that these changes fragment rather than complete the foundational suppositions of classical Marxism. However, rather than simply abandoning this fragmented Marxism, Laclau outlines the ways in which postmodernity can retain a living and productive dialogue with a Marxism that has given up its foundational claims.

Laclau concludes that abandoning the myths of immediacy and foundationalism leads to the postmodern proliferation of discursive structures and positions that further radicalise the emancipatory possibilities of modernity. Modernity's foundational narratives are thus replaced by the antifoundationalism of a postmodernity that opens up new horizons for action and debate.

Notes

1. Martin Heidigger, *Being and Time*, trans. Linda Russell (Oxford, 1985), p. 40.
2. Ibid., p. 22.
3. The example is from J. Lyons, *Introduction to Theoretical Linguistics* (Cambridge, 1968), p. 69.
4. It would not be correct to argue, given the functional character of the discursive, that every discursive sequence presupposes language; this is no doubt true, but language in turn also presupposes vocal chords. Thus, rather than define the abstract conditions of existence of something, we should define the structural totality in which these conditions are articulated.
5. That there are, here and there, hints of a different perspective in Marx's work is undeniable; for example, the well-known letter to Vera Zasulich on the possibilities opened up by the Russian peasant communes. But they were only hints; there can be no doubt that his thinking moved in the opposite direction.
6. Ernesto Laclau and Chantal Mouffe, *Hegemony and Socialist Strategy: Towards a Radical Democratic Politics* (London, 1985).
7. As I said above, this argumentative fabric is not solely verbal; it is also interlaced with nonverbal actions to which it gives rise. Thus, every nonverbal action has meaning, and, reciprocally, every verbal argument has a performative dimension.

Glossary

Note: Words or phrases given in italics are also defined in their alphabetical place in the Glossary.

aesthetics Aesthetics is the philosophical study of beauty in art and nature. More generally, it refers to the whole process of human perception and sensation. In debates around modernity and the postmodern, it can be used both in the restrictive sense of a philosophy of art and in the less well- defined sense of a logic of sensation.

Althusser, Louis French Marxist philosopher who developed a theory of *ideology* that brought together Marx's ideas about society and French theories of subjectivity (particularly those developed by *Jacques Lacan*) to challenge the humanist idea that the *subject* is a free agent capable of determining her or his own identity and ideas. This theory is set out in 'Ideology and the Ideological State Apparatuses: Notes Towards and Investigation', in *Lenin and Philosophy and Other Essays* (2nd edn, London, 1977).

avant-garde The vanguard of artistic innovation that, through stylistic experimentation with the possibilities of representation, creates the newest developments and ideas in art or culture.

deconstruction A term derived from Jacques Derrida's philosophical processes of reading texts. By uncovering traces of *difference* or otherness within what appears to be self-identical, deconstruction seeks to disrupt the hierarchies that have often structured thought. Unlike *dialectic*, deconstruction does not seek to resolve the disruptions it uncovers in a higher synthesis.

dialectic The term 'dialectic' comes from the Greek for conversation, and in the work of Plato is presented as the correct method of philosophical enquiry in which the opposition between a thesis and its antithesis is reconciled through argument in a synthesis. *Hegel* develops the Platonic account of dialectics to form the basis of his speculative philosophy. Hegel's dialectic involves three steps: (1) a concept is taken as fixed and sharply defined, but (2) on closer analysis contradictions emerge which, when worked through, result (3) in a higher concept that includes both the original concept and its contradictions. The third stage is frequently referred to as the *sublation* of the oppositions. Hegel's idealist account of the dialectic is taken up by Karl Marx and given a material basis in his political philosophy.

difference A term developed from *Saussure*'s linguistics. While for Saussure, meaning is based solely on the differences between linguistic elements, for much contemporary thought difference forms the basis of all notions of identity: identity can be derived only according to its difference from other things or people.

Enlightenment (Aufklärung) A philosophical movement that came to the fore in the latter part of the seventeenth and throughout the eighteenth century. Enlightenment thought sought answers to questions of human existence, meaning and morality in

174

reason and scientific experimentation rather than in religious faith, superstition or mysticism. Central to the Enlightenment tradition is the idea that history is the narrative of human progress towards a more informed and just future.

ethics A philosophical analysis of moral behaviour and choices which either instructs on what should be done, or explains how it might be done, or sometimes both of these.

epistemology Also known as the theory of knowledge, epistemology is the strand of philosophical enquiry which investigates the grounds and possibility of knowledge.

eschatology The study of the ends of history and last things. Eschatology can have either a religious (as in, for example, Christian revelation) or secular (in, for example, Marx's projection of a classless society) structure, but in either case the end is presented as the completion of a linear developmental history in which the problems perceived to be facing society are resolved.

Hegel, G. W. F. Hegel (1770–1831) is the main representative of German Idealist philosophy and a crucial thinker of modernity. For Hegel, the world is comprehended by *dialectical* philosophical thought that presents reality and history as rationally explicable and conceivable in terms of a system of ideas.

hegemony Like *ideology*, hegemony designates the ways in which a political system functions by the consent as well as the coercion of its *subjects*. This consent is generated through civil institutions like, for example, schools, the media, trades unions and churches. For Marxists such as Antonio Gramsci, a key part of the revolutionary struggle is the transformation of a bourgeois hegemony through the education of the proletariat.

ideology An ideology is a set of beliefs and attitudes held (often unconsciously) by a *subject* that shapes her or his understanding and attitude towards the society in which he or she lives. Although frequently defined as false consciousness of the material conditions of existence, ideology can also refer to the entirety of the subject's consciousness of the world.

Kant, Immanuel German *Enlightenment* philosopher (1724–1804). Immanuel Kant is frequently cited as the thinker who provides the first formulations of philosophical modernity. Kant's three *Critiques* (of 'pure reason', 'practical reason' and 'judgement') split thinking into three spheres – knowledge, justice and taste – which correspond to the three orders of philosophical enquiry: *epistemology*, *ethics* and *aesthetics*. In his discussions of aesthetics, Kant formulates a theory of the *sublime*, which is crucial for many of the postmodern thinkers in this book.

Lacan, Jacques French psychoanalyst who read Freud in the light of *Saussure*'s theories of language and *Hegel*'s philosophy. His theory of subjectivity has been very influential for subsequent thinkers, including many of the writers on postmodernity who are included in this book. For an introduction to his work, see Malcolm Bowie, *Lacan* (London, 1991).

ontology The philosophical analysis of being which asks questions about the nature of existence. An ontological property is one that relates to a being's existence.

poststructuralism Originating as a reaction against *structuralism*, poststructuralism challenges the assumption that self-sufficient systems and structures are possible or necessary for knowledge and action.

referent See *sign*.

Saussure, Ferdinand de The Swiss linguist, Ferdinand de Saussure (1837–1913), laid the foundations of modern linguistics in a series of lectures that were posthumously published as the *Course in General Linguistics*. According to Saussure, meaning (signification) emerges from the differences between *signs* rather than language's relation to objects that already exist outside it.

sign A sign is a unit of meaning such as, for example, a spoken or written word. According to *Saussure*, a sign is made up of a signifier (the sonic or written image) and a signified (the concept) whose relationship is arbitrary rather than natural. This being the case, meaning arises from *differences* without positive terms. The *referent* is the object that is denoted by a sign.

structuralism A form of analysis developed from *Saussure*'s linguistics to become a critical approach that investigates the structures and formal relations that are seen to underlie a wide range of cultural phenomena from anthropology to film and television. Whatever its subject material, structural analysis seeks to make explicit the formal elements shared by different instances of the type of phenomenon under consideration.

subject The term, 'subject', derives from the Latin 'subjectum', meaning 'that which lies under'. It therefore defines that which persists through change and acts upon objects. In grammatical terms, the subject is that part of a sentence that initiates actions, but at the same time 'subjection' implies submission to an external force. In modern thought, the subject is the active human agent who is capable of reflecting upon her or his own existence. Perhaps the most famous formulation of this idea of subjectivity is Descartes' statement, 'I think therefore I am'. In recent thought, Descartes' notion of the subject has come under attack from, among other discourses, psychoanalysis and deconstruction that challenge its foundational status. Questions about the position of the subject are crucial to many of the debates about postmodernity in this book.

sublate / sublation See *dialectic*.

sublime Along with beauty, the sublime is a central category of *aesthetics*. An experience of sublimity occurs when an experience is overwhelming, and almost too much to be taken in. It arouses both fear and exhilaration, and is the most extreme form of aesthetic experience. Because of its potential to disrupt everyday knowledge and expectations, the sublime is a crucial aspect of many accounts of the postmodern.

teleology The study of the ends and goals of nature and human action. Teleology asks questions about the purposes of actions and events. A teleological account of history would therefore provide a theory of the ends and goals of historical development and progress.

Notes on Contributors

Jean Baudrillard is former Professor of Sociology at the University of Paris (Nanterre). He has written extensively and influentially on many aspects of postmodern culture and politics. His books that have been translated into English include *For a Critique of the Political Economy of the Sign* (1981), *Simulations* (1983), *America* (1988), *Cool Memories* (1990), *Fatal Strategies* (1990), *Seduction* (1990), *Symbolic Exchange and Death* (1993), *The Transparency of Evil* (1993), *The Illusion of the End* (1994), *The System of Objects* (1996), *The Perfect Crime* (1996) and *Paroxysm* (1998).

Homi K. Bhabha is Professor of English and Chester D. Tripp Professor of Humanities at the University of Chicago. He is also a visiting professor at the University of London. His publications include *The Location of Culture* (1994) and *Nation and Narration* (1990). He is currently completing a history of cosmopolitanism, to be entitled *A Measure of Dwelling*.

Judith Butler is Maxine Elliot Professor in the Departments of Rhetoric and Comparative Literature at the University of California, Berkeley. She is the author of *Subjects of Desire: Hegelian Reflections in Twentieth Century France* (1987, 1999), *Gender Trouble: Feminism and the Subversion of Identity* (1990, 1999), *Bodies that Matter: On the Discursive Limits of 'Sex'* (1993), *The Psychic Life of Power: Theories of Subjection* (1997), *Excitable Speech* (1997), as well as numerous articles and contributions on philosophy, feminist and queer theory. She is currently finishing a manuscript on Antigone and the politics of kinship.

Jacques Derrida is Director of Studies at the Ecole Normale des Hautes Etudes en Sciences Sociales in Paris, and also a Visiting Professor at the University of California, Irvine. English translations of his many works include *Memoirs of the Blind* (1993), *Aporias* (1993), *Spectres of Marx* (1994), *The Gift of Death* (1995), *Politics of Friendship* (1997), *Monolingualism of the Other* (1999) and *Adieu to Emmanuel Levinas* (1999).

Terry Eagleton is the Thomas Warton Professor of English at the University of Oxford. His numerous books include *Criticism and Ideology* (1976), *Literary Theory: An Introduction* (1983), *The Ideology of the Aesthetic* (1990), *The Significance of Theory* (1990), *Ideology: An Introduction* (1991), *Heathcliff and the Great Hunger* (1995), *The Illusions of Postmodernism* (1996) and *Crazy John and the Bishop: Studies in Irish Culture* (1998).

Jürgen Habermas is Professor of Philosophy Emeritus at the University of Frankfurt. English translations of some of his publications include *Knowledge and Human Interests* (1978), *The Theory of Communicative Action* (1984–7), *The Philosophical Discourse of Modernity* (1987), *The Structural Transformation of the Public Sphere*

(1989), *The New Conservatism* (1989), *Postmetaphysical Thinking* (1992), *Between Facts and Norms* (1996) and *The Inclusion of the Other* (1998).

bell hooks is the author of a series of influential books on race, gender and cultural politics. These include *Ain't I A Woman: Black Women and Feminism* (1981), *Talking Back: Thinking Feminist, Thinking Black* (1989), *Yearning: Race, Gender and Cultural Politics* (1991), *Black Looks: Race and Representation* (1992), *Outlaw Culture: Resisting Representations* (1994), *Killing Rage: Ending Racism* (1995) and *Bone Black: Memories of Girlhood* (1997).

Linda Hutcheon is University Professor of English and Comparative Literature at the University of Toronto. Her publications include *A Theory of Parody* (1985), *A Poetics of Postmodernism: History, Theory, Fiction* (1988), *The Canadian Postmodern: A Study of Contemporary English-Canadian Fiction* (1988), *The Politics of Postmodernism* (1989), and *Irony's Edge: The Theory and Politics of Irony* (1994), and with Michael Hutcheon, *Opera: Desire, Disease, Death* (1996) and *Bodily Charm: Living Opera* (2000).

Fredric Jameson is a Professor in the Department of Literature at Duke University. His books include *Marxism and Form* (1971), *The Prison-House of Language* (1972), *The Political Unconscious* (1981), *Late Marxism* (1990), *Postmodernism or The Cultural Logic of Late Capitalism* (1991) and *The Cultural Turn: Selected Writings on the Postmodern* (1998).

Alice Jardine is a Professor of Romance Languages and Literatures at Harvard University. Among her publications are *Gynesis: Configurations of Woman and Modernity* (1985), *Shifting Scenes: Interviews on Women, Writing and Politics in Post-68 France* (1991) and, with Paul Smith, *Men in Feminism* (1987). She is currently completing a book entitled *Blooming: A Millennial Memoire*.

Ernesto Laclau is Director of the Doctoral Programme in Ideology and Discourse Analysis in the Department of Government at the University of Essex. He is author of *Politics and Ideology in Marxist Theory* (1977) and *New Reflections on the Revolution of our Time* (1990) and *Emancipation(s)* (1996), and co-author with Chantal Mouffe of *Hegemony and Socialist Strategy: Towards a Democratic Politics* (1985). He has also written a wide range of influential essays on politics, philosophy and critical theory.

Jean-François Lyotard was Professor of Philosophy at the Collège International de Philosophie and Professor of French and Italian at the University of California, Irvine. English translations of his publications include *The Postmodern Condition: A Report on Knowledge* (1984), *The Differend: Phrases in Dispute* (1988), *Heidegger and 'the jews'* (1990), *The Inhuman: Reflections on Time* (1991), *The Postmodern Explained to Children* (1992), *Lessons on the Analytic of the Sublime* (1994) and *Postmodern Fables* (1997).

Richard Rorty is University Professor of the Humanities and Director of the Theory Seminar at the University of Virginia. He is the author of a number of influential books which bring together neopragmatism, continental philosophy and critical theory. His books include *Philosophy and the Mirror of Nature* (1979), *Consequences of Pragmatism* (1982), *Contingency, Irony, and Solidarity* (1989), *Objectivity, Relativism and Truth* (1991), *Essays on Heidegger and Others* (1991), *Truth and Moral Progress* (1998) and *Achieving our Country: Leftist Thought in the Twentieth Century* (1998).

Index